CAMPUS CHILLS

CAMPUS CHILLS

Edited by Mark Leslie

Introduction by Robert J. Sawyer

STARK
PUBLISHING

ISBN: 978-0-973-5688-1-3

First printing October 2009

Printed and bound in Canada on the *Espresso Book Machines* at

> *Titles Bookstore McMaster University*
> Hamilton, ON

> *University of Waterloo Bookstore*
> Waterloo, ON

> *University of Alberta Bookstore*
> Edmonton, AB

Cover design by UW Graphics

Published by Stark Publishing in conjunction with Titles Bookstore McMaster University, University of Waterloo Bookstore & University of Alberta Bookstore

To all of the teachers, instructors and educators
who inspire, coach and nurture young minds

Particularly, to Jim Turcott
Teacher, mentor, friend
1951 - 2008

TABLE OF CONTENTS

CAMPUS CHILLS

INTRODUCTION

BY ROBERT J. SAWYER

What is scarier than leaving home for the first time?

What's more frightening than facing a tyrannical professor?

What better way to raise goose bumps than by walking past empty classroom buildings late at night?

Welcome to the world of campus chills! Prepare to have your blood run cold, your heart race, and your brow bead with sweat: this anthology of horror stories ranges from the starkly terrifying to the tantalizingly creepy; there's something here for every taste—so long as that taste runs toward the dark side of life. There's magic mixed in with the chalk dust, evil lurking in the textbooks, malevolence biding its time in the labs—and probably something even more horrifying in the student cafeteria!

The authors in this anthology range from *New York Times* bestseller Kelley Armstrong to brand-new writer Brit Trogen (who won *On Spec* magazine's recent young-writers' contest), from Bram Stoker Award winner Edo van Belkom to multiple Aurora Award-winning science-fiction superstar Julie E. Czerneda, from cult horror favourites Nancy Kilpatrick and Sèphera Girón to award-winning short story masters Douglas Smith and James Alan Gardner. Indeed, it's hard to think of *any* anthology published in 2009—including the Year's Best volumes— that has a more prestigious roster of contributors. That they all happen to be Canadian just goes to show how preeminent our writers are in the speculative-fiction fields.

3

But that should come as no surprise. We are a big, empty nation, full of howling winds and dancing auroral skies, a place where—as everyone who has read Margaret Atwood's *Survival* knows—the very land itself will try to kill you . . . if it can.

Publishing has changed a lot since I myself entered Ryerson University thirty years ago (and had my very first story published in my campus literary journal, the *White Wall Review*). There are all sorts of new ways to bring work to market, and what you're holding in your hands is an example of one of the most exciting methods. *Campus Chills* is being produced exclusively at McMaster University, the University of Waterloo, and the University of Alberta, via print-on-demand through Espresso Book Machines, a revolutionary technology. Because of its limited distribution, this book is bound (that's a pun!) to become a sought-after collectors' item.

It's a brave new world of publishing—the dawn of a new age for reading—and editor Mark Leslie should be commended for being on the bleeding edge; that he was able to bring such an amazing group of writers together (and that he was able to pay them professional rates!) is a testament to how much the landscape has changed

So, turn the lights down as much as you can, bolt the door shut, pull the blanket up around your neck—and dig in. Terror—and wonder—await.

HARBINGER

BY KELLEY ARMSTRONG

As hard as Jenna tried to concentrate on the professor's words, all she could hear was water dripping off the drowned girl behind her. She'd even tried threading her ear-buds up through her sweater, popping them in, and cranking the music as loud as she dared. But she could still hear it. That relentless *plip-plop, plip-plop*.

Jenna fought the urge to look over her shoulder again. She'd done it so often now that the students behind her had started to squirm and glower.

There was no use looking because she knew what she'd see. The dead girl, naked, her white and wrinkled skin hanging from her arms and legs like an oversized suit about to slide off. Long, dark hair hung to her shoulders. Her lips were blue. Part of her nose was missing, and one ear. But it wasn't any of that that made Jenna shiver. It was the girl's eyes. Empty and dead, staring straight into hers.

More than once in the last six hours, Jenna had considered the possibility that she'd lost her mind. Yet it seemed to her that if you were truly crazy, you wouldn't consider that possibility. You'd see a drowned girl sitting behind you in Philosophy and ask if she had the notes from the lecture you missed last week.

When class ended, she called her roommate, Bree. No reason. She just wanted to talk, make a connection, preferably with someone alive.

It took four rings for Bree to answer, and even then she sounded groggy, her voice thick with sleep. Jenna turned her back on the drowned girl and concentrated on hearing only Bree's voice through the cell phone.

"Don't tell me I woke you up again." Jenna forced a laugh. "I swear, you're worse than my little sister."

"Mmm, no. Just resting my eyes." Bree yawned. "What's up?"

"Not much." Jenna struggled to think up an excuse for calling. "Have you changed your mind about the party tonight?"

"Nah. I need to study."

Jenna couldn't argue with that. Bree was barely passing most of her courses. They'd both struggled at first—university was so different from high school—but it seemed that as Jenna started catching on and catching up, Bree only fell farther behind. One could argue, though, that Bree was still coping better than she was. At least *she* wasn't being followed by a dead girl.

"Jenna!" a voice called.

She turned as the teaching assistant from her Classics course cut through a gaggle of students. Jenna struggled for his name, distracted by the water pooling around her feet.

"Just the girl I was hoping to see," he said with a smile. Trey. She was pretty sure that was his name. He looked like a Trey, anyway—gleaming blond hair, crisp preppy clothes, blindingly white teeth. Not your usual teaching assistant. He certainly didn't look like he needed the money. Maybe Daddy had cut him off after he totaled the Beamer. The snark was totally uncalled for, but she couldn't help it. One look at Trey, and all Jenna could think was, "I bet he never needs to worry about being followed by dead girls." Live girls, sure. Dead? Never.

"I just read your essay this morning," Trey said. "I wanted to talk to you about it. Do you have time for a coffee?"

"Is something wrong?"

"No, no. It's great." His smile oozed reassurance. "That's what I wanted to talk to you about."

A soft, sighing hiss sounded behind Jenna. She glanced over her shoulder. The drowned girl just stood there, staring, empty-eyed, dripping, water puddling at Jenna's feet, murky now, a thick brown rivulet trickling in from a stream off to the left.

Another hiss, and Jenna followed the sound to the source of the brown water. Another drowned girl. This one was bloated, like a grotesque doll inflated to twice its normal size, gray skin straining the seams of her sundress, decomposing flesh pillowing over the neckline. A faint pop, skin breaking, gas hissing out.

"Jenna?"

She turned back to Trey.

"You okay?" he asked, full lips pursed in concern.

"S-sorry. I thought I heard someone call me. Coffee, you said? Sure, coffee would be great. Lead the way."

The dead girls fell in behind them, floating above the floor, water trailing in their wake.

According to Trey, Jenna's essay was amazing. Which was bullshit. It was a B-plus effort, and that was stretching it.

If the guy didn't look like he belonged on a prep-school brochure, she'd have thought he was hitting on her. As it was, she figured he was just trying to do his job. *Overdoing* it, but she couldn't fault him for that. He poured on the praise, encouraging her, then asked about her day, her week, being friendly, taking an interest.

Not the most stimulating conversation ever, but it took her thoughts off the dead girls, who stood against the next table, dripping into the coffee cups of a laughing couple. Eventually, though, Jenna's mind wandered back to them and she began to wonder if the girls were actually ghosts. The possibility didn't shock her as much as she supposed it should. She'd grown up in a world where such things were always possibilities, where family and friends would tell stories of seeing Uncle Mike minutes before getting the call that he was dead or seeing Grandma by their bedside, telling them not to grieve for her. They didn't necessarily believe the dead walked among the living, but they were willing to concede that they could return, briefly, to console the living or to pass on a message.

After coffee, Trey left for his last class of the day. Jenna walked through two buildings, then into a courtyard. In fall, it had been jammed with students, studying under the ancient maples, tossing Frisbees, grabbing a few minutes of fresh air before another stiflingly hot class in the old buildings. Passing through it earlier today, she'd noticed a few kids braving the March chill. Now, though, past five, sun dropping, it was empty. Just Jenna and the dead girls.

She found a spot under the biggest maple, tucked out of the way of anyone stepping from the building. Then she turned to the girls.

"What do you want?"

They stared at her, eyes as empty as ever, no indication they'd heard her, no indication they'd even seen her lips move.

"Do you think I know you? Do you think I had something to do with your deaths? Is that what you're trying to do? Haunt me?"

The only answer was a hiss of gas, a fissure splitting on the bloated girl's arm.

"The only person I've ever known who drowned was a guy who rented the cabin beside ours. Got drunk. Dove into shallow water. I was five."

They continued to stare.

"Do you have a message? Something you need me to pass on?"

No reaction.

"Is it a message for me? Is there something you're trying to tell me?"

A *plink-plink* as a puddle formed around the first girl's bare feet.

"I can't do anything if you won't tell me what you want. You can stare at me all you want. I'm not psychic. I don't understand."

Jenna waved her hand in front of each girl's face. They didn't give any sign they noticed. When she stepped to the side, though, their gazes followed her.

She leapt forward, trying to startle them. Nothing.

She turned on her heel and headed back inside.

Jenna called Bree and said she was heading to the library. She wasn't hungry, wouldn't bother with dinner.

"Are you still going to Jackson's party?" Bree asked.

"Probably not."

"Why?"

I think I'm going crazy. I'm being followed by dead girls and I have no idea what to do about it, but I really don't think a party is the answer. She sputtered a small, ragged laugh.

"Jen?"

Jenna turned the laugh into a cough. "I just think I'll skip it."

"Hey, I'm the one who has to study. Go have a few beers for me, meet some hot guys, let me know what I'm missing. You could use it." A pause. "You've been a bit off lately."

"Have I?" She looked at the bloated girl. That might explain a few things . . .

"Go. That's an order."

"Maybe. I'll hit the library first."

Jenna considered herself a serious student. But that day's three-hour study stint was definitely a record. She was hiding; she knew that. Hiding not from the dead girls, but from what they portended and what she planned to do about it. She'd breezed through her day, trailed by spectres. Surreal. Ridiculous, too, but if she stopped, then she'd have to act. Better to just bury her head in a book stack and hope they went away.

She immersed herself in research, cranked up her iPod and eventually the *plink-plink* and the hiss faded into background noise. She was deep in a microbiology text when a crimson drop hit the edge of the table. She didn't look up to see where it came from. She didn't dare.

Another drop fell, next to the first. Then a third, joining the two into a tiny pool. A pool of blood.

Jenna steeled herself and looked up. The two drowned girls stood to the side of her table, silently, patiently waiting. A third figure had joined them. Another drowned girl, fresher than the others, looking no different than someone who'd been out for a long skinny-dip—naked and pale, with wet hair, skin wrinkling on her fingertips. Jenna couldn't see where the blood came from, only that it streamed down the backs of her arms and dripped from her fingertips.

10

"I don't suppose *you'd* care to speak to me either." Jenna tried to sound jaunty, but her voice frayed at the edges. She swallowed and looked away. A deep breath. Then she closed her textbook.

If she really was going crazy, then locking herself away like this wouldn't help. She needed someone else to judge. She needed to be around people. She needed that party.

When she got back to the apartment, Bree was taking a study break, napping on the couch. She hadn't changed her mind about the party, but she was happy that Jenna was going, helping her pick out clothes, making Jenna promise to tell her all about it, then retreating to her books.

As Jenna fixed her hair in the bathroom, Bree came back.

"That's a great shirt," she said. "But it really needs something." She held up her hand. Silver flashed in the light. "Something like this."

From Bree's fingers dangled her Celtic cross necklace, one Jenna had admired many times, teasing that if it ever went missing, Bree knew where to look for it.

When Bree reached to put it on Jenna, she protested, but Bree insisted.

"That shirt screams for a necklace." She grinned as she fastened it around Jenna's neck. "And if it disappears, I know where you live."

Jenna laughed, then glanced at the three drowned girls crowded into the bathroom behind Bree. Was it her imagination or were they eyeing the cross nervously?

"Thanks," she said.

"Anytime. Now go party."

If the necklace had any effect, it was minimal. The girls didn't go away. Didn't even shy away. She'd tried waving the cross at them. Even struck one in the cheek with it. The girl didn't flinch.

By the time Jenna arrived, the party was in full swing. She leapt in, almost hoping someone would say, "You seem a little off, Jen" or give her a strange look and find an excuse to retreat to the other side of the room. No one did.

No one noticed the dead girls, either, and Jenna was forced to admit *that* was really why she'd come to the party—the hope that with all those people around, the booze and dope loosening them up, someone would notice the girls.

As for the dead girls, if they even noticed they were *at* a party, they gave no sign of it. Just stood there, dripping, rotting, bleeding, leaving a trail on the carpet that no one else could see.

Trey was there, too. He'd come with friends and, while he did pop over and say hi, later bringing her a drink, he hung out with his buddies, only smiling and nodding if their eyes happened to meet.

The drink stayed untouched by her elbow, abandoned when she moved on to talk with a couple of girls she knew from high school. All things considered, adding booze to the mix didn't seem wise.

She tried hard to relax, but it wasn't happening. As long as she led the dead girl entourage, there was no way she could just kick back and party. Eventually she gave up, said her good-byes and slipped out.

Jenna paused on the sidewalk, taking a deep breath, icy air scorching her lungs, a bitter breeze bringing tears to her eyes.

Definitely a night for the shortcut home. Common sense, though, kept tugging her toward the roundabout route, along the well-lit roads.

The front door slapped shut.

"Leaving so soon?" a voice called.

She turned to see Trey on the steps. He frowned into the dark night.

"Please tell me you've called for an escort."

She shook her head.

He jogged down the steps. "You shouldn't walk home alone."

She looked at the dead girls and was tempted to say that, unfortunately, she *wasn't* alone.

"Okay, I'll save the speech," he said when she didn't respond. He took a card from his pocket and flashed it. "Luckily, you have a campus escort already here, ready for duty."

"No, that's—"

"I insist. Party sucks anyway. I was just going back to my place to study for midterms. Are you on campus?"

"Just off it." She waved northwest. "But it's a short walk, so you don't have to—"

"—miss much study time. I appreciate that. Come on. We'll take the shortcut."

They walked along the riverbank, talking about the party. Trey admitted his friends had only gone for the booze. He'd mentioned the party and there weren't many going on with midterms coming up, so they'd decided to crash and hang out with the sophomores for an evening.

It was a comfortable conversation, almost enough to make her forget the dead girls. She did glance back now and then, though, hoping they'd vanished. Once, as she twisted, her foot caught on a root. She stumbled. Her shoe slid on the mud. Trey grabbed her around the waist and yanked her back just as the edge of the embankment crumpled under her feet.

"Close call," he said as she stared down into the fast-moving, spring-swollen river.

She tore her gaze away and looked at the drowned girls. Was that what they'd been trying to warn her about? A premonition of danger?

Trey tugged her back onto the bank. "That drink hit you pretty hard."

She nodded, not saying she hadn't touched it. Better for him to think she was tipsy. As they resumed walking, though, he kept his arm around her. She tried, subtly, to slide away from it. His grip tightened. Her heart picked up speed, but when she glanced over, he smiled and said, "Steady there."

She nodded. A few more steps and his hand slid into her back pocket, which definitely *wasn't* okay and when she moved away this time, there was no subtlety about it. He didn't let go, though, fingers biting into her rear, tugging her so close she almost tripped again.

She realized, then, just how empty the riverbanks were, how far away the nearest buildings were. She thought of the drink he'd given her. Spiked with more than just vodka? And that escort card. She hadn't taken a good look at it—didn't even know if they *carried* ID cards.

She glanced at the drowned girls. They were no help, of course, just trailing along behind her like faithful hounds.

Keep going, she told herself. *It's not far now.*

After a few more steps, though, Trey swung in front of her, cutting her short, his other hand going around her waist. When he leaned in, face coming to hers, she backed up so fast she stumbled. He only tightened his grip, chuckling as he held her steady.

He leaned in again and she was ready to kick, scream, bite, whatever it took, but at the last second, he averted his face, lips going to her ear instead.

"About that essay, Jenna? I lied. It sucked."

She stiffened.

He continued, "That's what I was going to tell you earlier. Warn you, but then . . ." He chuckled again, his breath warming her ear. "I couldn't do it. You're too pretty to get a failing grade."

She tried to back out of his arms. He ignored her struggles and kept whispering.

"I noticed on your file that you want to minor in Classics. You can't do it with essays like that. But I'm willing to give you a little . . ." His fingers slid under her shirt, skating over the back of her waist. ". . . assistance. That's all it'll take. A few weeks of tutoring. And, in the meantime, I can make sure you don't fail that essay." He lifted his head then, teeth glittering in the dark as he smiled. "Or I can make sure you do."

Jenna trembled as his mouth lowered to hers. She forced herself to look up at him with terror-filled eyes. When their lips touched, she stood frozen. Then, as he relaxed and closed his eyes, she caught his lip between her teeth and chomped down with everything she had. Blood spurted into her mouth. He let out a yelp. She punched him in the stomach and wheeled to race away, but he caught her by the jacket.

"Stupid bitch!" He swiped his hand across his mouth, blood spraying. "Do you have any idea how many girls at that party would be happy to be out here with me?"

She wrenched away, dancing backward. "Lots, I'm sure. But that's not the way you like it, is it?"

She tried to run. He caught her again, and dragged her to the embankment. She kicked and punched, but he hauled her to the edge and when she looked down at the water racing by, she knew what the dead girls had been trying to tell her.

"That water's ice cold," he said. "You'll be dead before you know which way is up."

She lashed out, her foot hitting him square in the kneecap. His leg buckled. They struggled. She managed to get free and, with one hard, backward kick, knocked him over the edge.

As she raced away, she heard him cursing, scrabbling to get back up the embankment, splashing at the edge of the water.

Jenna didn't stop until she reached her apartment. She paused in the lobby to catch her breath. Only then did she notice the drowned girls, still following.

"It took me a while, but I figured it out." She managed a smile. "Would have been nicer if I'd been a little quicker on the draw, huh?"

They didn't answer. Didn't react. By now she didn't expect them to. She wasn't even sure they were ghosts at all, not in the usual sense. Just spectral images of girls who had died, unable to do anything but, by their presence, warn of impending danger.

Harbingers of death.

She shivered.

"I'm safe now," she said. "You can go."

They followed her up the elevator. Outside her apartment, she stopped again.

"There's more, right? You want to make sure I do something about it. Well, I will. I'm calling the police as soon as I get inside."

No answer. No reaction.

She sighed and opened the door. It was quiet inside. The apartment was tiny, only one shared bedroom and a kitchen/living room combo. Both were dark. She tiptoed to the bedroom door and peeked in.

Bree's bed was empty.

Had she gone out after all? Good. She deserved it. Jenna only hoped she hadn't decided to go to Jackson's party, expecting to catch up with her.

Jenna took out her cell phone. She was about to dial when, in the silence, she picked up a faint *drip. Drip. Drip.* Her gaze shot to the drowned girls. The first was still shedding water, but with a *plip-plop* so familiar Jenna had started to tune it out. This was a different sound . . . coming from a different room.

She stepped back into the hall. Her foot hit a slick spot on the wood and she had to grab the wall to keep from falling. She flipped on the light. There was water on the floor. A tendril stretched from the bathroom door.

"Bree? Bree!"

Jenna raced the few steps to the door. She grabbed the handle. Locked. Twisting it, she threw her shoulder against the wood. The door burst open.

The first thing she saw was the bathroom floor, a puddle of water around the old claw-foot tub. Pink-tinged water.

Drip. Drip. Drip.

Almost reluctantly, her gaze followed the sound to the tub. Water trickled over the side. Bloody water, the tub filled to the brim.

She ran, sliding across the floor.

Bree lay at the bottom of the tub, face barely visible through the red water.

Jenna dropped to her knees, reached in and hauled Bree up as best she could, but as soon as the cold, bloody water enveloped her arms, she knew it was too late.

Bree's head lolled back. Her eyes stared up. Dead eyes. Empty eyes. Eyes Jenna had been looking at all day.

Jenna turned on the drowned girls.

"Why didn't you tell me? Why didn't you warn me!"

Their eyes met hers. Then, the faint outline of a fourth girl materialized behind them, a girl whose dead eyes passed over Jenna without pausing, with no flicker of recognition. Then as one, the harbingers turned and drifted away, off to warn someone else, someone who might understand in time.

THE FOREVER BROTHERHOOD

BY JULIE E. CZERNEDA

brotherhood n. the relationship between brothers; the feeling of kinship with and closeness to a group of other people; an association, society, or community of people linked by a common interest, religion, or trade. *New Oxford Dictionary*

The engineering lecture hall was the largest on campus. Beautiful. New. Bright. With ergonomic seating, wide tables, and a coffee shop by the door.

This was not that lecture hall.

The two math lecture halls were the oldest on campus. They were dark, hollow rooms, with cracked concrete steps leading from the lecture stage to the upper level, each lined with chairs ranging from permanent tilt to full recreation of a medieval torture device. To make the recreation more authentic, attached to the chairs were ridiculously small side tables that swung over laps to trap occupants. When they worked at all.

Worse, the halls were identical and butted against the same corridor, lulling more than a few first year students into believing they sat in the right one – until their triumphant and happy daze was jolted awry by the realization that not only was the prof talking fractals instead of sonnets, but the hot girls in the front row were thus in a different class.

19

The math lecture halls were used for any class between 200 and 350 students, the upper limit having nothing in common with the actual number of functioning chairs. Latecomers sat on the hard steps. These halls were particularly favoured for first year classes. First year night classes. First year night classes having a three hour lecture component. Why? Rumours abounded. Perhaps someone in environmental science was correlating poor lighting, poor seating, and abysmal climate control on student performance. Did overheated brains work faster? Or maybe the psych department was recording the symptoms of sleep deprivation. It was true that by midterm week, pens, pencils, and texts routinely plummeted down the steps, released by oblivious fingers.

The favoured hypothesis postulated the university was torturing certain tenured profs to make them retire sooner – for a disproportionate number of late night lecturers seemed on their way to fossil. Unfortunately, those same lecturers typically appeared wide awake and able to blast out a lecture at hours that made even the rowdiest kinesiology student blanch.

On this night, a damp and dreary Wednesday night, Math Lecture Hall Two, not One (where a lively discussion on the significance of sex to chordates was anticipated but where horrified students encountered a pop quiz on readings they hadn't done), but Two, grudgingly filled with students taking PoliSci 101E. Political Science for 2nd year engineering majors.

Students who filed in and took their seats as though under a death sentence, aware tonight would be worse than usual. There was . . . a guest speaker.

Guest speakers, like chairs, varied in quality. The entertaining ones commanded the bright and gleaming stage of the engineering lecture hall. There might be food – a lure for starving students of any ilk.

Renowned visiting academics held forth in the library concourse to intimate groups of those likely to understand more than three consecutive words, as well as giving public talks in the neighbouring physics rotunda in the evenings. Followed by wine.

Alas, the majority of guest speakers in the math lecture halls were, to put it mildly, a challenge for the average student. They appeared like rotting ghosts in either One or Two, again causing no end of confusion and distress to those students who couldn't tell them apart, and their sudden appearance was tied to things like reports, critiques, and the dreaded attendance marks.

This was all well and good. Earning credit for sitting through a guest lecture, a break from the usual prof, a new voice and vision?

Right.

It was more like having ten marks you desperately needed clutched in the hands of someone who either mumbled for hours or spoke emphatically, with gestures, in an accent completely unrelated to any of the twenty-three you'd come to know on campus. And this if you were able to pay attention for, truth be told, some guest speakers rambled on, prompting snoring, while others hammered at the same point over and over and over again, again prompting snoring. The occasional outburst of passion or profanity rarely affected the end result.

But every so often, just rarely, maybe once in a lifetime . . . a guest speaker lights a spark.

Now a spark didn't appear likely this dreary Wednesday. Especially when the tinder in question consisted of aggrieved engineering students who might have been in the library studying for tomorrow's Calculus exam, thank you very much, if not for the marks glued to perfect attendance at the PoliSci 101E guest lecture series. It could be assumed that few in attendance had scores entering midterm week which would allow them to scoff at a mere 10%.

Students greeted by a shrill: "Hurry up. Get to your seats! They've only given me three hours. If we don't get started immediately, we'll have to go over."

At this dire possibility, five students grasped their books and did an about-face, that desperate look in their eyes meaning only one thing. *Fear of Calculus* had finally overwhelmed them. The rest teetered on the brink of stampede.

"Sit!"

The soprano voice of authority, albeit hoarse with use and probably a few million cigarettes, came in the nick of time.

To be fair, some were already in their seats. For all anyone knew, they always were.

The engineering lecture hall might be locked after hours, locked and cleaned and readied for the next day's classes, but math lecture halls were not. Why? Some believed Physical Resources, those mysterious beings in green allowed to drive on the grass, hoped to tempt furniture-less students to take the old plastic chairs so replacements would make the budget, a foolish notion since unbolting one took the sort of industrial equipment most students did not carry with them and, more to the point, no student would consider the chairs worth the effort. More likely, being used by every department on campus – including the biology club, whose members hadn't twigged to the availability of the back room of the campus pub in three decades – enough sets of keys had been misplaced over the years to remove any value to the locks in the first place.

So it was within reason to find students in a math lecture hall at any given moment.

22

Even students no one knew.

Or wanted to know.

Tonight, as always, a group claimed the uppermost two rows of Math Lecture Hall Two, clumped as far as from both stage and exit to the real world as possible. As always, none appeared to own books or laptops; tonight, metal chains and piercings glittered on black cloth and tattooed skin. In other years, they might have been in hockey jerseys or white tees. The look didn't matter. The thirteen were never seen to arrive. Or to leave.

When anyone noticed them at all, rumours grew. Perhaps they weren't students at all, but the mysterious entity called the Review Board, there to assess lecturer performance. The implied link between poor performance in front of students and tenure provided satisfaction to many.

During Frosh Week, however, rumours took a darker turn. The tale would spread of the very first term of computerized scheduling, and how these students had been scheduled into Math Lecture Hall Two – not for two classes, not for five, every hour of every day and night, never to be free again.

Or graduate.

Of course, no one fell for that. Frosh, clutching their shiny student cards, knew better. Older students felt their own mortality and refused to believe. Still, there were moments when dread crept down a spine, usually while trying to find a comfortable position in one of the plastic chairs. You felt eyes on the back of your skull and shuddered at the thought of being here, forever.

It was, after all, that lecture hall.

Tonight, as always, the thirteen spoke in low tones, with confiding looks. Stiff upthrusts of purple or green hair tipped this way and that.

They were interested in one another, nothing else, and no one was interested in them.

Save the guest lecturer. Dr. Smith, before losing interest, gave the group a sorrowful look.

Her face was prone to sorrow. It was built on it. Heavy brows that sagged in the middle and ends. Deep-set eyes of indeterminate colour. Skin much the same, wrinkled at each junction point. Her short straight hair was out-of-a-box black, capable of absorbing every known form of light. Her mouth was crayon red and turned down at the corners. Some of the red caught in the wrinkles beside her lips. She wore, of course, a dark blue skirt with a hem that dipped to the back, a wrinkled white shirt, and a dark blue cardigan stretched where she tried to tug it over her ample hips. Sensible, unpolished shoes completed the look.

"She's got a better moustache than you, Dougie!"

"Shut up." Dougie, who'd taken engineering in starry-eyed hope of courses like *Better Space Elevator Construction* and *Bridges To Make You Famous*, not that he'd admit it, stepped sideways along the fifteenth row. The seats were fixed to concrete steps wide enough to allow a four-year old child to sit without their knees hitting the head of the person in the next row down. Dougie, tall, lean, and eighteen, balanced his heavy backpack and tried not to imagine how he'd look somersaulting to the feet of the now-pacing Dr. Smith.

The impatient poke from behind didn't help. "Get going!"

Dougie grabbed the back of one of the plastic seats for balance, wincing as it gave under his weight. "Quit that, Putz."

Putz poked him again. In self-defense, Dougie lurched into the nearest seat, swinging his backpack forward and down between his feet in a practiced move that barely brushed the heads of the students in front and below him. He tried the side table – some still worked. Not this one. So he pulled out his Calculus text, some crumpled notes and a pen, then plopped his laptop on top of it all.

He wasn't alone. Dr. Smith watched in steely-eyed silence as student after student found private space in the shadowed top third of the lecture hall – as always, none too close to the group already there. Faces lit from underneath as one by one would-be engineers switched on laptops and concentrated.

Quiet descended. An ominous, waiting hush. If you didn't count the incomprehensible whispers from up and left. Or the growing tappitytaptap, *huuuummmmmm* of active keyboards. There was that faint wail from a set of earplugs in the top back corner. The hall did have superb acoustics.

"If you are quite ready?" Dr. Smith bellowed. "I'm here to edify you on the connections between human nature and political systems, a topic surely of – what are you doing?" This to the three students scrambling to close laptops, pack bags, and edge their unsteady way along the rows to the steps.

"Wrong room." "Sorry!" "'cuse me."

"Frosh," commented someone from midlevel.

Dr. Smith brought both hands in front of her rounded stomach, as if cradling her waist, and rocked back and forth. Back and forth. Back and forth. Dougie lost his focus on a troubling derivation, distracted by the motion. She looked like an android bomb about to explode.

"I do not plan to shout all night," Dr. Smith announced after the doors closed. "Sit in the first five rows or leave. Now."

"Think she means it?" Putz said, his expression one of rapture as he put away his pen.

A book tapped his head. "Yes. So you'd better move down."

Dougie swiveled to look up. "Hey, Bas. Didn't see you there." Not that he was surprised. Bas never cut a class.

Their schedules had thrown the three together from the start. From the choices ahead, they'd likely be together until graduation; had they made any other, they wouldn't have met. Putz knew everyone in rez by the second day and was on his way to knowing everyone on campus, including profs, by their first names, but he sweated math. Dougie swam through math, but had yet to talk to a girl – or prof -- without sounding like an idiot. While Bas?

The dark-eyed student was as brilliant as he was hard to pin down. He didn't use slang or party. Lived off campus with an elderly aunt prone to dollies and dusting. A good guy to have in group work or on your team in sports, just not someone to hang around with.

He made people nervous.

Like now, when Bas obviously knew Putz and Dougie were planning to take the excuse Dr. Smith offered to bail the lecture and study.

Which meant, of course, Dougie couldn't. "Move down, Putz," he grumbled. "Before we get kicked out."

As always, the group topmost, far left, didn't stir from their seats; they never did. They did, however, pay attention as the engineering students thumped their way down to the first five rows. Amused? Impossible to tell, had anyone tried. The group didn't smile. Or laugh.

They always whispered.

The lowermost seats were in better shape than those further back. This minor improvement did nothing to help the fact that those first rows were under the lights from the stage area, allowing Dr. Smith to peer directly into each and every pair of shifting, uncomfortable eyes.

Dougie sighed, doing his best to find a place for his feet that didn't kick either those to either side or the seat in front. Being compressed into five rows meant everyone had to sit side-by-side, making it awkward to find a place for his elbows as well. At least it wasn't winter, when everyone had to cram bulky coats into the limited space. The engineering lecture hall had hooks for coats.

This wasn't that hall.

"Are you brothers?" Dr. Smith demanded.

Every pair of eyes blinked. The silence stretched itself into cramps and the urge to either sneeze or giggle. Neither would have been an acceptable response, given the gimlet-eyed stare Dr. Smith aimed at each student in turn. Having skewered the rest into submission, she stared last and longest at Dougie. "Well," she prompted. "Are you?"

"Am I w-what?" Dougie managed, ignoring the strangled wheeze to his right as Putz tried to control himself.

"Brothers. You. These other two." As he opened his mouth to deny the very suggestion, she raised a crooked finger to stop his answer. "I'm not talking in the biological sense."

"Us? Oh, no," Dougie protested, not needing to turn to see Putz and Bas shaking their heads vehemently.

"You're classmates." She made a show of consulting a piece of crumpled paper drawn from a pocket in her cardigan. "Second year engineering students."

"Until tomorrow's Calculus exam," Putz blurted.

This prompted a chorus of snorts and rueful chuckles. They'd been warned. The midterm would sort those who'd continue from those who might as well drop out now.

Dr. Smith gave a tight smile and surveyed her captives. "You are gathered here, in this place, not by friendship or bonds of shared experience, but by a common purpose. A future goal. To become engineers. Is that a reasonable explanation for your being together?" As she dropped her gaze to Dougie with this question, he felt obligated to nod. "So. You are brothers, as in components of a brotherhood." Her eyebrows met and her lips twisted to one side. "Before the ladies in the room object, sisterhood as a term is equally gender-biased and there's no worthwhile meaning for my purpose in 'personhood' so lump it."

Lump it? Dougie sank as low in his seat as he could. He felt more than heard Putz groan.

They had hours of this to go.

Lump it.

"Now. Let's discuss brotherhoods as a form of non-government organization of overlooked significance to social structures within communities. What interests me are those brotherhoods which arise from the needs of individuals, thus are self-forming, rather than those imposed by outside agencies such as the drafting of young people for military service –"

"Frat houses!" Neighbouring students congratulated their outspoken comrade, who stood and bowed before resuming his slouched curl, feet on the chair below, head barely visible above his knees.

Dr. Smith's face took on an even more sorrowful cast, as if acknowledging her doom as well as theirs. "Yes, we'll be talking about fraternities –" she stopped the rumble of interest by tapping her foot smartly on the hollow stage "– briefly. But I want to consider longer and more lasting goals for a brotherhood than the attaining of panties and beer.

"So. This Calculus midterm." She looked along the first five rows; the topmost three might have been empty. "How many of you aren't ready? Hands, please." She gave a faint smile at the eager up thrust of arms. "Thank you. And no, I don't care.

"What I care about at the moment is the calibre of your brotherhoods. If you've joined a good one, that exam will be a snap. Commit to fools and sluggards, and why bother study at all? Come, come. Surely you all know each other's quality by now. Those you've chosen to sit with will determine whether you succeed or fail. As you will determine their futures."

Clearly, few in the hall had given much thought to the selection of an appropriate brotherhood until this point. The unsubtle swing of heads from side to side would have been comical, had there been any chance those who'd chosen poorly could infiltrate any more successful group by this point in the term. Or their full university career. And who would? With self conscious nods of camaraderie admitted, the students settled back in their seats. Hadn't they'd bonded over such telling moments as tasting the latest batch of purple Jesus and run as a glorious nude pack in the snow between the residences?

They would be friends forever, regardless how abysmally they failed tomorrow's midterm.

"A brotherhood that blends disparate strengths with a commitment to mutual success will be to your advantage," Dr. Smith droned on. "What sort will not?" Her voice wheezed to a stop. The ensuing stare, moving row by row, seat by seat, drummed into the slowest of heads that this was not a rhetorical, ignorable question. This was the worst sort of guest lecturer. One who expected answers. She wasn't to be encouraged. Everyone shrank back in their seats.

Not everyone. Bas leaned forward past Putz, as if Dr. Smith's babble meant something. His hand lifted, palm flat.

Putz shook his head. The rest of the class regarded Bas with horror. Who answered a guest lecturer? Worse, who answered in the first ten minutes? Before a Calculus exam? Dougie whispered, "Put your hand down!"

Not quietly enough. The Stare locked on his face. He felt his cheeks radiate heat.

Bas' dark eyes flicked over his friends, dismissed them both as idiots, then returned to Dr. Smith. "One that fails any member."

The red lips pursed with satisfaction, Dr. Smith whirled to the centremost of the three boards. The engineering lecture hall had screens and panels and lighting and speakers, all at the control of an alert, dedicated AV technician.

This was not that hall.

These boards were pulled down with a hooked stick. And required chalk. Chalk that left dust trails over the stage and, if used to excess, a cloud that lingered in front of the seventh row. Chalk like the thick yellow piece trembling with eagerness between her fingers.

Dougie groaned inwardly. She was going to write everything down. He just knew it.

"Where's the damn stick?" Dr. Smith muttered, bending at the waist in her hunt.

She was remarkably limber.

And had thick ropy veins leering above her black socks.

Dougie eased his spine down as far as he could with his knees locked.

It was going to be a very, very long night.

#

30

Each math lecture hall had a pair of analog clocks, rumoured to have been scavenged from a school house that pre-dated the university on the same site by a century. They hung on the wall, one to the left, and one to the right of the stage. The left clock in Math Lecture Hall Two leered a nightmarishly permanent ten to twelve. The right clock still kept time, but on each sweep, its secondhand would stick at twenty-two after the hour. Students would stare at the motionless hand and wait, hardly daring to breath. And wait. When all hope seemed lost – the lecture to never end – the secondhand would spring to twenty-five, then tick around the rest of its circle. Until twenty-two after the hour came again.

Lecturers, guest or otherwise, were spared secondhand death through the simple expedient of being unable to see either clock from the stage. No matter. If they didn't have a cell or watch to tell time, the growing shuffle of feet and closing of books as students stirred near the end was as good as an alarm clock.

Lecturers who weren't Dr. Smith.

Dougie watched the secondhand stop. Again. At nine o'clock, Smith had launched with enthusiasm into what she called a relevant tangent: the vulnerability of rural politicians to well-organized quilting groups. As far as anyone could tell, she hadn't left it. At nine twenty-five, when students stirred as students do, because the schedule said nine thirty and surely that meant the end, she merely raised an eyebrow. And her voice.

Nine thirty came and went. Putz whimpered.

Dougie scribbled another unreadable line, eyes back on the blurry page in case Smith looked his way. He'd long since lost the topic; words ran through his ears like wind through a bus window. Potent whiffs of fresh hand sanitizer assailed his nose without notice. Showers were optional midterm week; getting sick wasn't. At least the detested smell helped him stay conscious. Gentle snores and the occasional thud of a plummeting book filled the air whenever Dr. Smith paused for breath. She continued, her tone grimmer by the minute.

The second hand stopped at twenty-two.

Putz snored.

Bas and Dougie elbowed him in the ribs simultaneously.

The secondhand jumped to twenty-five.

Nine thirty came and went. Dr. Smith had violated the sacred trust between undergrad and printed schedule. She was running overtime. Bas, who had minimal tolerance for misbehaviour or social excess by anyone, tenured or not, began to pointedly check his cell whenever Smith looked his way.

She stopped looking his way. Her arm pumped like a weight lifter's as she drew sweeping lines across all three boards to connect phrases as readable as hieroglyphs, adding circles and triangles and nonsensical underlines. Chalk dust streaked her cardigan and coated her hair. It hung in clouds like a bar haunted by smokers' past.

At nine forty-five, the girl in the rightmost seat of the second row bolted for the exit, careening down the steps, hair flying behind her. The air rushing through the opened door was like an elixir. Students who'd been slack-jawed and half asleep moments before suddenly chattered like bright-eyed birds, packing their bags with reckless abandon. Freedom beckoned, if only the freedom to stay up all night to cram Calculus. Dr. Smith's red lips flapped indignantly, whatever objection she raised lost beneath the drum of moving feet. The escape was on.

"Give it a minute," Bas shouted in Dougie's ear, the reason obvious. Five rows of students spilled down the concrete steps at once, students who'd been trapped for over three hours in small plastic chairs of dubious quality. Those who didn't stumble, staggered. Broken limbs were avoided because you could only fall so far without landing on someone else anyway. Several someones.

Their haste, as Bas had predicted, was in vain.

In the engineering lecture hall, a series of wide doors swung open to the corridor beyond, each with inset glass to prevent collisions.

This was not that lecture hall.

The math lecture halls had two doors, only one of which actually opened. Without windows. An incautious exit would severely damage anyone making a simultaneous and incautious entry. Worse, it was physically impossible for more than three students to squirt through at once.

Dougie, Putz, and Bas weren't the only ones to wait for a better opportunity.

The thirteen who had been as far from the stage and door as possible sat in the middle seats of the sixth row, pale eyes bright.

As if they'd always been there.

In the second row, Dougie worked his feet from under the seat in front and stood, stretching with a relief close to pain. "My place?"

"What for?" Putz said with an air of gloom. "The exam's in twelve hours. It's hopeless. I vote for beer."

Bas snapped a light finger against the Putz's blond head. "You heard the good doctor. We're a brotherhood. We won't let you fail."

"It's too late for a brain transplant."

Dougie chuckled. "What you need is caffeine."

"What you need," Dr. Smith interjected from the stage, the hall having superb acoustics, "is to learn not to leave studying to the night before." She clutched a mass of notes and books; perhaps she'd expected a demand for extra reading. Guest lecturers were known for extravagant hopes. Dougie made sure he didn't look interested.

Bas grinned down at her. "Did you?"

Too-red lips twitched, the folds to either side deepening. Almost a real smile. "Me to know." Dr. Smith adjusted her armload. "Till next week, gentlemen." The anticipation in her eye was pure evil. "I'm covering Dr. Paul's intro to human geography series. Paternity leave. Triplets, poor bastard."

She headed for the exit. Her footsteps rang on the hollow stage floor like a tolling bell.

"We have her . . ." Putz swallowed hard ". . . for the rest of the term? Kill me now."

"Knows her stuff," Bas commented, drawing incredulous looks. "Well, she does." Defensively.

They were side-stepping along the row to the stairs when Dougie realized two things. First, Dr. Smith had paused to hold the door open. Clearly this was to goad them to move faster. Clearly, they had to obey. He moved faster, trying to catch up to Putz and Bas. He wasn't going to be the last one out.

Second?

He would not, in fact, be the last student to leave Math Lecture Hall Two.

Thirteen students sat in the fourth row.

How had he missed seeing them till now? The designs writhing at wrist and neck alone should have caught his eye. Dougie might possess no tattoos of his own – in part because he did possess a father who loathed them and in part because he himself loathed needles – but he wanted one. Or two. At least the Gates of Moira on his lower back.

The students weren't getting up to leave. They didn't speak. They only looked.

At him.

Their eyes were chips of glass caught by the sun. Trapped in reflections, Dougie froze, one foot on the next step. His blood crawled through his heart, thick and reluctant, each beat slower than the one before.

A tug on his shoulder strap broke the spell: Putz, swiping his cell again. "I'm getting pizza," his friend said, as if the world was normal and safe. "Ooh, and let's get garlic sticks."

With a grateful shudder, Dougie blinked and looked away. His arms and legs prickled. Pins and needles. "Sat too long," he muttered. He flexed his numb hands as best he could around his books. They should toss a football before studying.

He took the last few steps to the floor, aware of a constant pressure on the back of his neck.

They looked.

At him.

Creeps.

He wouldn't look back and give them the satisfaction.

#

Finals were written in the gyms, at solitary tables distributed on a grid of disturbing exactness, with chairs that broadcast the slightest movement. Midterms, on the other hand, were held in classrooms; classrooms that otherwise never had to fit the full complement of a course's registered students. When hundreds of previously invisible students showed up, schedules got ugly. A silent, but nonetheless bitter struggle continued between the giants – Psych 101 and Econ 101 – for the engineering lecture hall. Negotiating skills meant little against such tactics as preemptive sign placement. Regardless, what mattered to students the day of a midterm was where theirs was to be held.

Putz closed *Calculus* 14th Edition with a thump that drew frantic looks then scowls from those standing or sitting along the corridor walls. Unwise to disturb the concentration of the desperate. Friendships failed. Breakups were common. But Dougie did the same, if more quietly. What they didn't know by now, didn't matter.

Bas nodded. He leaned peacefully against the beige cinder blocks, one foot crossed over the other, a picture of sublime confidence guaranteed to chill the blood of lesser students. His text, if he'd brought it, hadn't left his backpack. He wore the same clothes as everyone else: jeans and a tee, but his aunt ironed them every chance she had. Everyone else was thoroughly rumpled, having either slept in their clothes, or not slept at all.

Rumpled and in need of soap. Dougie stood straighter to elevate his nose, though to be fair, he should have showered too.

"76%," Putz said in a low voice. "Any less and there's no point coming back tomorrow."

"You'll be fine." Bas stirred. "Finally. They're posting the room list."

Like chum tossed to starving sharks, the harried TA was instantly surrounded. He barely managed to staple the list to the board before being pushed aside. Students peeled away as they found what they were looking for, some breaking into a run. Exam proctors had a deplorable habit of starting on time even if no one was there yet to write.

Putz and Bas waited for Dougie, a head taller, to scan the list and find their section.

Fingers crossed for a biology lab – the only place where he could stretch out his long legs, Dougie looked.

He looked again, heart pounding in his chest, midterm forgotten.

Math Lecture Hall Two.

#

Writing an exam in one of the math lecture halls was not the worst thing that could happen to a student. Drunken idiots could fill your room floor-to-ceiling with leaky water balloons on the coldest night of the year. At Xmas, your parents could give your bed to a cranky great-uncle you hadn't known existed (and your game system to a cousin you did). Or your hard drive could crash the instant you were finally ready to print the most important report of the year, the one you'd always meant to back up.

Make it Math Lecture Hall Two, and it was the worst. Dougie had never experienced cold fingers of dread playing with his bones.

Until now.

He balked at the door, causing a minor pileup. "I can't –"

Several hands proved otherwise. Dougie staggered into the lecture hall. He stepped out of the flow, waiting his chance to leave.

"Space yourselves out," the proctor said without looking up from the table on the stage. "Empty seat to either side."

His friends stopped with him. "What's wrong?" Bas asked.

Putz blanched. "Isn't this the right room?"

"Section 4, Calculus," the proctor intoned, on cue. Four students scrambled from their seats and ran for the door.

"Right room." Putz shrugged and headed for the steps.

Bas stayed where he was. "What is it?"

An impossible question. Dougie didn't know himself. He forced himself to look up.

The top third of the lecture hall wasn't dim, it was dark. The proctor hadn't bothered to turn on those lights. The rows were marked by vague suggestions of chairs. Dougie couldn't tell if they were empty – or full. He couldn't tell if he saw or only imagined glints of reflected light.

When he blinked to clear his eyes, they were gone.

The lit portion contained nothing more terrifying than the classmates he'd had for the past six weeks. Granted, some faces were less familiar than others. A few hadn't bothered coming since the first day. Why come now was one of those mysteries of the human mind, right up there with a belief in personal immortality and why not snowmobile across a lake in December?

"Who are you looking for?"

"I don't know," he admitted.

"Take a seat." The proctor began handing out exam papers. "Leave them face down until I say to start."

Papers began flipping over. Voices died away. The proctor hurried.

The midterm. Calculus. Dougie focused with an effort. "Good luck, Bas."

"You too."

The class settled, other than those forced to move when their side tables wouldn't pull out. The left-handed tables, being less used, worked better and were in demand. Dougie eyed one, but moved over to let Bas take it. He couldn't contort himself enough to fit anyway.

"Two hours." The proctor, having done her duty, walked back to her table and opened a book, discouraging questions had any planned to ask. No one would. The disruption caused by walking between the cramped rows only to answer "yes, 'pick two of the following' means you don't have to do all three," would not be forgiven.

The math lecture hall took on that air of silent communion Dr. Smith had so longed to hear, except for the occasional whispered expletive as students hit question 5b and realized the so-called optional section of Chapter Ten wasn't so optional after all.

Dougie rolled his head on his shoulders, trying to shake the odd headache. It was more pressure than pain, cold and hard at the base of his skull. Not the exam. That was a gift straight from the text. Including 5b. To his right, Putz laboured steadily, making little happy grunts. To his left, Bas answered questions as quickly as he could move pen across paper. Student after student sat back and stretched, their posture going from strained to relieved. Which wasn't completely wise. At the halfway mark, someone snored gently. The proctor smirked as she read.

Dougie reached the end of the exam. He checked his answers. Twice. There was nothing left to distract him – other than Putz, who fidgeted when thinking. Fidgeted and chewed the end of his pen.

Were the creeps here? Were they still staring at him? Was that what he felt?

He had to know. Pretending to stretch, Dougie risked a quick glance behind.

Fifteen neat rows of students rose to the line of darkness, jean-covered knees together, heads down, feet on the floor for once. Every other seat was empty. It was a midterm.

Every other seat should have been empty.

But wasn't.

Dougie's heart heaved in his chest, trapped by nightmare.

The thirteen filled every other seat: five in the row immediately behind him, four above that, four above that. Why didn't anyone notice? It was a midterm!

The thirteen weren't writing the exam, like those they sat between. This close, sameness overwhelmed difference: dyed spikes on black hair, torn black tees, chains from jeans, piercings and tattoos on skin. Leather sandals, worn ones.

They weren't writing. They looked at him, pale eyes of ruined glass, taking life from the lights. With each breath that fled Dougie's lungs, they came closer and closer – or did the normal world fade back? They smelled strange. No. Familiar. New textbooks, that was it. Promising, fresh. Before being lugged in a backpack with gym clothes, being dropped on tables, being read and reread wore the newness away.

Dougie felt his blood thicken, could almost hear the strain of his heart to move it. The closest of the thirteen smiled.

Somehow, Dougie shut his eyes. Somehow he managed to turn his back on them, keep his eyes shut, draw deep, shuddering breaths.

Minutes crawled under his skin, sank into his bones.

He refused to open his eyes. They'd have him if he did. He knew it. Whatever they were.

#

"Psst. Dougie." A nudge followed the whisper. "Wake up. The exam's over." Another, stronger nudge.

He'd fallen asleep.

Dougie shuddered. A nightmare, that was all. Light-headed with relief, he opened his eyes and looked towards Putz, who was grinning happily at him.

A shape grew solid between them, tattooed and dark.

Dougie whirled towards Bas, only to find one of the nightmares already there, looking back at him. More were in front. He didn't need to turn to know he was surrounded.

They had him. Looked at him.

At him.

And smiled.

He couldn't move, couldn't speak. Air became heavy in his lungs; breathing an effort.

The one who blocked Putz from sight offered him a sheet of paper, pastel green stripes on white. The sides were rough, the print dot matrix. A schedule.

Gooseflesh rose on his arms. It was true, then.

The thirteen were trapped here, in Math Lecture Hall Two. Forever.

As he would be the instant his fingers touched the paper. He'd join them.

Dougie would have wept, if they'd left him tears.

On every side, students stood and walked down the steps, murmuring content or discontent, handing in their papers. Soon, the hall would be empty of life.

Dougie watched in horror as his hand lifted at their command, as it reached –

"Bas. D'you see Dougie leave?" Putz, puzzled, looking *through* him.

They whispered cheerfully among themselves; they'd taken his voice.

His fingers were about to touch –

"That's weird." Bas leaned forward *through* one of the thirteen. "His exam's still here." He frowned. "Guess we'd better hand it in –"

Later, Dougie wasn't sure what happened. Had Bas reached for the exam and missed? Had he suddenly seen what was happening and sacrificed himself? Or had the thirteen simply found a better victim?

Whatever happened, his friend's hand closed, not on Dougie's Calculus midterm, but on the ghostly schedule above it.

And at that instant, Bas was gone.

"Whew," Putz exclaimed. "Glad that's over. I'm buying!"

"Bas!" Dougie jumped to his feet. "Bas!"

"What?" A student, halfway out the door, stopped to look back. His head was topped with green-dyed spikes. Chain looped at both hips and piercings sparkled at chin and eyebrow. His eyes were a rich, dark brown against his pale skin, skin peppered with black and red tattoos from wrist to sleeve, and up both sides of his neck. His lips pulled from gleaming teeth. "Did I forget something?"

It wasn't possible. Dougie whirled to the top row. No eyes glinted back.

"Our mistake," Putz replied, scowling meaningfully at Dougie.

The student who answered to "Bas" gestured his opinion and walked out of the hall.

Free.

It wasn't possible. Bas couldn't have changed places with one of the trapped.

"Since when do we drink with Bas?" Putz shook his head. "You heard Dr. Smith. Pick the right brotherhood or else. Now can we out of here? Gives me the creeps, being last out of a room. Especially this one."

Dougie picked up his exam. It wasn't possible.

But it was that lecture hall.

#

The new optometry lecture hall was the largest on campus. Beautiful. New. Bright. With touch screens and swivel chairs. And a food court beside the entrance.

This was not that lecture hall.

One door didn't open. The other did. Yumi pulled it wide, then hesitated. The lights were off. The dark didn't bother her, but the air smelled strange. Like new textbooks.

Must be where the bookstore kept the extras in the month before class. She shrugged and felt for the lighting panel. "If you don't mind, Yumi?" she muttered to herself, doing a credible version of Dr. Carl's accent. "I left the laptop behind again." He'd leave his head behind if it wasn't attached.

Optometry lecture hall had skylights with remote controlled shades, plus individual lights for every student. Even the old engineering lecture hall had computerized lighting controls, with leds to mark the panels.

This was Math Lecture Hall Two.

Yumi's fingers found cold flat metal, with three protruding toggles. "Place is a museum," she commented as she flipped them.

She walked on the stage towards the podium, footsteps echoing, then began unplugging the laptop.

It wasn't that she heard anything. What would she hear in an empty room? But something made her look over her shoulder.

Thirteen students sat in the first row. Neat, tidy students, with pressed jeans and tees. The weird kind of students, who showed up early, and sat waiting for wisdom. As if.

"I didn't see you come in –" her voice trailed away. They were too much alike.

They looked at her, eyes of glass caught by the sun.

At her.

Then one held out a piece of paper.

And smiled.

PROSPERO'S GHOST

BY KIMBERLY FOOTTIT & MARK LESLIE

McMaster University - 1964

Dr. Marshall Emerson lost his balance as a student brushed past him in the stairwell, almost knocking the withered, leather-bound text out of his hand. Clutching the book to his chest, Emerson fell to one knee, sending a sharp pain up his side. With a grunt of annoyance, he checked the precious book to make sure it had not been damaged; he would sooner fall down the stairs than let it come to any harm.

"Sorry Professor Prospero," the youth said over his shoulder as he vaulted up the stairs. "I'm late for class."

"Rapscallion!" Emerson watched the youngster with the t-shirt and bell-bottom pants disappear through the doorway to the main floor of the library. "Always rushing. Never pausing for deep thought or study."

Still on one knee, Emerson looked at the collection of Shakespeare's plays in his hand. The pain in his bones receded quickly when his eyes rested on the rare tome.

This single volume of Shakespeare's plays represented much of his life's work and focus. And though he thought his simple alliterative nickname was immature, he allowed a small part of him to warm with pride whenever he heard it.

"Professor Prospero, indeed," he said, shaking his head and briefly allowing a smile to cross his lips.

The stairwell door opened again and the smile left as fast as it had appeared as a library assistant, this one dressed properly for an academic setting, rushed to help him. "Dr. Emerson," she said. "Are you okay? Let me help you up."

McMaster University - Present Day

Richard Hamill pulled the text from the display shelf, closing and locking the glass case. He turned the book over in his gloved hand, caressing the withered leather cover.

"I'm amazed at how well this has stood the test of time," he said to the young blond man beside him. "Look at how solid and sturdy the spine and binding still are."

"It seems the perfect candidate for the Kirtas scanner," the young man, Matthew Phillips, said, reaching for the book.

Richard held the text away from his reach. "Your gloves," he insisted.

While he watched Matthew put them on, Richard said, "This particular book was owned by none other than the world renowned Shakespearean scholar, Dr. Marshall P. Emerson.

"It's an 1861 reprint of the first folio edition of Shakespeare's plays and could easily fetch enough money to completely re-equip the William Ready Division of Archives and Research Collection here at McMaster."

"Wow. Really?"

"Absolutely. But I'd sooner die than see this book lost or sold, which is why I'm delighted we have the ability to scan and create a digital replication of it from which print on demand versions can be made."

"It allows others the ability to appreciate the text without having to handle the original," Matthew added.

"Exactly." Richard was always surprised at how the reverence for the printed word remained intact in someone so young during such technologically advanced times. "These archives aren't about the monetary value of the texts, but more about the cultural significance," the older man added.

And this one held plenty.

"On top of its standing as the first reliable printing of twenty of Shakespeare's plays in 1623, this book is held in regard from its final ownership by McMaster's own Dr. Emerson," Richard continued.

"Professor Prospero,"Matthew grinned, unable to hold back and wanting to display his knowledge. "The leading expert on *The Tempest* for over thirty years, and controversial in his proclamation that it was an example of one of Shakespeare's finest tragedies, despite the more popular supposition of the play being a comedy."

"Indeed he was," Richard said, bemused at how Matthew sounded as though he were reciting the facts straight from Wikipedia.

"Did you ever meet him?" the young man asked.

"No. I joined the university six years after he died."

"So you never witnessed if the rumours were true."

"The rumours?" Richard said, fighting the shiver crawling up his spine.

"That he carried this book with him no matter where he went."

Richard relaxed. "Oh, that. Yes. Yes, apparently it's true. He was said to be a difficult man, not love by his colleagues; yet when he passed on, his entire collection of books, including the much-adored text he always carried around campus was bequeathed to the library archives."

"And," Matthew said, his eyes brimming with curiosity, "what about the *other* rumours?"

Richard felt his shoulders tense again. "What *other* rumours?"

"The legend of Prospero's Ghost."

He averted his eyes from the young man. "Hogwash."

"Really? I've heard that the ghost of Dr. Emerson has been seen wandering the library halls endlessly searching for his lost book. You mean you've never seen him?"

"No," Richard said, his eyes not returning to his assistant. "No. Never. Those are just silly stories."

McMaster University – 1970

On his first week of work at McMaster, Richard Hamill not only saw a ghost for the very first time in his life, but he heard it, too.

Hamill was making the rounds on a Thursday night, ensuring the top floor of the library was cleared and that any books left in the study carrels were placed on the "to be shelved" carts in the main aisle. Though it was his first week, he'd become fond of the late shift and the wonderful quiet and solitude that came at the end of a long and busy day.

As he was passing an aisle he thought he saw someone out of the corner of his eye, just off to the left. It appeared to be an older man with grey hair in a dark jacket crouching to look at the books on the shelf second from the bottom.

Hamill turned on his heel and headed down the aisle prepared to politely ask the patron to retrieve their books and proceed to the checkout downstairs.

But there was nobody there.

He took a few steps forward to stand in front of the shelves where he thought he'd seen the figure crouching.

This was the drama section. The second shelf from the bottom held Shakespeare's works. Hamill had been in the section not two hours earlier, having resorted the previously unordered books.

But they were strewn about again. A complete mess, as if a child had been searching for something and been unable to find it.

He was furious. He was certain the figure he had seen had messed up the books. Dashing down the aisle, he looked left, then right.

On the periphery of his vision, a scrawny grey haired figure shuffled by on his left, quickly disappearing behind the shelves of the aisle he'd just been in.

"Excuse me!" Hamill said, racing in that direction, unashamed of the loudness of his voice in such a quiet place.

But, as before, when he got to the end of that aisle, nobody was there.

He looked left and right.

The stacks were quiet and still.

Then, just as he was about to head back to the mess and tidy it for the second time that night, he heard a distinct low voice echo across the library, coming from the drama aisle he'd just vacated.

"All . . . all lost, quite lost . . ."

The voice faded in and out like a radio tuned to a strange station from another world. At the same time the words reached his ears, a cool chill, not unlike a stiff fall breeze, settled over him.

But in the same manner the words faded, so too did the chill, leaving Richard Hamill alone in the library to mark that day, April 23rd, as the start of what would later become a life-long passion of studying Dr. Marshall P. Emerson.

McMaster University – Present Day

Placing the book carefully on the Kirtas APT 2400 scanner, Matthew reached up to adjust the focus of the top left camera.

While disappointed that Dr. Hamill hadn't stayed with him, as he had more questions and enjoyed listening to tales about the university's history from his mentor, he also found joy in the solitude offered by his role. Slipping the ear buds back on, he pressed play on his mp3 player and then adjusted the attachments that would hold the pages flat while they were scanned.

As Matthew turned toward the keyboard to enter specifications into the software that ran the machine, he didn't hear the creak of the door opening behind him.

He'd just entered the keystrokes to begin the process that would capture a digital image of each page, then carefully turn the pages until the entire book was photographed -- a process that took no more than about fifteen minutes -- when a shadow fell over him.

Matthew turned to see who was there.

#

It had been a long day at the library. Nancy Irving, rubbing the back of her neck with a tired hand, headed into the special collections section. Students could be so demanding some days. There was just one more book to return before finally calling it a day.

As she passed by the scan room, she noticed the light was on. Knowing Dr. Hamill was in his office, she could only assume that Matthew Phillips was still in there, tinkering around with the library's new toy. She stopped and checked her watch. It was well past Matthew's finishing time. She sighed. For such a bright boy, he could be so absentminded. If it wasn't his pass card, it was his water bottle or his glasses. Now it seemed his forgetfulness had moved onto leaving the lights on.

When Nancy entered the room, the machine was humming. She frowned as she noticed that the book still in the machine was quite old. This had to be more than just carelessness on Matthew's part. Dr. Hamill spoke so highly of him, and she had personally seen the boy with the books. He was always so careful.

She was about to reach for the mouse, to turn off the screen saver and start the shut down process when the figure in the corner caught her attention.

The young man was pushed into the corner, as though backing away from something until the walls had stopped his progress. The body was pale and rigid, but it was the look of sheer terror on Matthew Phillips' face that froze the scream building in Nancy Irving's throat.

He was dead.

Yet still standing – rigid, like a stone statue.

#

Dr. Richard Hamill ignored the carriage clock on his book shelf as it chimed the late hour. Without family to go home to, his office had been his refuge after many a trying day, but there was no peace tonight.

He stared into the amber liquid that swirled in the short square glass in his hand. It was usually a calming movement, meant to still the mind, but instead it just brought up more questions.

The police had long removed the body of poor Matthew Phillips and were now finishing up their crime scene investigation. He should be down there, making sure they didn't damage any of the precious and fragile editions that lay in the collection, but he couldn't bring himself to enter those rooms. Not yet.

Nancy Irving had been given a strong sedative and taken home by her sister who worked in the campus bookstore. Of all the people in the library, it would have to be the most sensitive and kindly of women to find a body. Had it been Mora Collins, the slightly gothic intern in the map room, perhaps there wouldn't have been quite the kerfuffle. Richard sighed. With Nancy's dramatics, it was guaranteed that the entire campus would know the elaborate version of the grisly discovery before the morning papers hit the doorsteps.

But it wasn't the bad press Richard Hamill feared. It wasn't the badgering of the campus and city police that pushed him to pull out his secret bottle from the bottom drawer of his desk and seek solace in its amber glow.

It was that book.

Professor Emerson's book of Shakespeare. That was the volume found in the machine by Nancy Irving before she turned and saw Matthew's horrified face. The computer had long since completed its scan before the young man was discovered. The information now waited for transfer to the bookstore so the book could be printed out on their new fangled book machine.

Professor Prospero's favorite volume. The jewel of his collection.

Richard took a swig of his drink, closing his eyes as it coated the heavy spot in his belly with a layer of warmth. But it didn't penetrate the feeling; the dread that had started growing there ever since Matthew had expressed an interest in the book's history.

Prospero had loved that book so, and now it seemed he had come back to reclaim it.

Richard raised his glass to the dim light around him.

"Welcome home, Marshall. Welcome home."

McMaster University - 1964

Alistair Rogers straightened his tie for the umpteenth time while he waited for Dr. Emerson – his two o'clock appointment. He wasn't sure why, but Professor Prospero had always intimidated him. It was laughable really, a man as old and frail as Emerson making him feel like he was a naughty schoolboy. The two men had started off on the wrong foot when the librarian had foolishly asked to touch the professor's precious volume of Shakespeare. The affront had carried through their relationship no matter how accommodating or ingratiating Rogers had tried to be.

That was about to change. He was sure of it.

Then there was a knock at his door and the eminent Professor was before him.

"Dr. Emerson," Rogers stood and came around his desk, hand outstretched. "I'm so happy you could meet me today."

"*Mr*. Rogers," the older man greeted, emphasizing the mister in his usual disdainful tone. He put out his hand and allowed it to be shook, but it was clear that it was a polite social gesture only.

Rogers chose to ignore the attitude and waved a hand to the empty chair in front of his desk. "Please sir, have a seat."

Emerson sat with a rickety grace, putting his worn leather briefcase on the floor with delicate care.

"Well Professor, I'll get right to the point," Rogers began, settling into his own chair. "As you may have heard the library has just acquired the new Xerox 2400. It's the latest in high volume copying technology. We now have the ability to preserve some of our oldest texts so we don't have to handle the originals and can make them available to a much wider student base for research purposes. We would be most honoured if we could borrow your volume of Shakespeare's works for the inaugural copy."

Rogers took a breath, waiting for the pleased, perhaps flattered, reaction to his proposal.

The silence was long as Emerson's face turned a deep hue of scarlet.

"I was unaware this institution was supporting mass copyright infringement," Professor Emerson finally replied, his tone cold, almost horrified. Reflexively, he reached for the briefcase, bringing it to his lap.

Rogers noticed the movement and guessed the edition in question was within its depths. "It's Shakespeare, sir. His work is in the public domain. It belongs to the world now, and is not restricted by modern copyright laws. None of the classics are." The librarian noted Emerson's

54

hold on the briefcase, the wringing of the bag's straps under gnarled white knuckles. "I assure you, no harm will come to the book."

Emerson rose, clutching the bag to his chest. "It is not merely a *book*, Mr. Rogers. This edition is a precious treasure. I certainly wouldn't expect you to comprehend its value."

Rogers stood as well. This was not going well and he had, yet again, offended the sensitive man. "But surely, Professor Emerson, you recognize the significance of making such a classic available to everyone."

"Such classic, unique editions should *not* be available to everyone!" Emerson turned to leave.

"With all due respect sir, Shakespeare wrote for the masses. It would be a shame to deny this generation such a treasure."

The professor turned back. "Shakespeare wrote for royalty, Mr. Rogers. And the masses of Elizabethan England were far more civilized and worthy of such art than the barbarous hordes of today with their long hair and loose clothing and rock and roll. Good day sir!"

The slamming of the door behind him punctuated his departure.

Rogers sighed as he sat back in his chair. His colleagues had laughed at him when he had made the suggestion at the last board meeting. They warned him against approaching the crotchety old eccentric, especially about anything regarding his precious volume of Shakespeare. He hated hearing "I told you so." Rumour had it that the old man was nearing retirement. Picking up the receiver of his phone and dialing the extension number of Frank Letts, the board chair, Rogers thought that day couldn't come soon enough.

McMaster University - Present Day

Alan Lester moved the mouse, manipulating the icon on the screen and clicking the button to start the next print job. He looked at his watch as the Espresso Book Machine started spitting out printed pages into the collector tray. Titles bookstore had been closed for a couple of hours and he was just over half done the order. All the drama at the library had delayed the transfer of the file, making him pull a late shift to get the copies needed for the students.

He sighed. That poor kid. He couldn't even begin to imagine what the parents must be going through. Didn't want to. Right now his own son would be out of the tub, a nightly pre-bedtime bath before heading off to visit the sandman. It was the best part of the day for Alan. Stretched out on the bed, his young son curled up under the covers, sharing a story or two. He couldn't imagine not ever doing that again.

The printer stopped and the carriage hummed to life, ready for the next step in the printing process.

Alan checked his watch again. With over half the order of the book already waiting in receiving, maybe he would get out a couple more copies and then call it a night. It wouldn't be the entire order, but he could easily come in early and print off the rest. Students never came into the store first thing in the morning anyway.

He was just about to write a note to Patricia Irving, explaining the missing texts, when he heard the distinct sound of shuffling through the book stacks. He frowned, paused in his movement, listened for the sound again. When nothing came, he shrugged it off. He knew he was in the store alone. Had been for hours.

He picked up the pen again, and heard the noise, this time closer.

"Hello?" he called out, turning from the machine, pen still in hand. No reply. No noise.

He chuckled at his own ridiculous behaviour. He really had to stop reading those horror novels before bed. He stopped when the noise came again.

This time, he didn't call out, but moved, walking slowly towards the sound.

Alan turned the corner, struck by the sight of an older man, slim and gangly looking in his grey trousers and dark tweed blazer.

"Excuse me sir, how did you get in here?" Alan asked, surprised at the steadiness of his own voice despite the rapid thudding of his heart.

The man turned, revealing a haughty facial expression dominated by dark blazing eyes behind silver rimmed glasses.

"He that dies, pays all debts," he said in an even voice.

Alan frowned. "Sir?" he asked. "Do you know where you are?"

"In the company of the Bard," came the reply.

The bookstore employee looked at the sign above the closest bookshelf and realized they were indeed standing in the Shakespeare section of the store.

He thought about it. While the store was cleared out by the closing staff, it was entirely possible for them to have missed one person, quietly loitering in an out of the way section such as this. Hidden away among the stacks, the poor man could have been locked in all night.

"We've been closed for quite some time, sir. Is there someone I can call to come and get you?"

"Hell is empty and all the devils are here."

Alan frowned again. It was obvious the man was quoting Shakespeare, but he couldn't remember which one of the plays the words came from. Despite his theatre background, the Bard had never been his strong suit.

Deep in thought, he didn't notice the older man's approach until he was close enough to touch. Alan started, dropping his pen on the floor, suddenly frozen with the chill of the air around him.

The man bent down with a rickety grace. Where he would have brushed the younger man's legs, there was only a cool breeze. He was speaking as he rose up.

"You taught me language; and my profit on't is I know how to curse . . ."

Alan, wide eyed and shocked, groped blindly for the source of the pain in his neck. His hand rested on his pen, thrust into his throat by a man that seemed like he had barely enough strength to stand. He tried to pull it out, but the flow of blood was too swift, and he felt the power and will drain from his own body. He slid to the floor, his last sight and sound coming from the old man, his figure shimmering with his last words.

". . . the red plague rid you for learning me your language."

#

Patricia Irving yawned as she pushed the big blue cart laden with texts down the deserted hallway. Despite the fact that she wasn't a morning person, she had to admit to herself that this was the best part of her day. The university was largely deserted at eight am, only the occasional groggy student shuffling to class met her in the hall.

She reached for the Tim Horton's cup on the cart, taking a careful sip as she walked. Usually that was all she needed – a coffee and a cigarette to face the day. This morning was different, however, having just finished her fourth cigarette and was now on her third extra large double double. Her husband would have a fit if he knew, but luckily she had left him to watch Nancy and drove herself into work that morning. What he didn't know wouldn't kill him.

She cringed at her involuntary choice of words. Poor Nancy. Normally her sister was someone who had a flair for melodrama, but last night her inconsolable fear and grief was genuine after finding that unfortunate Phillips boy. Patricia loved books, especially a good thriller, but after having heard the details of an incident so close to home in all their chilling glory, she was looking forward to shelving the business books rattling on her cart.

The elevator's final stop boomed, echoing into the high ceilings of the auxiliary bookstore commonly referred to as The Tank. It was a large space in the sub basement of one of the Arts buildings, once a water reservoir before the bookstore took possession of it in the late seventies. Cold and sterile, it had become Patricia's second home since she became textbook buyer in the early eighties. It was humid in the summer and cold in the winter, murals of sea life painted on the walls making it no less gloomy. Dust bunnies conspired in every corner and the fluorescent lights hummed overhead constantly. Still she loved it at this time of the day. Quiet and deserted, with only half the lights lit.

She left the lights as they were, knowing the cashier would turn them all on when she came down in a half an hour and another sales day would begin. Until then it would be her and the books, exactly the way she liked it.

Patricia flicked on the radio as she put her purse and coffee down on the text desk at the back of the store. Coffee alone wasn't going to keep her awake this morning after a night of soothing her excitable sister. The station sputtered through static before the tinny refrain of a song came through the speakers. It was the oldies station and Patricia smiled and hummed along as the music took her back to her youth.

In this manner, the business books came off the cart in no time. Accessing the computer, Patricia punched in the ISBN of the smaller paperback stacked on the bottom shelf of the cart. She frowned when she realized it was a Print On Demand book ordered for a course and half that order was missing.

After a futile search for a note of explanation, Patricia stood, trying to recall if she saw something on the floor in receiving. She sighed, remembering nothing and silently kicked herself for not making a stop at the EBM desk before picking up the cart and heading to the tank. The books were already being asked for by students eager to begin their studies, so Patricia pushed the cart to the appropriate shelf, making a mental note to send those students who didn't get a copy fast enough to Alan Lester. Let the store's Book Manager take the complaints.

As she maneuvered the cart between the high metal shelves filled with texts, the air seemed to chill. Patricia shivered, frowning as she pushed. It was only early October and while there was an autumn nip in the air that morning, it shouldn't be this cold, even in the sub basement.

Methodically, she began to stack the books on the appropriate shelf, trying to convince herself that the air wasn't getting colder with every text. When the last copy was in her hands, she looked down, her frown deepening as she read the cover. It was a folio edition of the works of Shakespeare.

From 1861.

The frown slid from her face as a picture of the original cover popped into her head. A book, worn and withered, grasped in the gnarled fingers of old hands, shoved into her face over forty years before. She remembered the day quite clearly, one of her first as a part time general books employee at the bookstore. She was as green as they come then, full of a passion for books. She never dreamed that she would make a career out of her part time job, and while she didn't regret her decision to stay, that one day had almost pushed her to the door. That wretched old man.

And that book.

The lights flickered, and the chill in the air grew as Patricia Irving stood frozen to the spot, still holding the book.

She never noticed the pale hand reach out for her shoulder.

"Morning, Pat," the cashier said, jumping a little and giggling when the older woman started. "Sorry, I didn't mean to scare you."

Patricia forced a smile, the lights on full and the chill in the air gone. "Good morning, Rose. You didn't scare me."

The young woman gave her a strange look. "Are you alright?" she asked.

"Yes. Yes. Just too much coffee this morning."

The cashier smiled and walked back to the front of the store, leaving Patricia at the book shelf.

"No dear," she said quietly, shelving the remaining text. "*You* didn't scare me at all."

McMaster University – 1964

Patricia Irving nervously pushed the cart out from the receiving area onto the brightly lit floor of the new bookstore. Having recently moved into the basement of the newest building on campus, the selection of general books had expanded, opening up part time positions in that department. Patricia, a part-time student cashier, now finishing her second year at McMaster, had been given a chance to prove herself by being offered a position on the general books team.

A lover of fiction, she was delighted with the opportunity to showcase her knowledge of both the classics as well as modern writers.

The bright wooden cart, filled with paperbacks from Pan and Penguin, vibrated due to a wobbly front wheel. Patricia frowned and bent low to examine the wheel as she kept moving forward.

The cart bumped into something soft.

"My word," a gruff voice sounded, and Patricia looked up at a dark eyed man with white hair that she immediately recognized as the professor for her class on Victorian literature.

"Can't you watch where you're going with that thing?" he asked.

"Sorry, Dr. Emerson," she said in a low voice.

His dark eyes fell on the cart of books and he let out a loud harrumph. "So this is what passes for literature today, is it? Mass produced pocket books manufactured like so much candy for the mind."

Believing she could impress him, Patricia held up the Pan books new release of Ian Fleming's latest novel, *On Her Majesty's Secret Service*. "Oh but, sir, this is such a wonderful novel, an utterly compelling read. I couldn't afford the hardback edition – but here it is, a compact, low cost option. Fleming is the master of the spy thriller."

Emerson let out a slow sigh as he glanced at the art on the cover. "A ring in a field of bloody snow? I fail to see how that can be a *wonderful novel.*

"The bard was the master of suspense and intrigue. He wrote tales from the richness of history, characters that live and breathe in the

62

minds of readers today. Not like this Fleming hack and his forgettable *Bond* character."

Patricia placed the book back on the cart, her face turning red and her eyes downcast.

"What other *treasures* does your cart hold?"

Feeling she might be able to redeem herself in the professor's eyes she remembered the series of Shakespeare's plays on the other side of the cart. She ran her hand along the spines until she found a copy of *The Tempest*. She pulled it out and held it to show him.

"Isn't this beautiful?" she said in a hopeful voice.

The professor was silent as he stared at the book.

Carefully, he leaned forward, plucked the book from her hand using the tips of his fingers, as if it were covered in mold or slime and flung it across the floor. Then he fixed his eyes on her.

"You mock me!" he growled. "Shakespeare was not meant to be published in such a low quality mass produced format."

"But sir . . ."

Emerson thrust the leather-bound Shakespeare book in her face, producing it from thin air.

"This!" he yelled. "*This* is fine literature. *This* is the way it was meant to be presented." He shook the book in her face. Despite the copy almost blocking her face, she could still feel drops of spittle from his lips land on her cheek.

"Shakespeare was never, *never*, meant to be lowered to this sort of mass production."

He slammed the fist of his free hand down on the cart, shaking his head, his face and neck turning a dark crimson.

"Why, oh why must this bookstore, this *campus* mock me?!"

He pushed at the uneven cart, the faulty wheel giving way. The cart tipped over on its side with a loud crash, spilling paperbacks across the tile floor as Emerson stormed out.

"Bloody stupid bookstore," he called out. "You'll not see me dare set foot in here again!"

Patricia stared at the books on the floor and began to cry.

McMaster University - 1973

Richard Hamill hadn't entered the library on an April 23rd since that first strange occurrence three years earlier. He'd always feigned illness or booked that week off work, whatever it took to ensure he wasn't around.

He knew enough to have determined that the specter he'd seen on the top floor of the library that April night in 1970 was that of Professor Marshall Emerson, Shakespearean scholar. There were enough clues and Hamill was a competent enough researcher to be able to hone in on the quote from *The Tempest* he'd heard the ghost utter, the significance of the date and the section of the library that had been disturbed.

But it wasn't any of the research or clues he'd put together that made him confident in his decision.

It was that portrait in the archives section of the library, down in the depths of the basement which he'd spotted the next day that clinched it. All those other clues were mere window dressing.

He barely glanced at the portrait when he walked past the first time. It was hung above a cubicle leading to the back of the archives – but a second after he passed it, he stopped, and the peripheral glance of the man in the photograph was enough to set all his hairs on end and give him a sinking feeling in his gut.

When he stepped back to look directly at the photo of Marshall Emerson he knew immediately. *That* had been the man he'd seen the night before on the top floor of the library; a man who had been dead for years.

Richard knew enough not to mention his suspicion to anyone. But he'd kept his ears open for any disturbing stories or tales, and jotted down anything that was even slightly out of the ordinary, just in case it had something to do with Emerson's ghost.

He kept his notes on these matters as well as the tons of research he had done on the man's life in a secret file that he simply labeled *Prospero's Ghost*.

And he was working on a note within that file on the second night he'd witnessed the apparition. He'd been sitting in the cubicle below Emerson's portrait, a cubicle he'd become rather fond of over the years despite that heavy feeling in his gut he experienced when he'd first seen it.

As he was making a quick note about a part-time student who had reported the Shakespeare collection on the top floor having been found strewn about the floor when a distinct chill encompassed the room.

Out of the corner of his eye, Richard saw a figure standing before him. When he glanced up, nobody was there, but he heard, very clearly, the following words in a gruff deep voice: "Knowing I loved my books, he furnished me from mine own library with volumes that I prize above my dukedom."

Richard paused only a moment before responding, almost by rote, since he immediately recognized the line as one the character Prospero said in Act I Scene ii of *The Tempest*. Once he started studying Marshall

Emerson he, in turn, studied the bard's works in detail, particularly that one play – the swan song of Shakespeare and apparently Emerson as well.

"Would I might but ever see that man!"

The response from the gruff voice was immediate. "Sit still and hear the last of our sea sorrow."

The chill immediately withdrew from the room and Richard was alone again.

He didn't have to make a note about this newly discovered fact.

Marshall could be pacified with the right words, the right response. Now he only needed to discover what the right response would be to rid the library of Prospero's Ghost forever.

McMaster University - Present Day

Titles Bookstore had only been open for about an hour and was still quiet when Richard rushed over to the Espresso Book Machine at the back of the sales floor. Ten minutes earlier, having returned to the Kirtas scanner room, Richard saw on the library's computer system that the Emerson Shakespeare folio had been uploaded to the bookstore's server.

Having been a regular customer for years, Richard was known to many of the full time staff at the store, including Melinda Harvey who was manning the customer service desk that day. He made small talk with the young woman, mentioning an order he had placed with the EBM staff. Might he have a look to see if it was completed? Melinda had seen the librarian plenty of times with Alan Lester and Patricia

Irving, playing with the new machine. She smiled and waved him by her desk.

Richard had observed Alan and Patricia enough to know the basics of how the machine operated. He quickly tabbed through the interface screens to see that the title had been added and had indeed been printed. Fifty-six copies to be exact. The print queue still had forty-four lined up to print.

The last copy had been printed at 9:20 PM.

Walking around the back of the machine to see if the books were anywhere nearby, he spotted Alan Lester's body slumped behind the Espresso Book Machine on a pile of paper boxes, a pen sticking out of his throat.

The young man lay face down, almost as though he had been dumped behind the machine so as not to be found. There wasn't a single drop of blood from his wound, yet Richard knew before he bent over to check for a pulse that the man was dead. Prospero had struck again.

He sighed as he looked down at the body. Alan had been a good friend. He was young, had a full life ahead of him. Richard offered a silent prayer and took a deep breath, trying to steady his nerves and slow the pounding of his heart as he turned away.

He knew that nothing could save the book manager now, and it would be useless to create a panic. It was with a surprisingly calm voice that he asked Melinda to call security. Her questioning glance was stilled by his stricken face, but when security picked up, she put her hand over the mouth piece of the phone, and asked:

"What should I say is the reason?"

"Tell them Alan Lester is dead. They need to come to the store now."

Her look of shock and fear made him step forward, put a slightly shaking hand on her arm.

"Now is not the time to panic, my dear. Just stay calm and wait for security."

He didn't wait for her response as he headed to the back entrance of the store, walking as quickly as possible without attracting attention. It was obvious to him that if the books weren't in the store, they had to have already been taken to The Tank. He knew the staff well, especially his good friend Patricia Irving. She would know where the copies were. As he cleared the store and began to run through the halls he only hoped he wasn't too late.

#

One of the benefits of having worked with someone for over 30 years was the inherent trust that allowed for communication short-cuts to be employed. When Richard found Patricia in the tank, it didn't take much to convince her what was going on, and despite the bizarre nature of his explanation, she immediately believed him.

Pulling the copies of the book off the shelf for English 3K06 they threw them onto a cart.

"Should we burn these copies?" Patricia asked. "Will that put his spirit to rest?"

"Probably," Richard nodded, then grinned and started to chuckle.

"What?" Patricia asked.

"In all the years we've known each other and shared our mutual passion for books, did you *ever* think one of us would suggest burning books as a good idea?"

A nervous giggle escaped from Patricia's throat. She had to admit, it felt good.

"I'd have said hell would have to freeze over first before I ever considered it."

"No kidding."

"Okay, I have twenty-four copies here. How many did you pull off?"

"Thirty-one."

They exchanged a dark look.

"There's one missing."

A low howl began to rise up from the back corner of The Tank. With nary a window or even glimpse of the outdoors, a cold wind blew down the aisles of the store as if it were in the middle of an open field.

"No," Richard said, running toward the front of the room with one of the books in his hand.

He reached the cash registers where Rose was serving a student. Richard pushed himself between the customer and the cashier, holding up the book.

"Did you sell a copy of this book this morning?"

Rose threw a confused look at Patricia who nodded, letting her know that Richard was not a threat despite the mad look in his eyes. The young woman took another look at the book. "No," she replied. "I haven't."

Richard turned back to Patricia.

"So where is it?"

The howling wind intensified. Papers and register slips near the cash register begin to swirl into the air.

"W-what's going on?" Rose yelled, as she and her customer began batting at the pages swirling around their heads. A few of them seemed to have nicked at their skin.

The flying pages nearest Richard sliced at his bare skin as well; dozens of paper cuts striking him at lightning fast speed.

The tempestuous winds raged louder as he ducked and tried to ward off the paper cuts. His hands and face were turning into a road-map of cuts. Barely distinguishable within the howling screams of the wind and the others in The Tank, Richard was able to pick out a gruff voice. "I will plague them all, even to roaring!"

From the far aisle, a student with a large backpack who Richard hadn't seen earlier bolted toward the metal stairs leading to the exit. He ran through the security gates, triggering the alarm with his passing, and leapt up the stairs. The heavy fire door at the top slammed shut with a thunderous bang just before he reached it. He pushed on the door's panic bar, but it wouldn't open.

"Hey!" Richard ran up the stairs with a surprising agility for a man his age and tore the backpack from the student's shoulder. He opened it, revealing three shoplifted textbooks, one of which was the replica version of Emerson's prized Shakespeare folio.

He held the book up as the pages continued to strike at his skin. He did his best to ignore the pain screaming to him from dozens of tiny cuts.

"This is the last one, Marshall!" he yelled into the storm. "No more blasphemous replicas of your text will be made. The offending bastard offspring will all be destroyed. This I vow to you." The flying papers continued to strike at his exposed flesh and the wind increased in intensity; enough to start lifting textbooks off the adjacent shelves and into a rising whirlwind.

Patricia, Rose and the student at the cash desk all scrambled for cover.

Still standing at the top of the metal staircase, Richard held the book opened at the midpoint, tiny trails of blood from his palms streaming onto the pages of the book. He grunted as he tore it in two. Several of the swirling textbooks slammed into his chest, shoulders and head, and he dropped the pieces as he stumbled to his knees halfway down the metal staircase.

"Marshall!" Richard screamed, holding onto the railing to keep from falling further. "I long to hear the story of your life!"

The wind immediately stopped.

The swirling books plummeted to the floor.

In the fresh quiet a gruff voice echoed from the far corner of The Tank. "I'll deliver all and promise you calm seas."

Richard got to his feet and walked down the stairs to stand beside Patricia as the papers that had been striking at them floated gently down to the ground.

As he reached her, more words could be heard, loud and distinct at first, but slowly fading.

"Now my charms are all o'erthrown . . ."

"It's over?" Patricia asked.

Richard nodded. "It's over. The final act." He took Patricia's hand in his own. "Rest in peace, Marshall. Be free and fair thou well."

#

University of Alberta – Present Day

"What's coming off the machine now?" Andy Todd, the bookstore director said as he walked into the lower level area where the University's Espresso Book Machine was located.

Laura Ryan smiled at him, not able to hear him over the sound of the hydraulic pump of the trimmer, but pretty sure she knew what he'd asked.

"It's a new file I just pulled off the EBM master server. It looks like Alan over at Mac downloaded it late last night."

"Is it another one of their library archive texts?"Andy asked, rounding the corner to have a closer look.The trimming process completed and the louder noise stopped.

"Yeah. A rare original printing of Shakespeare's complete works." She grinned. Though she'd operated the machine for close to two years, every new title she produced on the EBM gave her a quick thrill. "The first one is just about to come out."

They watched the book drop down the chute and out of the machine. Laura picked it up and quickly fanned through the pages. "Looks good," she said.

"Excellent," Andy said. "Okay, I'm heading home. Don't work too late."

"I won't," Laura grinned.

As they exchanged pleasantries and Andy turned to leave, neither of them noticed the dark shadowy figure in a brown tweed jacket lurking behind the closest set of bookshelves.

TRUTH-POISON

BY JAMES ALAN GARDNER

"How hard is it to analyze an unknown chemical?"

"Anywhere from trivial to impossible. Why?"

"There's this woman who's asked me a favor..."

"Uh-oh."

Rick and I sat on the patio outside Modern Languages. It's quiet there in the second week of May, when most Arts students have gone home for the summer. It's even quieter when the sky is overcast, and a cold spring wind blows at just the right angle to hit the gap in the patio's sheltering walls. In May, the University of Waterloo is supposed to be warm, with everybody wearing shorts and T-shirts . . . but when the clouds roll in and the breeze picks up, people hug their bare arms and hurry from building to building.

Huddling on the patio, I gritted my teeth and wrapped my hands around my coffee mug. Rick looked no warmer than me, but he refused to go inside—he said we needed privacy, and since no one else was stupid enough to sit out in the cold, we had the place to ourselves.

I didn't ask why Rick wanted privacy. Since our days together in high school, he'd always been connected: when I was in the market for something to smoke, or to keep me awake while studying, Rick could sell me whatever I asked for. In exchange, I helped him out—I was majoring in chemistry, and while I refused to manufacture anything illegal, I'd occasionally test pills and white powders to verify they were what they were supposed to be. Freezing my ass off on the patio, I assumed Rick had some new product to run through quality assurance.

"It's not what you think," Rick said. "It's totally legit."

"Oh sure, I believe you."

"No, really," he insisted. "This woman is doing her doctorate in anthropology. She just got back from some jungle where she and her supervisor lived for a year. The natives had a sacred plant..."

"Ah," I said. "And this plant has interesting properties?"

"So the natives claimed."

Centuries ago, people explored remote places to find gold and jewels. Nowadays, the same sort of people sought "traditional medicines"—extracts from plant roots, or leaves, or bark that natives used as home-brewed remedies. Most such concoctions didn't do much of anything, but a few were the real deal; they contained previously unknown chemicals with gigantic commercial potential. As a result, every drug company in the world hired "prospectors" to pester shamans in the hopes of hitting the jackpot: a moss that cured cancer, a berry that reduced cholesterol, a bean that prevented male pattern baldness.

I asked, "What does this plant do?"

"The natives said if you ate the fruit, it made you see the truth."

"What does that mean?"

"The natives wouldn't give specifics. This woman—her name's Catherine—said the tribe was all hush-hush. 'Our plant is sacred, outsiders mustn't learn our deepest secrets . . .' Yada, yada, yada."

"Sounds like it's a hallucinogen."

Rick nodded. "I'm thinking it's like peyote or magic mushrooms: take a dose, see the truths of the universe." He grinned. "That could be worth millions."

"If we've already got peyote, who needs something new?"

"Everyone," Rick said. "Look, I have contacts in the drug industry—not just dirt-bags, but people who wear nice suits and sit in boardrooms. The big boys in Pharma would *love* to get their hands on a hallucinogen that isn't illegal yet."

"Why?"

"Because loosening your brain can be therapeutic. There've been studies, like using Ecstasy on post-traumatic stress. It works, it really works, but the government is all, 'No way we'll ever legalize E.' Same with marijuana and lots of other stuff: they all have useful medical applications, but they'll never get approved because politicians don't want to look soft on drugs. On the other hand, if something new comes along . . . something the public hasn't been brainwashed into being afraid of . . ."

"I get it," I said. "Corporations give this new drug some clinical-sounding name, they test it against post-traumatic stress or whatever, and maybe it works as good as something illegal."

"Exactly. These days, most politicians realize that banning drugs has been a fiasco. They're too gutless to legalize the old stuff, but they don't want to repeat past mistakes by outlawing something new."

"Especially," I said, "when pharmaceutical companies make generous campaign contributions."

"Especially then," Rick agreed. "So I need you to test this fruit and make sure it *is* new . . . cuz if its active ingredient is just an illegal oldie like mescaline or psilocybin, then we're back to square one. But if it's something no one has seen before, then you, me and Catherine may be in for a huge finder's fee."

"Split three ways?"

His eyes flicked away. "First, let's know where we stand. Okay?"

"Give me a few days."

Chemically speaking, the job seemed do-able. The fruit's key ingredient was likely a complex organic molecule, and those could be excruciatingly difficult to analyze in full detail. However, comparing it to a few known hallucinogens was much easier; instead of mapping out the complete chemical structure, I only had to look at a few simple properties. They'd be enough to reveal meaningful differences.

"Great," Rick said. He reached into his pocket and pulled out a baggie containing a black lump the size of a prune—puckered, flat, and damp with oily sweat. The lump had left greasy marks on the inside of the bag, as if it had been crawling around the plastic in search of a way out. "The sacred fruit," Rick said. "Ugly sucker, isn't it? Like a turd from some animal you'd never want to meet."

"And the natives ate those things?"

"That's the funny part," Rick said. "According to Catherine, the natives never touched them. They grew the plants in special gardens, walled in by bamboo fences that were painted with sacred symbols...but she never saw anyone go inside the fences. She figured maybe medicine-men were the only people allowed to eat the fruit, and they only did it when no one was watching."

"So how did Catherine get the fruit?"

"Stole it. Duh. Filled a bag with several dozen while the natives were distracted. All in the name of science, of course."

"Did she ever take a nibble?"

"Are you kidding? The stuff may be poison—especially to someone who hasn't grown up eating it. Or it may be rough trade . . . like that wicked strain of peyote that always gives you a bad trip." Rick gave me a look. "You weren't thinking of trying it, were you?"

I took the bag and tucked it into my pocket. "Hey. I'm a professional."

76

#

To tell the truth, I *was* a professional: people paid me to do chemistry. More precisely, people paid a certain professor, and he paid me ten hours a week to deal with chores too menial for Ph.D.'s. Other chemistry students did the same—we washed a lot of test tubes, but we also got to participate in cutting-edge research. Even better, many of us were given keys to campus laboratories and small sections of worktable where we could experiment on our own.

I wasn't the only person who snuck in on weekends to pursue less-than-respectable projects. Your typical chemistry geek grows up making stink bombs and high-powered acids because dangerous stuff is *fun* . . . and when we get to university, we don't suddenly turn into saints. Almost everyone I knew dabbled with mild explosives, and a number of us indulged in pharmaceutical pursuits. The geek mentality loves to trespass: as soon as someone says, "There's a line you shouldn't cross," geeks take it as a challenge.

So late that Saturday night, I made my way to the lab, ignoring lights leaking under doors of five other labs along the hall. I'd planned my activities in advance, so I went through half a dozen tests in quick succession—mass spectrograph, gas chromatograph, and so on—which let me narrow in on my target. Unsurprisingly, the puckered black fruit contained dozens of organic compounds, but most were old familiars . . . the same substances you'd find in a sun-dried tomato. Only one chemical stood out as unusual: an alkaloid with a remarkable quantity of zinc in it. I knew that alkaloids often have psychoactive properties (morphine, nicotine and curare, just to name a few), so I figured I'd found what I was looking for.

Next step: testing Alkaloid X against known hallucinogens. I won't bore you with the details—just take it for granted I know what I'm doing when it comes to drug comparisons. By four in the morning, I could confidently say the tiny amount of juice in my pipette had never been banned in Canada.

Was it truly a hallucinogen? That question was harder. People have made computer models for predicting what a chemical will do to humans, but no one puts much faith in them. The only truly effective method for seeing what a drug does is to try it.

Yeah.

You have to realize, it was 4:00 a.m. To pull my all-nighter, I'd been guzzling Red Bull, plus some little green pills I'd got from Rick. At that hour of the morning, it made perfect sense to say, "If malnourished jungle natives can eat these ugly prunes without dying, how bad would it be if I touched my tongue to the end of the pipette and let a little Alkaloid X soak in?"

Chemistry geeks don't play safe. When I muttered, "This isn't the stupidest thing I've ever done," the saddest thing was that I was telling the truth.

The truth.

A single droplet of Alkaloid X leaked onto my tongue. The truth leapt down my throat.

#

At first, nothing happened. I had time to clean up my work and chuck out what remained of the fruit: tiny heaps of charred ash, miniscule quantities of juice, and so on. I dumped solids into the garbage and liquids down the sink; no one would notice such small amounts of nondescript leftovers. I washed my hands, packed my gear, and stepped out of the lab.

The corridor was dark. Officially, the building had been closed for hours, so most hallway lights were off; only the stairwells were still illuminated, at opposite ends of the corridor. The other Saturday-night geeks must have finished earlier than me, because lights no longer beamed under most of the lab doorways. There was just one still shining a few rooms away—a single night owl left.

It was quiet in the darkness. Shadowy silence. As I locked the door behind me, the world suddenly refocused.

Those of you who wear glasses know something of the experience: that moment when you put on your lenses, and the blur goes away. Everything becomes clear and sharp. But this was more than that. Colors grew more intense—gradations of light and shadow seemed to stretch through a wider spectrum. Noises intensified too; I was suddenly aware of equipment humming behind closed doors, sounds I'd previously ignored. The odors of chemicals sifted through the air . . . all my senses were keener, but not overwhelmed. For the first time, I felt I was perceiving the world as it was.

And I perceived the world was empty. Barren. Untended.

I'd never believed in God, but I wasn't militant about it—I didn't much care one way or another. Now, though, I realized that some part of me had always nursed naïve beliefs about the universe: that it followed laws . . . that its laws were understandable . . . that despite the constant atrocities of history and the evening news, on balance, the universe was *fair*.

Somehow I'd believed that. I'd blinded myself to reality. But now my sight had cleared and I saw the truth.

No comfort anywhere. The universe was indifferent—maybe actively malign.

I recognized that this sensation came completely from the drug. Magic mushrooms could make you see God; Alkaloid X apparently made you see God's absence. I knew that what I sensed was no more objective than the light-shows you get from LSD. On the other hand, I was a pro when it came to psychedelics: I could appreciate the illusions without buying into them.

This was different—my mind seemed so *lucid*. No dizziness. No buzz on. My pulse wasn't racing or dragging its heels. I felt absolutely ordinary . . . except that I'd finally been freed of ludicrous fantasies.

The universe had no plan, no higher purpose. There was no lofty reason why humans lived or died. Shit just happened. That was all.

Several paces in front of me, a lab door opened spilling light into the hallway. Someone stepped out: a fellow student named Beth. She was one of many candidates on my "Maybe I should get together with her" list—tall and embarrassed about it, but not bad-looking. Long thin blonde hair. A soft sweet face that she hid behind big glasses and an always-tentative smile. The sort of beanpole who hunches her shoulders in a lame effort to disguise her height, and doesn't say much around people she doesn't know. I'd sometimes watch her in class; she looked good in turtlenecks. But as I gazed at Beth in the darkened hallway, all I could think was, "She's going to die."

I couldn't tell if this was an immediate prospect or just a long-term inevitability. I simply sensed death infusing her, like an eye-catching new color I'd just learned to see. It was the morbid brown color of meat starting to rot, but it was *interesting*, not gross. At the same time, I thought (with a twinge of pity), "She doesn't know." Beth didn't realize she was mortal . . . didn't realize the universe was a merciless place that no one survived. She was still in a sheep-like state of blindness, believing soporific lies.

"Hey," Beth said with that tentative smile. "Finished for the night?"

"Yep." I knew I ought to say more, but nothing came to mind. Mostly, I was trying not to blurt out, *Wake up! The world is an abyss, and you'll soon be worm-food.*

"What were you working on?" she asked.

"Something for a friend," I said. "How 'bout you?"

"Stuff for my prof. She's been off at some conference and she left me things to do. She gets back on Monday . . . but honestly, this is the first chance I've had to even start . . ."

On and on, as words tumbled out of her. It was the most Beth had ever said to me. I wondered if she too was pumped up on Red Bull. I also wondered how she'd just happened to emerge at the moment I was leaving . . . but then the phrase *meaningless coincidence* popped into my head. That was all the answer I needed.

Eventually, her talk trickled to an end: "But I'm starting to get sloppy. Too tired, you know? I should fold up for the night and come back tomorrow."

"Sounds smart," I said. I couldn't stop looking at her. She was standing in the light of the open doorway, but I knew that even in the dark, she'd be mesmerizing. You might think the rot-brown of death would be disgusting or scary, but just the opposite. Beth's mortality was an arousing confirmation of what Alkaloid X kept telling me: the universe sucks. I *loved* staring at Beth and seeing death upon her.

"Which way are you going home?" I said. "I could walk you."

#

81

She had a car, so I walked her to the parking lot. We talked on the way—nothing noteworthy. As I recall, conversation flowed easily . . . but since I was under the influence, my memory shouldn't be trusted. (How many people feel charming and witty when stoned, only to be told differently in the morning?) We didn't kiss or even touch when I left her at the car, but the undertones were there; it seemed like the start of something.

For me, though, sexual attraction was only part of it. What I felt most was pity: I wished I'd kept some Alkaloid X to help Beth see the truth. I keenly wanted to free her from warm fuzzy delusions.

#

When I got home, I wondered if I'd be able to sleep—sleep is a biochemical state that some drugs make impossible. I hit the couch and turned on the TV to search for something good. Next thing I knew, it was almost noon, with the sun shining brightly outside.

I took stock of myself: a stiff neck from falling asleep on the couch, but otherwise no ill effects. The "high" (if you could call it that) was gone; I could remember my razor-sharp feelings of emptiness, but they were no longer present. Like remembering an orgasm—I knew it had been great, but the actual sensation was dim in my mind.

Aloud, I said, "That was weird."

Thinking the world was harsh and lonely might sound like a bad trip; I hadn't been upset at all. In fact, I'd felt liberated—it was so *right*. My thoughts had been coherent, filled with pure clean benevolence toward Beth and anyone else who hadn't yet realized the truth. Now, although the drug had worn off, I still felt like I'd seen the light. I took pride in knowing just how bleak existence was.

Smug cynicism. Intellectual superiority. I didn't know if Alkaloid X would interest pharmaceutical corporations, but sales would be dynamite on university campuses.

#

I texted Rick and set up a meeting: the barbecue pit beside Laurel Lake, across the ring-road from the Psych building. There wasn't much there—just a few concrete benches and the barbecue itself—but it was the sort of meeting place Rick liked: out in the open and seldom visited. We wouldn't have to worry about eavesdroppers . . . except, of course, a horde of Canadian Geese, whose cranky attitudes and copious droppings would keep human interlopers away.

When Rick arrived, he had a woman with him—trim, late-twenties, short brown hair with expensive highlights. She had a deep dark tan, which I assumed came from a year in the tropics; this had to be Catherine. Seeing her with Rick, I wondered how they'd found each other. He was in his 4A term, the same as me. She was a doctoral student, several years older. Most likely, when she got back to Waterloo with her stolen fruit, she'd made discreet inquiries about the drug scene on campus and eventually found her way to Rick.

Was their relationship any more than business? Something told me it was, despite the difference in their ages.

A voice in my head whispered, *She's using him.* Strange—I didn't usually make cynical snap-judgments. But Catherine wasn't an angel, was she? She'd stolen sacred fruit from her native hosts. Now she wanted to sell it and make herself rich. Whether or not she'd actually broken any international laws, the university's ethics committee would go ballistic if they found out.

Catherine gave me a bright white smile when Rick introduced us. We shook hands, and hers lingered in mine a heartbeat longer than necessary. *Oh yeah, the worldly doctoral student is working us dumb undergrads.* Rick must have noticed what Catherine did, because there was an edge to his voice when he asked me, "So what did you find?"

"The drug's new," I said. "Not even close to any old standbys. I call it Alkaloid X."

Catherine said,"The Huaropo called it Gweenjiru. In their language, that means Truth-Poison."

That gave me a jolt. "They called this stuff poison and you thought it could become a saleable drug?"

Catherine waved her hand dismissively. "I'm sure they invented the name just to scare people away. You have to understand . . ."

She stopped. I said, "What?"

She didn't answer for a few seconds. Then she sighed. "I guess I should come clean." She gave Rick an apologetic look. "I kind of shaded the truth when I first talked to you. The Huaropo—the natives I stayed with—are total Puritans. We're the chosen servants of God and everyone else is damned' . . . that sort of thing. As if they've re-invented old-time Calvinism."

"So they believe in God?" I asked. That didn't fit my image of people who cultivated Alkaloid X. Wouldn't the drug stamp out blind faith?

"The Huaropo are fanatic monotheists," Catherine said. "Which is rare in such tribes. They call their god Temmas and he's ordered them to protect the world from Truth-Poison. To the Huaropo, the plant is a demon that Temmas wants imprisoned. He's appointed them its jailkeepers."

"So when they fenced in their gardens," Rick said, "they were trying to keep the plant from breaking out?"

Catherine nodded. I asked, "Why don't they just rip up the plants and burn them?"

"Apparently, that would set the demon free," Catherine said. "He'd escape in the smoke, or something." She rolled her eyes. "The Huaropo think the only way to lock up the demon is to keep some of the plant growing at all times. They say it buries the demon's feet in the ground so he can't run away. You also need to wall off the plants with magic fences so the demon can't ooze out."

"Which worked perfectly well," I said, "until a certain anthropologist stole some."

She glared at me. "You don't know the Huaropo. They're uptight self-righteous prudes. They don't drink, they don't dance...they disapprove of anything remotely resembling fun. You want to know why my supervisor and I were the first to study them in depth? Because other anthropologists couldn't stand them." Catherine made a face. "Spend a year in Huaropo territory, and you'll start to think, 'If these guys say Truth-Poison is evil, that's a big fat mark in its favor.'"

Since I'd already sampled the drug, I knew she was right. Puritanical natives would *hate* the effects of Alkaloid X; religious zealots might invent all kinds of shrill myths to prevent anyone from trying it. The shrillness itself should have been a hint that Truth-Poison wasn't so bad.

Rick didn't have my inside knowledge. "But what if it *is* a poison?" he asked.

85

"It isn't," I said. "At least not in tiny quantities." Which was stupid for a chemistry student to say, since strychnine and arsenic are safe in tiny quantities too. Dosage makes all the difference. "Look," I said, "I have a confession . . ."

"You tried some?" Rick said. "Dude, you're out of control."

"What was it like?" Christina asked, learning forward eagerly.

I considered describing the sensation, but worried I'd sound like some cultist. *I've seen the ultimate truth of the universe! Join me and be saved.* "It was awesome," I said. "Different than anything you could imagine. You have to try it."

Rick said, "Are you kidding?"

Catherine said, "The sooner the better."

#

She had another Truth-Poison fruit in her purse. She whipped it out; I thought she was going to pop it straight into her mouth. Then Rick said, "Whoa, whoa, whoa!" For someone who sold illegal drugs, he'd never had much sense of adventure. "Let's not rush into anything," Rick said. He looked at me. "How *much* did you take?"

"A little drop on my tongue."

"Then for God's sake," he said to Catherine, "don't eat an entire fruit."

Rick had a point. Even if I'd proved that one drop was safe, for all we knew two drops might be lethal. Anyway, two drops were *unnecessary*: if one lick was enough to show someone the truth, then two could enlighten *two* people. Double the benefit—because I deeply wanted to share the effect with as many people as possible.

I said, "How about this: we head to my lab and I extract the Alkaloid X from that fruit Catherine has. It won't take long—I can skip the analysis and go straight to the harvest. Then we can all have a drop."

Rick said, "I don't think that's such a great idea."

"Of course it is," Catherine said. "Do you know how long I've waited to try this stuff? A year with the damned Huaropo; nothing to do but think about what lay behind those fences."

"Forbidden fruit," Rick muttered. "That never works out well. Why don't we smoke some weed instead?"

"A drop of this stuff won't kill you," I said.

"Right," Catherine agreed. She took Rick's arm and lifted him to his feet. "Remember, if Truth-Poison is as good as advertised, it's worth a lot of money."

Rick grimaced, but let her lead him back to the ring-road. I thought of Adam being led by Eve. Did that make me the snake?

#

An hour later, I had a pipette containing purified Alkaloid X. There wasn't much—maybe ten droplets—looking as clear and harmless as water.

"Is that all?" Catherine asked. She sounded disappointed.

"What did you expect from one fruit? You get a lot less opium from a single poppy."

She frowned. "It'll take a whole whack of acreage to grow a significant crop."

"Whoa!" Rick held up his hands. "Who said anything about growing this stuff?"

"It's a fruit," Catherine said. "Each one has seeds. I've already planted some on my apartment balcony."

Rick groaned.

"It's not illegal," I assured him. "And trust me, the stuff is good." I stuck out my tongue and licked a droplet from the pipette's tip. "See?"

"Me next," said Catherine. She took a drop, then looked at Rick. "Are you in or out?"

He didn't look happy. But whatever relationship he had with Catherine, he obviously didn't want to look chicken in front of her. Under other circumstances, I might have come down on his side . . . told her to not to pressure him. But a voice in my head whispered, *This is for his own good.* I held out the pipette. Reluctantly, Rick took a hit.

"So how long before it kicks in?" Catherine asked.

"Five or ten minutes," I said. "You guys wait here. I want to check something."

I walked out into the hall. The building was quiet: nobody else anywhere in sight. I went and knocked on the door of Beth's lab. As I'd hoped, she answered—still working on whatever her prof had left her. "Hey," she said, this time with a real smile instead of a tentative one. "You slaving away again?"

"Sort of. I read an article on a new artificial sweetener and I thought I'd make a batch." I held out the pipette. "Want to try?"

Beth's smile faltered. "I don't know . . . I have allergies . . ."

"This stuff is allergy-free. That's one of its selling points." I held out the pipette again. "Go on."

She still looked doubtful. "Have you tried it?"

"Sure. But it's not sweet to me. Apparently some people can't taste it—you need the right genes." I gave her my most winning look. "Come on, help me out."

She tried to smile. "Okay. Just a drop."

"Tongue out."

She gave a nervous giggle and stuck out her tongue. I dabbed it with the tip of the pipette. Beth licked her lips, then shrugged. "I don't taste a thing."

"Huh. I guess we both have the wrong genetics. Or else the formula . . ."

I stopped. The Truth-Poison I'd taken a few minutes earlier had just kicked in. Heightened perceptions. Sharp-focused mind. I looked at Beth and brown color of death was upon her like a skin disease. Her tall bony body seemed more skeleton than flesh.

I must have been staring at her, because she gave me a curious look. "What?"

Before I could answer, I heard movement behind me. Rick and Catherine surged out of the lab, their eyes glittering. I could tell the drug rush had hit them too. They seemed surrounded by a phosphorescent glow, like deep-sea fishes prowling the bottom of the ocean. Nary a trace of the brown rot that infected Beth.

"Wow," said Catherine. "It's amazing, isn't it? I'm thinking this stuff affects the right temporal lobe of the brain—that's where spiritual feelings live—but it must also touch the pleasure centers. Maybe it stimulates production of dopamine: that's always good for a positive emotional response."

Beth shrank back slightly; I remembered she was shy with new people—especially ones saying things that would make no sense to her. I told her, "This is Rick and his friend Catherine." I turned to them. "This is Beth."

Rick and Catherine gazed at her keenly. Were they seeing the brown death upon her? Beth cringed back a little more, withdrawing

89

into the lab doorway."Well, maybe I should let you and your friends – " She stopped, cleared her throat. "Hey this is . . ." She cleared her throat again. "Oh no."

She turned as if intending to run from us. Then she crumpled. I managed to grab her before she totally collapsed, but her body was deadweight in my arms. "Epi-pen," she gasped, gesturing weakly toward a desk inside the lab. Her purse lay on top of it. "For allergies," Beth whispered. "Epi-pen."

I lowered her to the floor. Her breathing sounded bad: a wheeze that grew tighter with every breath. I stepped over her body and moved toward the purse. Then something made me stop and look back.

The corruption enveloping Beth had grown so thick, she was a dark brown heap on the floor tiles. Rick and Catherine appeared in the doorway. Phosphorescence still surrounded them, so bright it cast shadows. The drug had embraced them . . . but Beth, poor Beth, had been rejected.

Were her allergies to blame? Were life and death that random? Or was Beth simply too *nice* for Truth-Poison?

The other three of us weren't nice. You couldn't call us evil—not compared to the absolute scum who sometimes surfaced in the human race's gene pool—but if Truth-Poison contained a demon, then Rick, Catherine and I would be more to the demon's liking than poor choking Beth. We had the right flavor.

Inside my brain, something said, *If God doesn't exist, how can a demon?* I found myself laughing at the absurdity. Demons were another pathetic invention of people who wanted the world to have meaning— people who would rather have evil supernatural overlords than no overlords at all. But demons were bullshit: no more real than a drunk's

90

pink elephants. Everything I was experiencing boiled down to soulless chemical reactions in my brain.

Beth whimpered and pushed weakly against my ankle, trying to shove me toward her epi-pen. I took a step in that direction, but something stopped me. *Why save her if she'll never see the truth?* Her allergies meant she could never successfully take Truth-Poison...so she'd spend her whole life in foolish gullibility. *Isn't it a kindness to save her from that?*

I glanced at Rick and Catherine. They stared at Beth, totally fascinated—as if watching a show put on for their entertainment. If anyone was going to do something, it had to be me.

I took another step toward the desk that held Beth's epi-pen. As I did so, my senses began to lose their precious clarity—colors, sounds and smells faded back to ordinary drabness. *Damn,* I thought, *I'm resisting the high.* Had I built up a tolerance to Alkaloid X, so that the kick didn't last as long?

I still had the pipette in my hand. Almost without thinking, I took another drop.

Heightened perceptions flared back immediately.

I never did get around to finding the epi-pen.

#

When Beth died, the rot on her skin vanished like a bubble popping. She became uninteresting.

We left her where she was, closing the lab door behind us. Someone would find her corpse sooner or later, dead of anaphylactic shock. There'd probably be an autopsy, but could the coroner detect a single drop of fluid that had dissolved on her tongue several minutes before she died? And even if the drug was noticed, it would only be a miniscule trace of an unfamiliar alkaloid—far too little to allow a complete analysis.

Still bright with enlightenment, Rick, Catherine and I strolled around campus. We talked about extracting more Alkaloid X, so we could share it with people we knew—people who could handle it, as opposed to innocents like Beth. Rick was eager to pass on the fruit to his contacts in big business; he was certain they'd love it, and do what they could to disseminate it globally. We also made plans to grow pots of the plants on our balconies, so we'd have plenty for personal use.

The more Truth-Poison the better. People would thank us for it.

I wondered if, when the drug wore off, I'd feel bad about what happened to Beth. I didn't think so. A voice in my head said, *The truth will make you free.*

CAN YOU SEE THE REAL ME?

BY SÈPHERA GIRÓN

York University, Stong College, 1982

Tia stared out the window, her brow furrowed. Her thick chestnut brown hair was pulled back into a pony tail and she wore black, thick rimmed glasses over her dark brown eyes. She leaned closer to the glass, her breath fogging the window as she strained to gaze at the crowd of people walking far below, looking for *him*.

Dana's lean lanky form strutted quickly along the path, his gait stern with an air of determination. He was easy to spot as he bobbed in and out of the throng of the class change traffic, pulling the collar of his coat up tighter to block the sudden bite of the sporadic wind.

Dana strutted closer to the building and then Tia lost him. She stepped back from the window.

Tia loved living on the thirteenth floor. From there, the view was akin to being a princess in a castle. She could observe the kingdom below and lay judgement upon her subjects. Even better, she could watch for Dana's return from class the one day a week when she had a spare and the dorm was almost empty.

The view from the common room was the best for watching the class changes. The Stong building was at the far end of the campus. Long stretches of tarred pathways led from the residence buildings towards the main academic buildings. Stong was situated rather far back from most of the buildings and the students had a fair hike.

During class changes, the paths were filled with moving people that scurried along like ants and beetles up and down the hill.

As the weather shifted from fall to winter, the path from the Ross building to Stong had to be the coldest in the universe. The wind gusted sporadically through the tall buildings and across the bare field. Tia wondered how cold and miserable the wind would be in the coming winter. She couldn't bear to consider it.

She turned back into the common room and turned off the large screen television. The soaps had started and she wasn't really interested in them.

Tia returned to her room down the hall, passing the elevators on the way. She lived in one of the few single rooms and in fact, had applied to Stong because she wanted a single room and Stong had more singles than the other residences. The corner rooms were the only doubles on the floor.

The idea of a co-ed dorm had seemed rather daring when she moved in, but as the first month passed, she had come to realize that a coed dorm was a fabulous idea.

She hummed softly as she left her door partly open. As she leaned over to put a record on the turntable, she caught a glimpse of herself in the mirror above her desk. Her eyes had a look of intensity behind her thick glasses and she fluffed her hair. After placing the needle on the last track of the album, she turned up the volume. The strong guitar riffs surged into "Listening to You" from The Who's *Tommy*. Tia smiled coyly and picked up a tube of dark red lipstick. The floor vibrated slightly signalling the arrival of the elevator.

She stood behind her dorm door, listening carefully. The elevator doors heaved open and then clapped shut. As the car vibrated up to the next floor, she put her hand on the door knob and pulled the door open. She stepped out and bumped right smack into Dana. Her rather large frame bounced his lean body nearly into the wall. He steadied himself, slipping his knapsack from his shoulders.

"Oh, sorry," Tia said as she headed for the co-ed washroom across the hallway.

"No worries," he said as he fished for the keys in his pocket. He walked the few steps towards his own room as she pushed open the swinging door into the washroom.

She headed for one of the seven stalls and locked the door. She listened as the sound of his key slid into the lock and the tumblers clicked on his door down the hall. She sighed as she pretended to pee and rustled some toilet paper between her fingers before she flushed the toilet. As she emerged from the stall, Dana entered the bathroom. He headed for one of the stalls.

"See you later," she said as he shut the door.

"Sure," Dana said as the sound of his fly unzipping echoed through the bathroom. Tia grinned and headed back out the door. She went into her room and grabbed her makeup bag; she counted to ten and headed back into the bathroom. Dana was at the sink washing his hands.

"How's it going?" she asked him, rummaging through her bag for a hair brush. She let her hair down from its pony tail and shook it. It fell loosely to her shoulders and she tossed it as she gazed at herself in the mirror, fluffing it with her fingers. He scrubbed his hands with the soap and glanced over to her.

"Quite well. My last class was really great. We explored the possibilities of what the brain would look like if we could see the patterns of consequence and conscience."

Tia sighed as he spoke. She loved listening to the lilt of his Irish accent even if she couldn't understand what he said half the time.

"That sounds intriguing. What do you think about it?"

"I think that the less guilt and remorse a person feels regarding immoral actions, the less electrical energy would be detected. Guilt and remorse are emotions of a higher evolution."

"I would think that all that restraint would build up electrical currents. You'd think there'd be more activity if the brain is constantly going."

"That's certainly the direction the debate went. I guess as technology grows more advanced, we'll get more answers."

"And what difference does it make if we get answers? Will the world change in any way?"

"Of course not," Dana said as he shook his head. His bright blue eyes danced teasingly as he caught Tia's dark ones in the mirror. Her breath caught in her throat as she locked her gaze with his for a moment before brushing her hair once more.

The direct gaze into his eyes caused her stomach to spasm and she was giddy with giggles. As she laughed, Dana stared at her.

"I'm sorry," Tia said. "It's not like the world would change for anything, let alone for some dry bit of science."

"Well, there are no definite answers yet for so many things. Who knows what could lie in store?"

"I guess . . . I think . . ."

"If there was no conscience or consequence then how can you determine moral standards?"

"Who sets these moral standards anyway?"

"Science. Society. Theory."

Dana turned to look at her. She swung around, tossing her hair, her eyes steadily watching him. He had a long narrow face, with chiselled features and was rather rugged. She wasn't sure of his age but figured he was likely in his early twenties. His eyes were bright sapphires against the fading tan on his face.

"Do you want a beer?" he asked her. Tia grinned.

"Why not? My classes are done for the day."

She followed him to his room, and he indicated the bed. She sat down on his neatly made bed and looked around the room. The rooms were all the same. Bed, desk, dresser and closet. The curtains were open and the rolling expanse of storm clouds spread for miles. He opened his small fridge and pulled out two bottles of beer. He popped them open with an opener and handed her one.

"Do you have a favourite class yet?" he asked her as he swallowed several mouthfuls of beer.

"Not just yet. Just when I think I like one, the teacher does something dumb or I just can't get things figured out." Tia said. Dana patted his pockets and at last found a pack of cigarettes. He plucked it out and offered Tia one. She took it hesitantly and placed it between her lips. He lit it with the click of his bic and did the same for himself.

"I have a couple of classes like that too. It's all part of the process," Dana said, breathing out a puff of smoke. He watched it circle and plume in front of them then float up in a spiralling ball. Tia watched the smoky spheres dance and disintegrate and joined her own smoke cloud with his. They spent a few minutes, smoking and drinking the beer.

Dana stood up and went through his milk crate of albums. He pulled out *Quadrophenia* and slipped a record out of the case. Tia grabbed the album cover while he started the record. With focused precision, he gently placed the needle right on the plaintive cries of "Is it me? For a moment . . ." from Dr. Jimmy and Mr. Jim.

Dana looked up at Tia with wide blue eyes. They were so vibrant and clear, large with sadness, troubles unspoken. He stared at her for a moment as if he wanted to say something, but kept silent. He stood up and went to get them both another beer. Tia hadn't finished hers yet so she quickly drank it up.

He sat back with a heavy sigh. His mood had shifted so swiftly that Tia wasn't sure what to say. She hummed along with the song, enjoying the fact they liked the same music.

"You know, I summered not far from there a few times," Dana suddenly said.

"Where?" Tia already knew he was from Ireland but this album was based in England.

"Near Brighton. In a tiny little town. But it was fine." He nodded. "It was fine for most of the times I was there on holiday. But then one day, something strange happened." He leaned forward and blew out another puff of smoke. "A darkness descended on the town and life was never really the same. There were whispers of things in the dark. Horrid evil things."

"Get out," Tia said. Dana nodded.

"My family didn't believe me when I said I didn't want to go anymore. However, they figured it out soon enough."

"Just like that?"

"It was like out of one of those movies where the small town is invaded by something not quite right. And that one was."

"And what happened . . . exactly?"

"I don't know. I just know that the darkness follows me and sometimes I dread it . . . the thoughts I have." Dana leaned back on the bed. He drew his feet up so he was half sitting and drank deeply of his beer. Tia sat up in her chair, eager to hear more.

"What thoughts?"

"Disturbing thoughts. Sexual thoughts of obsessions beyond my control."

Tia leaned towards him with great curiosity.

"Do you ever act on them?"

"I don't want to go to jail."

Dana drank more of his beer and stared at the poster.

"What about other creatures?" Tia asked. "Are there leprechauns? Fairies?"

Dana shrugged and looked bewildered.

"There is no more to say, I guess," he sighed. "There's more and there's no more. I'm picking no more. "

They passed the time in silence, humming along to *Quadrophenia*.

He lay on the bed, pillows under his back staring at the ceiling, his arm propped under his head so that he could continue to drink his beer. Tia looked at his long lean form stretched along the covers. He was so slight that he looked like he could blow away in one of the gusts of wind that rattled the windows. The view from Dana's window was of a vast field and the city of Toronto beyond. The CN tower glinted in the distance on sunny days. This day, there was far too much turbulence to see the lake. Everything was in flux. The shift was coming, the preparations were nearly ready.

The window creaked from the pressure of another gust, lifting the curtains slightly. A whistling pierced through the windows, rattling the glass and she realized that the wind had picked up immensely in the short time they had talked. It pressed in-between the window cracks and she rubbed her arms at the cold intrusion. Clouds rolled past the window, casting shadows along Dana's face. Still his blue eyes glowed as he dreamed of something else, beer clutched in one hand, cigarette in the other. There were large psychedelic posters across his walls. Rainbows and zodiac signs, constellations and waterfalls vibrated, beckoning relief from an aching world.

His look of intense concentration sent lusty shivers down Tia's spine and into her throbbing groin. A shrink would have said she was attracted to that which she couldn't have but she didn't really know that she couldn't have him. She was here, wasn't she? Listening to the autumn wind howl, watching him think. She was alone with him when no one else was. The opening strains of "Love Reign O're Me" were starting up. That had to count for something.

Her body hummed with anticipation. She had waited so long and today was the day the planets were aligned in perfection. Today she would lose her virginity. She looked hopefully at Dana who continued to stare, seemingly at a kaleidoscope poster in defiance of her presence.

He finished his beer and took another drag of his cigarette. The smoke plumed above him swirling into many tiny orbs. Tia stood up and reached into the fridge. She opened another beer and handed it to him. He didn't even look at her as he brought it to his mouth.

She knew how he was. His mood swings. They had known each other mere weeks, but had formed an unlikely bond on Friday afternoons when the dorm floor was pretty much empty except for them. When others were around, Dana was a social butterfly, plugging in conversation holes with jubulous tales of his boyhood exploits in Ireland and England, hugging the girls, taking a different one home every few days. He was a womanizer, a comedian, a mysterious stranger that she couldn't shake from her bones.

Dana gazed at nothing, sullenly, as if his mind was bulging with thoughts he couldn't dismiss. Tia wanted to speak but didn't want to annoy him. As he lay there, Tia wanted to curl up beside him, feel his long slender fingers cupped around her large fleshy bosom, her own arms hugging his narrow chest to hers. The beds were narrow and she wasn't but he was so slender they could both fit easily. He had many a woman in that narrow bed of his and she dreamed that one day, she'd be the next one. Maybe even on one of their Friday afternoons. Maybe today when the planets were perfectly aligned. She trembled to be thinking about it.

"I guess I should be going," she stammered. He turned his head as if suddenly realizing she was there.

"I appreciate your company, Tia," he said.

"Thanks."

Tia left him to his musings and returned to her room. She shut the door. The album had been over long ago and the arm of the needle bobbed gently against the spinning cardboard center of the record. She hoped that she hadn't worn it out but she could buy another copy of *Tommy* if worse came to worse.

The elevator rumbled and she heard voices of people returning from their last class of the day. It would soon be time to go eat in the cafeteria.

She wasn't feeling very hungry.

She pushed her typewriter as far to the side of the desk that she could and piled all the papers on her bed. She pulled a red velvet cloth from the top drawer as well as several small white candles. Reaching up to the shelf over her desk, she pulled down a large black candle. She also pulled out a little metal cauldron and a small bag of herbs. A piece of charcoal was placed in the cauldron. She wiped out her metal skull hand goblet to remove any dust that might have fallen in. A small amount of red wine was poured into the goblet. A large athame was taken from a wooden box lined with velvet on the shelf.

Tia organized the items on her makeshift altar, humming quietly as she did so.

More elevator rumblings, more chattering students flooded the halls. She was grateful for the noise as she sang softly.

She pulled a large book out from under her bed. She hefted it onto her chair and opened the binding. It was old and the leather that wrapped around it was splintered. She carefully turned the pages until she found one with foreign words. There was a large painting beside it of a man and woman kissing.

At last, it was time to light the candles. One by one, tiny flames flickered on her desk. She lamented the brightness of the afternoon and leaned over her bed to pull the thin curtains shut. It was darker but not by much.

She rang a small bell and proceeded to light the charcoal. As the flame surged from the mini cauldron she sprinkled a pinch of herbs into it. The colors sparked and for a moment she worried that the whole thing would set her room on fire, but it didn't. With a grin, she watched the flame subside. Words came out of her mouth as she chanted in a rhythmic pattern. The air in the room shifted. Her arms tingled, surging with electricity. Blue sparks began to shimmer along her, bouncing freely as her energy grew stronger.

She closed her eyes and imagined Dana standing in her doorway. She spoke the foreign words quickly and quietly. The candle flames flickered and the room filled with a mist where oblong phantoms danced. The images puckered and pulled, morphing into faces and wispy torsos. Long fingers pointed while arms lifted towards the door.

The mist heightened with activity as a small army of phantoms assembled. The heat of the room made her brow sweat and she opened her eyes in time to see a quick fog streak towards the door and then through it.

She smiled and extinguished the charcoal and the candles with her snuffer. She folded up the cloth and put it back in the drawer. She closed the big heavy book and slid it back under her bed. She put everything back where it had come from and turned the record over.

Within minutes, there was a knock at her door. She giggled a bit to herself and checked her face in the mirror. Her eyeliner was a bit smudged so she lifted her glasses to fix it. Other than that she looked rather presentable.

She opened the door to Dana. He clutched four beers and walked firmly into her room. She closed the door behind him, wondering if he could smell the charcoal and candle wax.

"Hey, I feel bad I zoned out on you. Let's have some more beer." He said. Tia took the opened beer from his hand and drank deeply from it. She stared at him while he paced around the room, circling once, twice, looking at her posters and her knickknacks.

Finally, he plopped down on the bed and patted the spot behind him.

"Have a seat. I don't bite, much," he joked. Tia's lips curved into a half smile as she sat beside him. She was trembling and hoped he wouldn't notice.

"So why are you here?" Tia said at last. He'd never been over to her room before.

"To drink some more beer. Just had the urge to do it with you," he winked. He held up his bottle. "Here's to drinking buddies."

"To drinking buddies," chorused Tia. She clicked his bottle. Dana cocked his head.

"Hey, that's *Tommy*," Dana said. "I love this album."

"Me too."

They sang along with the album for a while, Tia feeling his warmth wonderfully close to her as they harmonized with The Who.

"You hear about the murder the other day?" Tia asked.

"Yeah, god that's the fourth one, isn't it?" Dana said. "Wonder how many it takes to close down a campus."

"I guess no one should try to go anywhere after dark," Tia said.

"Yup. There's never been so many," Dana said as he swigged on his bottle.

"You know, I did some research on it. I remembered hearing stories when I was a kid."

"About this place?"

"Yep, and though this place isn't very old, there's been a hell of a lot of mishaps."

"Really?"

"You don't really hear much about it. The handbook certainly doesn't tell you."

"What?"

"Every seven years. It's a cycle. There's going to be three more killings before this is done."

"Seven killings every seven years?"

"Back in the seventies, people thought it was wild animals. There was lots of farm land around and thought maybe they were wolf attacks. Rabid and random."

"Killing people?" Dana raised his eyebrow.

104

"Sure. But this was more than wolf attacks. There's always seven. Can wolves count to seven?"

Dana shook his head, his eyes growing distant once more.

"Not that I'm aware of. Maybe this is something more like cult activity."

"But a cult wouldn't be so obvious . . ."

During the Christmas song, they opened more beer and Tia's head began to swim. She thought about seven killings in seven years. The killings had to stop. Side One was over and she flipped the record over to Side Four. She sat back down beside him, nervously sipping her beer.

Dana smiled at her and she tried not to gasp as he gently touched her face. She looked at him with large wanting eyes. He leaned forward to kiss her lips softly. The press of his lips against hers was all she had dreamed of and more. As she hungrily leaned into him, he wrapped his arms around her.

"You're so delicious," he whispered.

"I'm so glad you're here," she sighed. His kisses grew stronger and more urgent. She ran her fingers down his back, his muscles rippling beneath her touch. A wave of flesh and sinew knit between her hands, pulsing as steady as the tide, his lips losing grip as his tongue commandeered the kissing.

She pulled her hands back and sat away from him. His face was changing. Growing oblong and narrower. His nose was elongating as his teeth grew sharper.

She gasped and stared down at his hands. They were covered with fur, his fingers larger and meatier. He reached for her hand, firmly gripping it. She sighed again, his eyes hypnotising her as she squirmed.

"Kiss me," he commanded his voice low. She hesitated, wondering how she could touch that morphing face with her mouth once more. Yet there was still enough of Dana in the shift that she kissed him again. He transformed beneath her lips, his mouth growing more canine until she couldn't kiss him anymore. His clothes ripped as his chest expanded, his legs growing well muscled.

She noticed his pants were splitting from the massive protrusion from between his legs. She was hypnotised by the size of it as it sprang from the ripped seams of his trousers.

He grabbed her hand and placed it between his legs. He pushed her hand up and down, his head thrown back in pleasure.

She grimaced as his breath grew laboured but didn't try to pull away.

Outside the door the last class of the day survivors hooped and hollered with the sound of popping beer caps. Friday before dinner was the noisiest time of day as the stress of the week was gleefully obliterated by booze. A shriek of piercing laughter from a giggling girl in the hallway startled Dana from his hedonistic euphoria. He panted, his tongue lolling from his mouth.

"So it's true," Tia said, her hand still holding firm.

Dana snapped up his head and stared at her with red glowing eyes. He held her gaze for a moment but lost focus as she continued her seduction, her hand steadily distracting him.

His voice was rough and deep when he spoke.

"The legends," he pleaded.

"Yes, you're a werewolf." Tia grinned. Her hands pumped him faster and he growled in pleasure softly.

"You can tell," he said sarcastically, his face speckled, fur growing from it practically in front of her eyes.

"Always a comedian," she sneered and leaned closer to him. She held on to him, tough and quick, his pleasure visibly mounting.

"I've always wanted to meet one of you," she smiled. "Your legends always intrigued me."

"Which part? The taking of virgins or that our bite can make you one of us?" he leered. She squeezed him tightly and leaned closer to his face. She whispered.

"What do you think? I've waited my whole life to give myself to any mortal?" She licked him long and sensuously along his face. "I've been waiting for the likes of you," she murmured breathlessly into his ear.

She released her hands and sat back. He groaned with the sudden loss of pleasure.

Getting his bearings, he shook his head and then reached for the bottom of her t-shirt. He pulled it over her head and swiftly unbuttoned her jeans. Tia was impressed how dexterous he was with such contorted fingers. *He probably did that to all the girls.* She didn't care. She was warm and ready to continue on with what needed to be done. Her body surged with an anticipation that heated her flesh.

She helped him wriggle off her jeans and her bright red panties brightened the dimming room. Long orange fingers of sunset streamed through the gap in the curtain. The room was still hot, the warmth of their bodies making it more so.

He snatched off her panties and buried his face between her legs. She cried out at first with fear not certain if he meant to eat her or *eat her*. Soon she cooed with pleasure as his long wolf tongue explored her inner recesses. The heat of the room was overwhelming and she pulled breath heavily in and out of her lungs as she pushed him off of her. Without explanation, she crawled across the bed to open the window.

A swirl of cold air rattled in, sending the curtains flapping and the papers on her bed flying. She rushed to gather them up, assorted notes and rough drafts of stories shuffled around in the breeze. Dana lay back on the bed, his furry belly sticking out from under his torn t-shirt.

"Just give me a minute," she said as she gathered up her work. He leered at her with red glowing eyes. She tried to meet his gaze but didn't enjoy the pull she felt when she looked into them. She averted her gaze only to find his pleasure was obvious. She turned away from him and resumed paper picking. Once more she had a small stack and put them back on the desk where they had started in the first place. The circle was complete. Her lips curved into a secret smile.

As she kneeled on the bed, Dana pulled her down. He roughly parted her legs and touched her with his large knobbly paws.

She succumbed to his rhythmic ministrations, his hot breath on her shoulder. She was ready for him. Or maybe not.

"Just a minute," she said, pushing him away. He leaned back, anxious but not impatient.

"Protection," she said.

She went over to her desk and took down the large wooden box. She opened it without him seeing what she slipped into her hand. She took off her glasses, shaking her hair seductively. Her breasts bobbed as she walked. She returned to him, staring into his eyes, hands behind her back. The last remnants of sunset painted the walls as she sat on the bed beside him.

"Come back down, baby," he cooed.

She leaned over to kiss him. One hand stroked his raised brow as she marvelled at his elongated mouth and sharp teeth. She ground her hips against his, squeezing him between her thighs. His eyes closed in ecstasy. Away from his sharp eyed glare, she raised her other hand, brandishing the athame. She dragged her knife-free hand down his cheek, stroking along his long furry jaw. She massaged his tongue firmly with her fingers. He groaned as she pulled on his tongue, her fingers wrapped around it gripping tightly.

She writhed herself against him and craved to feel him inside of her. *Not just yet.*

She rubbed his tongue some more, sucking on it with her lips. His gasping snarls weren't heard in the chaos of the partying going on outside of her door. "Listening to You" was just starting up and her body pulsed to the rhythm.

Dana moaned as she sucked harder, his hips moving wildly in a frenzy. The moves made her want him more and she finally lowered herself onto him. Her fingers clutched his tongue, holding it rigidly in her hand. With the other hand, she brought the knife down and into the fleshiest part of it, just inside her mouth. His panicked twitch thrust him deep inside of her and she cried out in exquisite pleasure mingled with a sharp piercing pain as she sawed through his tongue with the athame.

He howled as blood flooded her fingers. Her grasp on his tongue grew tenuous and eventually slipped away. The knife was nearly through and she clawed at the flesh with slipping fingernails. She clutched his tongue long enough for the last final slashes to break it away. She cried out orgasmically as she raised the tongue above her head before it slipped from her fingers.

Dana bucked his hips up high as he reached for her with his large taloned paws. She arched her head back, pulling every inch of him deep inside of her as she savoured the pulsing flood of sensation flooding through her.

When Tia collapsed forward, she thrust the athame hard into his chest and the smell of burning flesh filled the room. His first shuffling thrashes of escape didn't last long as exhaustion overwhelmed him. He jerked and spasmed and then was still.

Slowly Tia lifted herself from him and plucked his tongue from the bed. She went over to her desk and wrapped it in paper. She lit a candle and said a small prayer.

When she was done, she turned back to him. His body rippled as flesh molded and sank in upon itself, fur shedding to the bed and floor. He was soon going to be recognizable as himself once more.

She slowly pulled her clothes back on staring at him in awestruck wonderment.

The record had long been over and she placed the needle back on the big *Tommy* finale. "See me, Feel me" cried plaintively over the speakers as she stared at his pulsing body. As the strains of "Listening to You" started up, his transformation to man was complete. Tia walked over to him and straddled him as he lay back on the bed. He was panting, his gasping breaths punctuated with shrieks as he caught his breath. At last his breathing subsided and Tia watched him carefully as she ground her jean clad groin against him.

He stared up at her with wide blue eyes.

"What the fuck?" he asked, his speech slurred. Tia stepped off of him and to the floor.

She went over to the dresser and unfolded the tongue. It was sticking a bit to the paper and she did what she could to pick the bits off. She handed it to him and he stared at it.

"What am I thupposed to do with thith?"

"See if it grows back."

He stared at her with exasperation and held the tongue inside of his mouth. She waited for a few minutes while he fussed and fiddled with it. He took his hands away and stared at her in disbelief.

"I think it worked." He said.

"I cured you," she said with a wink and she placed her hand around the athame that still protruded from his chest.

"You did. How?" He winced as she slowly pulled the knife out.

"Magic," she said coyly, carrying the dripping knife over to her desk. She opened the drawer and removed the velvet cloth she used for her athame. She wiped the knife with it.

Dana touched the wound that was rapidly healing. He shook his head in disbelief as he stared at the dried blood on his finger. He put his fingers into his mouth and pulled out his tongue. Much shorter but a tongue just the same.

"I'm cured?"

"You won't have the curse anymore."

"Well . . . thank you," he stammered sitting up. His shreds of clothing clung to him as he put his face in his hands. "Wow."

"You won't be tormented by your transformation when you get horny anymore. The downside is that you're stuck with me forever. But that's okay. I picked you very carefully."

"What?"

"You mated with a virgin during the spell in the circle. I am yours." He stared at her with glassy blue eyes, his pupils tiny black pricks. As he pondered her words, his pupils grew large and dark. His mouth curved into a smile. He reached over to her face, cupping his hands around her cheeks and pulled her towards him. Tia's heart thumped so loudly that she hoped he couldn't hear it.

"You cured me." He stated still in wonderment. Tia trembled, anxiously worrying about what he might say.

"Yes."

"Then I am yours forever." He pulled her towards him and kissed her roughly on the mouth.

There was a loud knock on the door and then a rattle as someone tried the door handle. Tia looked over at the door but declined to do anything about it. She returned to the urgent lips of her lover. Dana's hand gripped her leg as the door burst open. A huge wolf like creature covered in a large black cape rushed in and lunged at Tia. There were screams from the hallway as people watched the beast smash through the door. It tore at Tia with large gaping jaws, sharp jagged teeth tearing holes easily through Tia's flesh. The wolf creature shook her head from side to side as Dana tried to simultaneously pull at Tia and beat at the beast.

Nothing was working. In the hallway, people panicked and fled down the fire escape stairs by the elevators. A few men looked into the room but in seeing the size and savagery of the beast chose to flee quickly. Tia screamed and beat at the beast. It gnawed through her back, teeth gnashing and snapping. Dana jumped on the beast's back, hitting her with his fists. She quickly threw him off. His human form was slight and no match for the mammoth behemoth of snarling teeth and snatching claws that were making short work of Tia.

Dana edged towards the door and slowly kicked it shut.

"No sense in scaring everyone when what you want is right here, I guess." Dana said, staring intensely at the beast.

The beast turned towards him, Tia's severed arm hanging loosely from her dripping jaws.

"You want me?" Dana asked.

The beast spit the arm out onto the ground. She picked up Tia's head and examined it, tossing it from paw to paw. The beast was twice the size that Dana had ever been in his other form. He stared in awe at her.

"Those kind are messing with nature. Curing werewolves, indeed."

"I think it might be kind of nice," Dana said.

"Nonsense," the beast said. "Her price was you were tied to her forever. And ever. That's the cure, that's the spell. More so then beauty and the beast. Is that what you wanted?"

Dana shrugged. "I didn't know her. She seemed pleasant enough."

The wolf tossed Tia's head back onto the bed where it rolled sideways until her vacant eyes were staring up at the ceiling.

"I saved you," the wolf beast said. "She tried to remove the curse. I removed her. Now you truly are free."

"Wow," said Dana, trying to act braver then he felt. The bloody saliva dripping from her jaws did nothing to make him feel free or saved. "I guess I should thank you . . . ?"

"It doesn't matter. First she saves you, and then she would get bored of you. Next thing you know, she's hunting more of us. Maybe for sport. Who knows what spells she's capable of casting? Better to be rid of her before we find out."

Dana stared at Tia's head, at the half closed eyes that had looking so longingly at him mere moments before.

"What good am I now that I'm not a werewolf?"

"You will always be a werewolf," The beast said as she swiped her claw along his arm. Dana cried out with pain. As blood poured from the fresh wound, Dana shook his head in disbelief. The beast licked the wound with her long wet tongue, bloody saliva mixing in with the fresh blood that spilled out.

"For fuck's sake . . ." Dana moaned.

The beast grabbed Dana's face with both of her hands and stared into his eyes.

"You're back to who you were and now it's back to work," the beast said, her wolf form shifting slowly into human. She was very tall, over six feet, and broadly boisterous. Her hair was long and golden and she had deep green eyes. Her body was round and heavy and she stared expectantly at Dana, kissing him full on the mouth with her blood soaked lips.

"Your work is important."

"Work . . ." Dana echoed.

"You're the gatekeeper, whether you know it or not. You found the first virgin here who wants to hunt us and believe me, there will be many more."

The tall large woman gathered up her black cape and slung it over her shoulders. She pulled the hood over her head and opened the door. There was no one around, everyone had been frightened away.

In the distance, Dana heard sirens.

"I have more work to do before the cycle is finished," she said. "Stay out of my way, and I'll stay out of yours."

She ran through the hallways and disappeared down a stairwell. Dana stared after her and then turned to stare at the mess in Tia's room.

He wasn't sure what to do. He stared at the body parts and the pooling blood. The bed was dishevelled and he noticed a huge book wedged under the bed. He pulled it out and saw that it was old and full of beautiful paintings and foreign writing.

Since no one was around, he scooped up the book, quietly walked out of the room and shut the door. He crept down the hall until he was back in his own room. He locked the door tightly behind him and with shaking hands, opened his fridge. Grateful to see more beer inside, he grabbed two and opened them both at once. He quickly drank from one and the other until he had calmed down. He stared at the bloody gash on his arm, the gash that was already healing.

He couldn't think about all that had happened. He couldn't think about what would happen when Tia's decapitated body was found. He'd have to say something and everyone saw the beast.

In the distance, he heard the howl of a wolf blending in with the approaching sirens. He wiped his face and hands on his towel and tossed it in his closet. Putting *Quadrophenia* on Side Four, he sat on his bed and carefully opened the old dusty book.

York University, Stong College, 2010

Dana stepped from the elevator and rounded the corner. A young, plump woman bumped into him on her way out of her room.

"I'm sorry," she stammered, her round acne scarred face flushed a scarlet hue as she tried to meet his gaze. Dana adjusted his knapsack and stared at her. Thick black glasses, shaggy brown hair with streaks of purple, round shape that had never been touched by a man. A vague scent of incense clung to her.

"No worries," Dana said as he continued down the hall and towards his dorm room. He heard her go into the bathroom and knew the cycle had started one more.

DIFFERENT SKINS

BY MICHAEL KELLY

Gary had no use for ghosts.

"They covered her over with mud and sticks," Will said.

Carmen sipped her beer, licked the foam off her lips, and placed the glass on the scarred wooden table. "That's awful," she said.

Gary had been transfixed by Carmen's small pink tongue, the way it circled her mouth.

Will punched Gary's arm. "Wake up," Will said. "I was talking to you."

Gary shrugged. Will was always talking, telling stories. When Gary had first arrived at the University of Toronto, Will was seated beside him in Philosophy 101. Carmen was in front of him. The three of them were new to the University, new to the city. Chatty Will had struck up conversations with them. Since then they spent a good amount of their evenings together at the University's Hart House Pub. Gary went along because of Carmen. She seemed enthralled with Will's tall tales.

"Sorry," Gary said. "I'm a little pre-occupied. What were you saying?"

"Ghosts," Carmen said. "We were talking about ghosts. Don't you ever pay attention, Gary?" Carmen chided. "Even in Philosophy class, every time I turn around you're daydreaming. Or staring at me."

Gary blushed, hoped it didn't show in the dim light. He swallowed some beer, said "Some of us are talkers, some of us are thinkers."

Will and Carmen exchanged a look; they laughed.

Gary flushed again, this time with anger.

117

Carmen said, "Sheesh, relax, Gary. We're not trying to take the piss out of you."

Gary had faces, like skins, like personalities, for every occasion. If you could put on a face, you could get whatever you wanted. He tried on his most sincere face, stared at Carmen, unblinking. "Sorry, C, you're right." He glanced at Will. "Go on, Will. Start again. I'm listening."

Will sighed. "Sure," he said. "I'm going to tell you about the ghost of Taddle Creek. The Lady of the Sticks. You both know Philosopher's Walk, don't you?"

Carmen nodded.

"Of course," Gary said. Philosopher's Walk was the large green space that meandered over much of the University's campus. It was mostly lawn and trees and scenic footpaths. If Gary had no use for ghosts, he had even less use for parks and songbirds. He didn't come to the city to get back to nature. He stared at Carmen. She was looking at Will, expectant, waiting. Her aquiline profile and pouty lips were perfect. No, Gary thought, she's the reason I came to the city. You didn't see girls like Carmen in Wilkie, Saskatchewan.

"It's a little-known fact," Will continued," that the footpaths of Philosopher's Walk follow what was once a small river called Taddle Creek. There are traces of it still, along the walk. The small ravine bordering the path is what's left of the creek. The ghost of Taddle Creek haunts Philosopher's Walk. She's a young woman, 21 or 22-years-old, our age, who drowned in the creek in the 1880's. She's been spotted on the footpaths, dressed in denim coveralls dripping water. Her hair is cut short, in a fashion that suited the men of that era. Some have said her skin is translucent green, covered in algae, and that at night you can see her essence moving along the various footpaths, like

118

some macabre lantern. Leeches and moss crawl along her green skin. Sometimes people have seen what looks like wet footprints appearing and disappearing on the paths, followed by the sounds of rushing water and strange gurgles.

"Other eyewitnesses have said she isn't green at all, but is a creature of mud and sticks, shambling along the footpaths at night, as if she is searching for something."

Gary snickered. "Yeah, a hot bath."

Carmen shot Gary a withering look. He was about to apologize, then thought "Fuck it," it's only a joke. When did the world get so serious, so damn politically correct?

"Why?" Carmen asked. "Why is she here, haunting the campus?"

Will leaned toward Carmen. She inched closer to Will, looked at him all dreamy-eyed. It was as if Gary weren't even there. As if he didn't exist at all. He might as well be back in Wilkie.

"Do you believe in ghosts?" Will asked. Carmen nodded, uttered a breathy "yes."

Will turned to Gary. "What about you?"

Gary shrugged, said "Not really. Do you, Will? You believe all this stuff?"

"Yes," Will said. "I do. I've seen her, The Lady of the Sticks, once, very briefly, late at night, sloshing along the creek bed, a walking bramble of sticks and thorns. It was early one morning. I was getting a run in before classes. I saw movement down in the little gulley, so I stopped running, walked to the edge of the footpath. I thought, perhaps, there was a coyote or groundhog or something down by the creek. Peering down, I didn't see anything, at first. Then a figure appeared to separate from the bank of the culvert, materializing from the mud, and tottered along the creek bed. I blinked. It was early, I'd not eaten, and I was breathing heavy from the run. I'd convinced myself I was seeing things. But the stick creature seemed to sense my presence, and it turned, slowly. Though it hadn't a proper face, it stared right at me, dark hollows for eyes. I saw a mouth, stuffed with mud, moving noiselessly in the middle of that dark countenance. It cocked its head, as if sizing me up, then turned back – with a forlorn resignation, I thought – to the creek. It trundled up the shallow bed of water and disappeared around the bend. In hindsight, it seemed a pitiable thing."

"Wow," Carmen said. "Incredible. Nothing like that has ever happened to me."

Will smiled at Carmen. "I got the distinct impression it was searching for something. That it wanted something from me. Some sort of help, perhaps. It was trying to tell me something, but its mouth and throat were clogged with dirt."

Gary grinned. He knew what Will was doing. He was trying on a different skin, one that would impress Carmen. He knew the game and could play along. "Impressive story, Will," Gary said.

Will frowned. "It's true."

Gary drummed his fingers on the scarred tabletop. "Of course," he said.

Carmen glanced at Gary, turned back to Will. "You found out what it was?"

"Bet you did some research on it, eh, Will?" Gary said.

"Yes," Will said. "After the experience on the footpath, I started poking around the reference library, looking at old newspaper clippings, books, etc. Here's what I discovered.

"It was the 1880's," Will said. "Times were tough. It was a hard world, especially for a single woman looking for work." He took a swallow of beer. "There was a city work crew commissioned to bury Taddle Creek and convert it to an underground sewer system. Pretty advanced stuff for the time.

"Anyway," Will continued, "it was a big project, and everyone in the city knew about it.

"One day this young man shows up at the work site, looking for the foreman. This *man* is young, scrawny, dressed in overalls, his hair cut straight and short; a billed-cap on his head protects his face from the sun, and from the curious crew."

Will stopped, slurped some beer. The ambient noise of the pub; hushed conversations, clinking glasses, and raucous laughter, buffeted their table like some live thing. Will cast an inquisitive glance at Gary and Carmen. Gary thought Will's gaze lingered overly long on Carmen.

Will grinned, said "Of course our thin young man with the strange haircut wasn't a man, at all, but a young woman posing as a man to try and find gainful employment."

"Of course," Gary muttered. "That's what women do."

Carmen glared.

Gary tried on one of his many faces. "A joke, Carmen. Just a joke."

Carmen looked away.

"Anyway," Will continued, "the young lady was of independent spirit. She'd come from a small town to the big city to make her mark." Will turned to Gary. "Like you, Gare."

Gary hated to be called 'Gare.' He conjured his Cheshire cat face, the one that promised to eat you alive, fixed it on Will. "Whatever you say, Will." Then, to himself: *Always. Whatever you say.*

"Taddle Creek is the biggest construction project in the city," Will said. "It's ambitious, and even though times are tough, as they are now, day labourers are needed to help get the city's new sewer system done in a timely fashion." He sipped flat beer. "So, suitably disguised, our young lady is handed a shovel and hired."

"How did she pass for a man?" Carmen asked.

Gary forced a smile. "It's easy. We all have different skins."

Carmen blinked at him. Gary continued smiling at her until she looked away.

"That's the tragedy," Will continued. "One day, the men in the crew found out there was a woman in their midst. Maybe her hat slipped off. Maybe there was something decidedly different about her movements, her size, and her voice, how she carried herself. Who knows? Either way, the crew found out. And they were none too happy."

Will looked at Carmen. "Back then," he said, "men were inherently crueler to women."

"Not much different these days," Carmen said.

Gary couldn't be sure, but he thought Carmen's eyes flicked his way.

"Apparently," Will continued, "this happened near the completion of the sewer system. One of the lasts days. There'd been some test runs. So the men decided they would have some fun with the poor woman. It was a Friday. Pay day. Near the end of her shift, the foreman sent her down into the belly of sewer with a shovel. She was told to literally shovel shit, keep it moving."

Like you, Will, Gary thought. *You and your tall tales. Shoveling shit.*

Will rubbed his chin, blinked, and moved closer to Carmen. "So the young lady went down the hatch, hauling a shovel. Once she was down there, though, they closed all the hatches, locked them. The men thought they would put a fright into her, keep her down there in the dark, wet, and smelly sewer."

Carmen shuddered. "I can't imagine," she said.

"Truly appalling," Gary said, feigning disgust.

"The crew had a good chuckle, then decided to break for lunch. What harm could there be if she spent an hour or so down there? So they headed to the nearest pub, money in their pockets, and proceeded to partake of the local establishment's libations. Hours later, drunk and lighter of pocket, they trundled back to the work site. It was only upon returning that they recalled they'd left the woman down there. So they unlocked the hatches and waited for her to come up. But she didn't emerge from the darkness. Nothing did. At least not right away.

"Eventually a few of the men went down the hatch. They stumbled about blindly in the semi-darkness, calling. And they found her, nearly tripped over her, half-buried in a pile of mud and sticks, her mouth agape as if she were trying to scream or catch one last, desperate breath. Dead."

Carmen trembled. "O-Oh, my," she said.

Gary thought Carmen was going to cry. He grinned unpleasantly.

"The crew decided they would leave her down there. They figured no one knew about her. She was a day labourer and the records, if any, were spotty at best. So the men in the sewer pushed her body into the mud and covered her over until there was no trace of her.

"As far as we know, she is buried there still. Only her spirit walks along the paths of the campus. Her bones are deep in the mud."

"A mouthful of mud," Carmen said. "Silenced forever."

Gary thought about putting something in Carmen's mouth.

Will reached over, patted Carmen's hand. "Yes."

Gary sighed.

"What is it?" Will asked.

"Nothing, Will. It's a good story. You like telling stories."

"You're not convinced?" Carmen asked.

"No," Gary said. "It's all nonsense. Mumbo jumbo."

"There were news accounts of a missing Toronto woman," Will said. "And mentions of an industrial accident during the final days of the sewer's construction. I've pieced this account together from various sources."

"I'm sure you have," Gary said. "It's the ghost stuff. Hocus-pocus. I don't believe it."

"But I've seen her," Will said. "So have others."

Gary groaned. "*I* haven't."

"Not yet," Carmen said. "Maybe we should look for her."

Gary was about to mock Carmen's idea when he caught himself and slipped another skin on. "That's a great idea, Carmen," he said. His voice was treacle. This was an opportunity to show her that he was every bit the man Will was, and more. "I'll go one better. I'll spend the night down in the gulley. If this stick ghost is down there, I'll find her."

"Why on earth would you do that?" Carmen asked.

Gary shrugged, smiled. "Why not? I'll go to the source. Try to prove you right, Will." *Or wrong*, he thought.

Carmen and Will looked at him. "Sure," Will said. "This'll be a fun exercise. When?"

Gary stared at Carmen until she glanced away. "Tomorrow," he said.

#

Gary was wearing a different skin today. It was thick and tough. Impenetrable. Like him. It registered on his face, where a half-sneer perched like a leashed predator.

Carmen, Will, and Gary stood on the curving path of Philosopher's Walk. Save for a few straggling late-night students, the campus was empty. Parallel to the path was a small trickle of water, the remnants of Taddle creek. The creek snaked slowly through a culvert of high, muddy banks. The culvert twisted away, around a bend, south, through a stand of elms and oaks, toward Toronto proper, to empty into the vast and frigid Lake Ontario.

Will pointed. "Down there," he said. "That's where she's buried. In the mud. The creek banks were the sewer walls."

It was dusk, the sky blue-black. The sodium lights along the path, at least the ones that hadn't been smashed by vandals or drunken frat boys, threw garish orange light along the walkway. The creek and muddy culvert disappeared in the encroaching darkness.

"Okay, then," Gary said, flicking on his flashlight, "off I go."

"How will we know if you find her?" Carmen asked.

"I'll tell you, won't I?" Gary said.

Will shuffled forward. "Even if you don't see her, it doesn't prove anything."

Gary frowned. "Well, I'm willing to give it a try. That's something, isn't it?"

"It's true, Will," Carmen said. "He's open to it so cut him some slack."

Gary smiled. This was brilliant, this concerned sensitive type. He'd have to wear this skin more often. Tomorrow, he'd be golden.

Will scratched his head. "Sure. Of course. Good luck, Gare."

"Adieu," Gary said, then turned with a flourish and, sweeping the flashlight before him, moved along the path, down the bank and splashed into shallow Taddle creek. He stopped, looked back, saw Carmen and Will watching him, so waved and hurried through the creek-bed and around the bend. Out of sight, he climbed back up the muddy creek bank and squatted. He'd wait half an hour, give Carmen and Will time to get back to the residence, then he'd take the rear footpath along the campus back to his dorm. Then, in the morning, he'd wake early, throw the muddy clothes back on, and sneak back down to the creek, where Carmen and Will would find him.

He smiled. It was a good plan. Ghosts, he thought. He had no use for them. He had even less use for Will. Always glomming onto Carmen. Always talking. You couldn't shut him up. A mouthful of dirt would keep him quiet.

Gary lay back on the bank, stretched. He turned off the flashlight. It wasn't quite dark yet. The sky was a shifting mass of pearled clouds. The wind pushed them south, toward the lake. And the night-wind sang through the autumn trees, low and sad. Another sound reached Gary's ears; a slow gurgle of water. The creek. Then a sloshing sound like some *thing* moving through the shallow water, slow and deliberate.

He sat up, blinked. Momentarily, Gary thought he saw a dim shadow move across the creek-bed. Then that gurgling sound again, only this time it came from behind him, and it was more of a gasping or choking sound. He was about to peer around when two figures crested the creek bank opposite him. He squinted into the near dark. Carmen and Will. They were holding hands, staring down at him, silent as ghosts.

Gary tried to stand, but he'd been squatting too long in the same spot and his feet had sunk deep into the mud and were stuck. He attempted to pull a leg free, but he only sank further. The ground below him shifted, rippled, made a wet sucking sound. Gary put his hands on the ground to try and get some leverage and boost himself free. His hands sank into the runny mud. It seemed as if the ground pulled at them greedily.

On the other bank, the two figures hugged, blending into one shadowy shape. *Why aren't they helping me?* Gary thought. "Hey," he called. "Down here."

The ancient wind moaned, moved along the creek-bed. The air thrummed, smelled of dead leaves. The ground swelled, pulsed as if alive, and lapped at Gary. He struggled, and fell further into the moving mud.

"Help!"

Beneath Gary something hard and angular poked through the mud, as if he were laying on a pile of broken twigs or a heap of bones. The bone-sticks broke through the ground and two appendages encircled him like the arms of a long lost lover.

"Help."

Gary writhed. And the mud and bone thing pulled. He sank. He opened his mouth to scream and mud and sticks filled his mouth. The further he descended into the creek bank, the more the black mud crawled over him. And just before he sank beneath the surface, he was nothing more than a skin of mud.

#

Hand in hand, Will and Carmen turned away, walked along the footpath back toward the campus. Carmen looked at Will, half-smiled, squeezed Will`s hand, said, "Life is full of sacrifices, Will. There's nothing to feel bad about. You helped her. Set her free. Sacrificed one to save many."

Will grinned. "Oh, I don't feel bad about it. He was always talking about people having different skins. He's wearing a new one now, I suppose."

"In a way," Carmen said, "he was right. We do have different skins. Some of us don't wear them on the outside."

Will leaned over, kissed Carmen on the mouth. "Amen to that," he said.

Down the footpath, around the bend, through a shallow creek-bed, and up a muddy creek bank, something stirred. A dark, vaguely humanoid shape wrenched itself free of the creek bank. It stood in darkness, blinked dirt-encrusted eyes, to be met with darkness still. It opened a mud-filled mouth, but no sound emanated from that dark maw. Then the mud-thing turned and shambled blindly through the shallow water, its black mouth issuing screams that no one could hear.

SARA

BY NANCY KILPATRICK

Ashley trailed the group of seven as they entered the stand-alone Victorian structure known as the Redpath Museum. Her heart beat wildly. She was about to meet Sara!

She just could not believe that she was really here, finally, about to begin four years at Montreal's amazing McGill University, away from her mom, from Saskatchewan, from the past. And plowing towards the future goal she'd harbored since childhood when she'd visited the Royal Tyrell Museum with her parents and sister. As far back as she could remember, Ashley had *always* wanted to be a paleontologist and if this wasn't the perfect place to get her undergraduate degree, she didn't know where that was.

McGill was *so* prestigious. She'd been lucky to get in, and to win a partial scholarship, but then her marks were excellent. And she just *knew* that after four years of piling on the biology and geology courses, she would be accepted into McGill's MA program. McGill and the University of Alberta had an exchange program for Masters students and she could go back and forth on summer digs. Once she had her MA she'd go for a PhD, then a full-time job at—

"This is the skeleton of a Plesiosaur, a prehistoric aquatic reptile, and over in this case is a modern-day Japanese Spider Crab," Sylvie Laroche said. She was leading the freshman group tour through the Redpath. Half turning towards the enormous crab skeleton, she went on to relate that the ten legs of this species can span four meters, they

129

are known to live to 100 years, and these giants dwell at the bottom of the ocean and feed on shellfish and dead animals.

Ashley was mesmerized by Sylvie, who possessed only the trace of a sexy French accent. The seriously chic graduate student wore a layered outfit in shades of grey and taupe. A charming smile spread over her full lips, giving her lovely face a warm human quality that Ashley hadn't really twigged to up until that moment. Clearly in her element, Sylvie was the woman Ashley saw herself as becoming. Someone with confidence, not troubled by the past. A woman marching into the future, who was doing what she loved; in Ashley's case that would be working in the field of dinosaur bones.

As she glanced around the museum, at the wood and glass cases of minerals, and the skeletons of prehistoric animals hanging from the ceiling or still imbedded in rock placed along the walls, Ashley could clearly see what a huge leap this was for a farm girl from Saskatchewan. A girl with dreams, and Ashley had plenty. The big one was to one day work at the Royal Tyrell Museum in Drumheller as a Paleontologist.

Ashley could picture her life in the future, returning for a visit to her hometown, no longer shy but a sophisticated woman who had studied in the big city and traveled the world, giving talks on the latest finds to her peers. Who now was in charge of digging up bones and reconstructing skeletons of the enormous creatures that prowled the planet long before human beings even got here—

"If you'll follow me this way," Sylvie said, and the group started up the steps.

They skipped the second floor and went up to the next level, passing on the landing a taxidermic grouping: Gorilla, lion, some sort of antlered animal that hadn't been labeled. Sylvie explained that "This is a Victorian-type display. In the past, natural-history museums often mounted dead animals brought back from foreign lands. It's not really in vogue anymore."

As they studied the display then started up another flight of steps, Ashley thought about her first trip to the Tyrell when she was thirteen. Sure, she'd seen movies, and lots of pictures of dinosaur bones, but viewing the bones for real . . . There were so many skeletons, almost all of them found in Saskatchewan and Alberta, and she felt proud that she was from out west, the place where dinosaurs once walked, crawled, swam, flew—

"That is awesome," a girl in front of her said as she turned to Ashley. "I mean this stuff is so *old*. Wouldn't you just *love* to have a pair of those?" She pointed to the elaborately embroidered red Chinese slippers just three inches long, made when wealthy Chinese girl children had had their feet bound because tiny feet were considered beautiful.

The girl, dressed in goth black, with short black hair and reddish makeup around the eyes, looked at Ashley seriously, and then her face broke into a grin. "I'm Jessica. Everybody calls me Jess. I'm over at New Residence Hall."

"No way! Me too!" Ashley said. "I just got in two days ago."

"I've been here like all week but I went to stay at my brother's place on the weekend."

"He lives here?"

"Yeah. So does my mom. She's on the west island."

"How come you don't live at home?"

Jess stared at her for a moment, one penciled eyebrow lifted. "Like, why would I want to live at home?"

Ashley felt stupid, her practical prairie roots exposed. She'd have to watch that. "Yeah, right. Why?"

Sylvie was talking about the African masks in another case. This 'floor' was really a narrow balcony that went around the entire room with a huge opening in the center that looked down to the Dawson Gallery. Ashley could see Sara from above. She felt excitement bubbling and just wanted to get all these cultural artifacts over with.

Finally they headed back down. Sylvie walked to the center of the room and pointed out the Albertasaurus skeleton and then the skull above a display case with antlers that must have reached eight feet across. And finally, she gestured towards the enormous skull. "Anybody know what this is?"

Ashley couldn't stop herself from raising her hand. She heard Jessica snicker behind her. "It's a Triceratops horridus. Well, the skull of the dinosaur. Triceratops means 'three-horned face'."

"Somebody's been doing her homework," Sylvie said. "We call her—"

SARA

Ashley was startled. The name, of course, she knew. But the *voice*! It wasn't Sylvie's. She glanced around quickly to see if anyone else had heard anything odd, but from the looks on faces, she was the only one. She figured it was the name that made her imagine the voice.

"Sara was likely a teenager when she died, between ten to fifteen years old. This Triceratops could have lived to twenty-five or thirty years. She probably weighted three to five tones and measured about six meters long. Her skull is two meters and it alone weighs 275 kilograms. Sara died in Saskatchewan about 65 million years ago—"

"Where in Saskatchewan?" Ashley stammered, then felt her face redden.

"A small town called Eastend. Actually, about an hour from there, in the Badlands."

'I'm from there!' Ashley almost cried out, but blew out air instead of words. She didn't want to sound like a *total* idiot. And besides, the dinosaur's name was Sara, and . . .

But the skull caught her attention in the here and now. It was amazing! Ashley hadn't seen a Triceratops since she was thirteen, at the Tyrell. She knew they weren't the superstars of the dino world, not the terrifying T-Rexes, the ferocious Raptors, or even the colossal Mammoths. But the gentle, vegetarian Triceratops' were special. And Sara even looked like a teenager. "She's beautiful," Ashley murmured.

Jessica, behind her, snorted, but Ashley moved closer to the barrier-less specimen. Even though this was only a cast of the skull and some of the pieces of the actual skull bones were in a case behind, Ashley just wanted to touch Sara. To feel the shape of her, to connect in some way . . .

"These two goat-like protrusions on the top of her head are eye horns," Sylvie said. "And this rhinoceros-like nose horn juts from her nasal chamber. Her mouth, as you can see, is beaklike—she was a vegetarian. But Sara's most impressive feature is the frill, here at the back. It contained blood vessels, like an elephant's ears, and was composed of bone with a layer of keratinous over that—much like a human's fingernails. The frill changed shape as the triceratops aged and we think it was used for courtship displays."

Just then a man entered the group and Sylvie introduced him as Dr. Hans Larsson, the Palaeontologist at the Redpath. He gave a brief talk, explaining that Sara's skull was collected in 2007 and 2008 and that it took his field team ten days to recover the 400 fragments which were imbedded in eight tons of rock.

As Ashley listened, she could well imagine herself working with Dr. Larsson when she went for her MA. Everything seemed to be falling into place.

Ashley wanted to ask Dr. Larsson a million questions but couldn't risk becoming known as some kind of bone nerd! And then he was gone and the group began looking at other specimens around the room. But Ashley stayed with Sara.

She felt as if Sara was smiling at her, wishing her well, and that made Ashley happy. And weepy, because suddenly she thought of her twin sister, and sadness fell around her like a fog.

"Over here . . ." she heard Sylvie say, but Ashley couldn't move. She tuned Sylvie out and tuned in to the past.

They had left their farm in Eastend just as the sun was rising over the vast Saskatchewan horizon, the tent and other camping gear packed into the small white trailer their old Dodge truck pulled because the truck bed was filled with other stuff, especially food. Mom never wanted to leave home without a couple of coolers, "Just in case anybody might starve to death or die of thirst," Dad always joked.

Mom and Dad rode in the cab, Ashley and her sister in the back of the pickup, facing backwards, the wilting August prairie sun tempered by a hot-but-bearable breeze whipping their hair and skin as the flat black-tar highway streaked away from them.

They had just turned thirteen, and had reached the point of desperation, at least Ashley had; she wanted to do things apart from her sister. For the last year Ashley had made an effort to dress differently, and cultivate different friends, even a boyfriend, although in Eastend there weren't that many kids their age so she couldn't be too picky. But going their separate ways, to the extent that Ashley had, only drew her sister closer to her, and that was getting

134

annoying. They could even read each other's thoughts, and finish sentences, much to the amazement of their parents and to Ashley's growing despair.

The twins sang along with some of their favorite songs on the old 'suitcase radio' their mom had been given by her dad when she was a teenager, at least they accompanied the singers until the batteries died, then they had just sang every song that came into their heads for the rest of the five hour trip to Drumheller.

The Tyrell was amazing and the family spent hours inside. Ashley did not want to leave. That's when she decided what she would do with her life. As if reading her mind, her sister said, 'Let's dig up dinosaur bones together when we grow up!'

Rather than end the trip early, Dad had decided they'd return to Saskatchewan and camp out in the Badlands overnight...

"Earth to Ashley!"

"Uh, sorry. I was daydreaming."

"Well, the tour's over," Jess said. "I'm headed back to the dorm. You coming?"

"Yeah, sure."

Just as they exited the building, a tall, lean guy approached, also dressed goth style, though Ashley suspected that the word 'goth' wasn't used anymore.

"This's Matt," Jess said. "He's from where you're from."

"Eastend?" Ashley asked, not recognizing Matt; she would have been totally surprised if there was another student from Eastend, Saskatchewan at McGill, especially somebody with Matt's style.

"Calgary," he said, smiling down at her. "She thinks everybody west of Ontario's from the same place." Black hair, cute mouth turned up at the corners, summer-sky blue eyes that seemed to reach inside her . . . Ashley felt her face burn in embarrassment, partly because she had blurted out the hick town she came from, and partly because he was scrumptious and she hoped he didn't notice her noticing.

"Hi," she said quickly, looking at her shoes, realizing how last year these old runners were, and then said to Jess, "I guess the dorm's that way, right?"

"Yep," Jess said. "The campus is pretty straight-forward."

It was a sunny day, warm for September, although maybe it was always like this in Montreal. Ashley had thought it might be snowing already. Sometimes it did this early in Eastend.

They circled the 'bowl', a grassy depression in the earth with a fountain of three life-sized nudes dripping water. Surrounding them stood the imposing buildings, both old and new, that composed most of the campus. McGill, she had learned, was almost a city within a city, with its own rules and regulations. There were few cars, but plenty of bikes on the narrow streets and paths that swirled around the university.

As if reading her mind, Matt said, "This is the only place in Montreal you can buy a hot dog from a street vendor's cart."

"Really?" Ashley said, although she had never seen a street vendor selling hot dogs or anything else in Eastend.

They left by the east gates and walked along rue Prince Arthur. But instead of turning left at avenue du Parc to get to New Residence Hall, Jess and Matt kept going east. Ashley didn't want to ask where they were headed, but maybe they were expecting that she'd leave them alone. She wondered if Matt was Jess's boyfriend. They were both really cute, tall, slim, none of the baby fat that Ashley knew she had to ditch if she ever wanted to grow up. Working on a farm all your life made a girl stocky, or so she'd read in the in-flight mag on the plane.

She made a split-second choice to follow and eventually the trio reached boulevard St. Laurent. Ashley had been warned about this street by one of the fourth years who was moving out of the dorm room as she was moving in. "Hang out on St. Laurent and you'll lose your mind, plus your grades will crash and burn. This school will drive you crazy enough!"

Jess and Matt headed across the main street and went south, stopping at the *Shed Café*. "In or out?" Jessie asked.

"Both!" Matt grinned, and Jess slapped his arm.

Ashley felt like a fifth wheel. Maybe she should excuse herself and be on her way. This was so awkward.

"Out here okay with you?" Jess asked Ashley, but she was already pulling a third chair up to the small café table.

"This is one of the cool places, and you should see it at twelve!" Jess said.

"I guess everything picks up around lunchtime," Ashley commented, just to say something and try to get into being here. But for her efforts, Jess and Matt stared at her a moment, then looked at each other, and then burst out laughing.

"What?" Ashley asked.

"Like, twelve at *night*," Jess told her.

Again, the fiery cheeks. Ashley hoped she'd figured things out soon. She picked up the menu the waitress had just dropped off and raised it high enough to hide her face.

While she tried to focus on the burgers and nachos and other listed food that she didn't feel hungry for, even though she hadn't eaten since breakfast, Matt said, "So, Ashley, how come you're at McGill?"

She tried to think of something clever to say, something that would make her seem worldlier than she felt, but then she looked up and met his dreamy eyes. Suddenly, she remembered her sister saying, 'We'll go to McGill. There's all these cute boys that go there.'

Ashley couldn't very well say that. Instead, she went the geek route. "They have great sciences programs and I want to study paleontology."

Instead of getting the eye roll she expected, Matt said, "Cool. You might end up working in Drumheller. Ever been there?"

"Yeah, with my family. When I was a kid. That museum is incredible! You been?"

"Sure. A couple times." And so it went. They talked for about thirty minutes, even when two more frosh joined them. And when the afternoon and the sangria came to an end and Ashley felt a pleasant buzz that let her see the world as colorful and magical and pretty much her oyster, Matt said, "I'm walking back your way, if you're going soon."

"Yeah, I am," Ashley said, grabbing her backpack.

They headed along rue Prince Arthur to Parc where they stopped and he said, "I'm going south. You're going north, right?"

"Yeah. I guess." She did *not* want to be saying goodbye to Matt!

"Listen, you should come out to *ReSemble* tonight. It's the best club. Jess's coming. Why don't you come with her?"

This was where Ashley wanted to ask if he and Jess were together, but she figured they weren't, or Jess would have blown a fuse when they left, or come with them, or whatever. Still, she had to know. "Are you going with Jessie?" she asked, meaning, to the club.

But Matt laughed. "With my sister?"

"Jess's your sister?"

"All my life."

"But she said her brother had an apartment here, where she's from, and you're from Alberta."

"I do. Have an apartment here. When our parents split, she stayed with Mom, I went with Dad, but I'm here now, for school, and other things. Anyway, gotta run. See you later?"

"Yeah. Sure. I'll be there."

He turned and left her at the south corner of Parc and Prince Arthur, waving goodbye. Ashley felt stunned. Did she have a date? It wasn't her first, but it was close. And she'd sure never had a date with such a hot guy!

She had just stepped off the pavement when suddenly she heard a sound, far away yet near, coming from the west, and she snapped her head around and almost lost her balance.

ASHLEY . . . ASHLEY . . . EARTH TO ASHLEY! SARA HERE! WE'RE HERE TOGETHER!

She couldn't see the Redpath Museum but Ashley knew that's where the sound originated. Maybe it's just the wind, she thought, despite the rippling up the skin of her backbone.

That thought and all others vanished instantly at the blast of a car horn. Startled by the screech of tires, Ashley froze as the bumper missed her by inches. The driver, a middle-aged man, ranted at her in French while she repeated, "Sorry. I'm so sorry! *Désole*," resurrecting the word from high school French classes, and hurried across the street, rattled.

Once she reached the safety of the sidewalk, Ashley stood before New Residence Hall and hesitated. Impulsively, she changed direction, crossed Parc, and went along Prince Arthur, re-entered the gates of the campus and made her way to the Redpath.

It was after five and the doors were locked. She walked around the sides of the building, then climbed the front steps and sat against the door and waited; she didn't know what she was waiting for and wondered if she was going crazy. Well, it was crazy to be here, just sitting here. Clearly, she'd had too much sangria.

But the voice was familiar, likely from her head. But why now? Ashley knew the answer. She and her twin Sara had always planned on attending McGill together. Right up until that camping trip in the Badlands, where the landscape looked like the moon with striated layers of earth that created vast canyons . . .

Ashley and Sara had taken a walk together after dinner. "Carry sticks," Dad warned them, "for the snakes." They did. Not that snakes were the problem . . .

"Nice building, isn't it?" The smiling guy climbing the steps was a bit geeky but he had a sweet-enough face behind the wire-rims and seemed innocuous.

"Yeah, it's beautiful."

"Did you know they've got this dinosaur in there? From out west?"

"Yeah, I saw her today. Sara."

He sat beside her on the step but not too close. "She's amazing. I wonder what she ate."

"Probably had a lot of leaves and stuff. She was a vegetarian."

"Well, even the vegetarian dinosaurs sometimes ate meat."

Ashley had read that somewhere, so maybe it was true, although their teeth didn't encourage it. "I guess she might have had the odd mouse or something."

"Or person."

"Huh?"

"Well, she could have eaten a person."

Ashley laughed. "You're kidding, right? Dinosaurs lived way before people did."

The guy said somberly, "Not really."

"What are you talking about?"

"I guess you haven't heard the theory that dinosaurs and people walked at the same time."

"Well, if you mean that movie—"

"And the creationist museums."

Ashley just stared at him. "Dinosaurs and people didn't exist at the same time. They use carbon dating on the bones and soil and can prove that. The earliest humans only go back about 1.2 million years. The last dinosaurs died out about 65 million years ago."

"If you say so." He smiled and stood.

Ashley put her head in her hands and mumbled "Weird!" under her breath. But then, she was weird herself, sitting here on the steps of the Redpath because she'd heard a voice, a voice that sounded like her sister's. When she looked up, the nerdy guy was gone.

She stood angrily and strode towards the east gates. She had things to do before tonight, including finding something to wear that would make her look sexy and smart and modern and not the timid, remorseful small-town girl she wanted to evolve out of.

#

"So, like, we'll go around 11," Jess said.

It was 10:30 and already Ashley felt sleepy. She'd always been a morning person, up with the sunrise, but she'd have to change that if she wanted a social life here in Montreal.

Jess wore the most amazing outfit, a short skirt that showed her pierced naval, and a bare-midriff tank full of colorful sequins and beads. Her arms were adorned with iridescent bracelets up to the elbow and metal armbands snaked up each bicep. Ashley knew she would fall off those shoes, though Jess said they were platforms so not as high as they looked.

Ashley had tried to find something interesting in her closet but there was nothing even remotely urban. Finally, in desperation, she asked Jess if she could borrow something and the girl gave her an electric blue asymmetrical skirt with an elastic waist that just barely fit her. Bev, the girl from Rhodesia who was Ashley's roomie and closer to her size, loaned her an orange-striped poncho that disguised the bunching at the waist.

Jess had been drinking wine and passing the bottle around. "Cheap stuff," she claimed, "from the *dépanneur*." Ashley had figured out that's what they called corner stores here, but she wasn't used to corner stores anyway. In Eastend, there weren't enough corners to put more than one store.

Finally, Jess, Bev, another girl named Britney who was Jess's roommate, and Ashley all headed out to *ReSemble* which, like all of the best clubs, Jess assured them, was along St. Laurent.

As they turned the corner onto Prince Arthur, the thought of Sara's voice crossed Ashley's mind, but she didn't hear anything now and her thoughts quickly moved on to Matt.

She *really* wanted to see him again. The idea that such an amazing guy could be interested in her . . . Wow. She could hardly stand it. It took all her willpower to keep from pumping Jess about her brother. She did ask, though, "So what's Matt studying?"

"Well, he's kind of finished now, unless he goes for an MA right away, which he might do. Or he might go to Europe for a while. Anyway, he wants to work in psychology. I'm not sure. You should ask him."

I will, Ashley thought. That, and a lot more.

St. Laurent was alive as if it were rush hour. She had never seen so many people out this late at night. Snarled traffic couldn't get through on the street and the sidewalks were crammed. Shops were still open, and restaurants crowded with late-night diners.

Their little group must have passed a dozen clubs easily on their side of the street alone, some with manikin parts on display, an old radio microphone that stretched up to the second floor of the building, even a club designed to look like a church, with a steeple, stained glass, the works!

Music blasted from every doorway, and some clubs had lineups to get in, with big bouncers keeping the hordes behind the velvet ropes.

ReSemble was about halfway up the second block and much to Ashley's surprise, a triceratops head composed of twisted rusted wire loomed over the door. She loved it!

At least three dozen people waited to get into *ReSemble*. Jess, though, knew the bouncer, a huge guy with a bald head and pirate earrings in both ears, and he let the four girls in. The place was jam packed, the clientele around the same age. "Is everybody here a student?" Ashley yelled over the din to Jess, who said, "Pretty much."

The music varied as the DJ played house, modern rap, electronic, trance, synth. Ashley was quickly caught up in the mood. Everyone seemed happy and half drunk already, as she felt herself to be. What an amazing place!

She looked around, hoping to see Matt, but there were way too many people. From behind her she heard, "Hey!" and turned with a big smile on her face. But instead of Matt, she found the nerdy guy from the museum. It took some effort to keep smiling.

"Great seeing you again," he yelled, but she heard him.

Maybe she should pretend she didn't.

Jess tapped her on the shoulder and yelled in her ear, "I'm, like, headed to the ladies, then the bar."

"I'm coming," Ashley said, turning away from the nerd.

The toilet was unisex and there were few stalls with doors. Ashley didn't have to go anyway. The bathroom was graffiti- coated, and some computer circuit board parts had been glued to the walls. She thought it looked cool. The washroom was almost empty when they came in and the only other person—a guy with red hair and arms laced with tattoos—left.

Ashley stared in the mirror for a moment then took out a small comb and tried to get her hair to do something but lie flat in what her mom called a 'page boy', but it was too late. Maybe she could get a haircut, try to look a bit more modern.

Try not to look so much like her sister.

They had been identicals, so much so that sometimes even dad hadn't been able to tell them apart. Even their eyes were the same shape and color. Ashley was just slightly taller, "by two centimeters," they had laughed. If only her sister could be here now, with her.

I AM HERE!

Ashley jumped and gasped at the same moment that Jess burst out of the cubicle. "Man, it's so hot in there, like they have the heat on or something." Jess picked at the little spikes she'd created in her hair with some super gel.

144

Ashley wasn't sure but she had to talk with someone. "Do you believe in ghosts?"

Jess didn't pause. "Sure. Why not?"

"I mean, like ghosts following you from one place to another."

"Well, yeah, it makes sense, right? I mean, this whole crap that they're locked into the spot where they died, I don't buy it. They're, like, spirits, right? Not physical. They should be able to go anywhere they want to. It depends on what they have to do, you know."

Ashley said nothing, just looked at Jess in the mirror.

Finally Jess noticed the scrutiny. "How come you're asking?"

"I . . . I don't know. Just curious."

Jess pulled up one more spiky tip and then announced, "I'm thirsty. Want a drink?" And before Ashley could say anything, Jess pulled her by the arm and said, "Come on."

Rattled, Ashley followed like a zombie. It had been her sister's voice. She'd know it anywhere. Her dead sister. Here, in Montreal. How could that be?

Jess ordered two *Boreal Rousse* and handed one bottle to Ashley, who tried to give her money, but Jess said, "You buy the next round. And here, take this." She pushed a pill between Ashley's lips. Ashley tried to take it out but Jess teasingly put a hand over her mouth and said, "Swallow, girl! You need this!" She lifted her bottle and said, "Santé!"

Ashley had watched Jess take two of these pills before they left, and another one just now. How harmful could one be if Jess had taken three? She raised her bottle, they clinked, and then drank. Then Jess moved away, swallowed by the crowd.

Ashley looked around her, suddenly feeling alone. *I'm going crazy, she thought. Why would I hear Sara now? Why why why?* As she scanned the crowd, she saw Matt and immediately all thoughts of ghosts and Sara vanished and her spirits soared. And then plummeted. He was with a girl! An attractive, slim girl with bright white hair that had blue streaks through it, a nose ring, and most of her slim body exposed by the short skirt and chain mail bra she was wearing. They both laughed suddenly, and Matt kissed her.

A wave of heat rushed through Ashley; she had to get out of here! She felt like she was imploding or exploding or both at the same time. The lights, the music, the crush of people. Matt . . .

Ashley turned abruptly and almost slammed into the nerdy guy, who grinned in her face and said knowingly, "They did! People walked with dinosaurs. And dinosaurs ate them. You know that's true!"

"Fuck off!" she screamed; a few people turned in her direction. She shoved past the crazy guy and raced towards the door.

The street was a blur of lights and people and noisy traffic, everything whizzing by at light speed. Ashley felt her heart pounding hard. She was burning hot and her skin clammy. Someone called her name and she knew who it was. Sara!

She found her way back to Prince Arthur and ran along the street, entering the campus pedestrian gate, the only one open at this hour. The guard only vaguely noticed her, and then went back to his book.

The Redpath Museum looked dark and brooding, partially illuminated by yellow lighting that might have mimicked Victorian gas lamps. Ashley felt an almost magnetic pull towards the structure and as she neared and began to ascend the outer steps, she heard a voice say,

ASHLEY! COME AND VISIT ME. I'M SO LONELY!

The voice chilled her to the bone but she knew she had to face this once and for all.

As she reached the top of the steps she heard the door being opened from inside and tucked herself into a shadowy corner of the wide entrance. A cleaner emerged carrying bags of trash. The woman did not look right or left but just headed down the steps. She had left the door open for her return and Ashley crept quietly inside.

The interior was lit but dimly, one florescent sputtering above the door. She raced up the steps quietly and quickly to the second floor and only stopped when she reached Sara. Up here, the lights were even dimmer, making the triceratops skull seem large and threatening.

All around Ashley the remains of these ancient creatures seemed to possess a sort of diabolical energy and suddenly she felt intimidated. She heard a bang from downstairs and thought that must be the front door closing. And locking!

She turned to Sara and said, "I'm here. What do you want?"

YOU! came the voice from the skull.

Ashley jumped back. "Why?"

YOU KNOW WHY

"It's not my fault. What happened to you, I didn't do it!"

DIDN'T YOU?

As if she were suddenly thrust back in time, Ashley remembered the walk she and Sara went on when their family camped in the Badlands.

Ashley felt tense as they walked and took snapshots of everything, just to avoid Sara's neediness. Her sister talked incessantly, tried to cling physically—would she never get to live without Sara practically attached to her hip?

Eventually they reached a wide canyon that must have been a quarter of a mild deep.

"Look at the colors!" Sara said about the striated earth.

147

"*Let me take you,*" *Ashley told her sister. "Move back a bit so I can get the canyon too. More.*"

Sara had. Right to the edge. And the ground gave way. Ashley watched through the viewfinder, horrified, as her sister plummeted over the rim.

For Ashley, it seemed that hours passed: she had gotten their dad, he climbed down, her mom drove for help, meanwhile Ashley stood at the rim of the deep crater in the earth, her eyes locked on her sister's dead eyes that stared up at hers, wishing that she had fallen and not Sara. But what horrified Ashley most was where her sister had landed. They told her later that Sara had fallen between the gaping jaws of a triceratops, the only part of the dinosaur sticking out of the ground.

YOU LET IT EAT ME!

"No. No! It wasn't me. It was just an accident. Dinosaurs don't eat people! They don't!"

ONE ATE ME!

Ashley fell to her knees, sobs wracking her throat. "I'm sorry. I'm so sorry!"

YOU'RE SORRY? YOU'RE ALIVE AND LIVING OUR DREAM. I'M NOT. I'M NOT ALIVE ANYMORE, ASHLEY, AM I? AND IT'S YOUR FAULT!

#

Ashley became aware of being lifted to her to her feet, voices asking if she was all right. The lights above her like the prairie sun the morning they had brought Sara to the surface.

The uniforms surrounding her spoke softly, kindly, as they led her away, as she tried to explain: "I can't leave Sara! I can't leave my sister! The dinosaur ate her; you've got to let me stay with her!"

Ashley was dragged kicking and screaming from the building toward an ambulance. She recognized Jess and Matt in the small crowd that had gathered, their faces shocked, saddened. And standing apart, the nerdy guy, whose lips formed the words, "I told you so!" but the voice was Sara's. She watched in horror as he climbed the steps of the Redpath, morphing as he went: eye horns growing on his head, and a nose horn; he turned slightly and his profile became Sara's; then turned again and Ashley saw the dark shadow of the triceratops; then his face; Sara's face; blending, fading, reforming, one into the other, the darkness of evil clinging to this demonic specter.

"That's Sara!" she cried. "He's Sara!" But no one paid any attention to Ashley as they strapped her to a gurney. No one but the fading, shifting creature mimicking Sara's voice, which suddenly vanished into the air like a vapor.

As the ambulance doors were closing, Ashley heard an otherworldly laugh, long, loud, sinister. Then the words: *Crash and burn! Crash and burn! Another freshman bites the dust!*

SOWN

BY SUSIE MOLONEY

Shara wondered if the Mac was ruined. The corner was dented as if it had been dropped from a height, like the top of a dining room table. There was blood on the corner that spread across the lid in a delicate spray that reminded her of the Magic Spin Art kit she'd had when she was little. It looked like batik. Groovy.

The Mac was brand new.

Hilary, on the other hand, looked used up and spent. She lay on her left side, arms out in front, on a pile of leaves and forest detritus where Shara had dragged her. Her eyes were open, staring up at the sky through trees.

There was a dent in her, too. The top right side of her skull was mashed in. Blood made her blond hair red.

Shara slumped to the ground beside the body, still holding the Mac. She was still shaking. She felt exactly as she did after masturbating, relieved and shameful. In fact, the whole thing was much like that: the exhilaration of arcing her arm over her head and bringing it down, full force, the meeting of force and flesh, and the knee-weakening result.

Leaves and earth clung to Hilary's bare midriff, where her top had dragged up. A single gold leaf and several shapely red ones.

Morus Rubra. Red Mulberry leaves. Kind of rare in Ontario. Some people thought they looked like oak leaves. The untrained eye thought that. Shara's eye was quite trained. Isn't that why she was here in the first place?

She didn't know what to do about the Mac. It was blood covered. She wondered if it would even still work.

It was shady where she'd dragged Hilary's body, but rays of sunlight cracked the treeline somewhere behind her. It was getting late.

Shara opened the lid and turned on the lap top. It sang awake, popping up a photo of what Shara knew was Hil's favourite flower. *Myosotis*. Forget-me-nots.

"Now your favourite flower should be a lily," she said to the corpse. "See that's a joke, Hil. I do *so* have a sense of humour."

The Mac still worked. She rubbed the blood off as best she could with Hil's skirt hem – a Stella McCartney. Hilary and her mom had made a trip to London that summer to buy school clothes. It was ruined now. But it left a lot of her flesh exposed.

The temperature was cool on the forest floor, Hil's body hidden by overgrown fern and ground cover. Shara heard rustling in the shadows to her right.

She left her like that, in the woods.

Shara had been driving Hil's car. They'd been sharing the driving, bickering off and on, like sisters, like girls who'd known each other too long to be objective.

I have to pee Hilary had said, right on the heels of *I work just as hard as you do. Why shouldn't I get it?*

She'd said it with that open-mouthed *duh, bitch* that she'd lately picked up using, after summer at tennis camp. Hilary had come back no better at tennis, but with a small tattoo that her mother didn't know about and a snotty attitude.

Shara had spent the summer at study camp, tutoring freaks in science, her first ever paid job.

Her student advisor at the U set it up. Shara had put off the inevitable in a persistent fog of denial for most of the previous year. Tuition had only been half-paid and she was wait-listed for a dorm room. Of course, Hil had invited her to stay with her at the apartment her dad rented for her off-campus. In return she could do Hil's laundry.

(*it's the least I can do* she'd simpered and Shara, remembering all the homework answers and French essays and class notes and assignments she'd given/done for Hil *aw c'mon please Shar-shar-shar you know I'd do it for you* – had thought that it WAS the least she could do for her)

It had all been settled.

I have to pee.

Shara driving had pulled over, maybe without thinking, her eyes scanning the horizon for just his copse of trees. She's written a paper on the area *Anomolies in Flora in the Canadian Shield*. She couldn't see what she was looking for from the road, but she stopped very nearly exactly at the spot. And they were talking about The Calder Prize for Botany. They were both up for it.

I work just as hard as you do, why shouldn't I get it?

There were so many answers to that. The thing is, it was about balance. A level playing field. Shara knew that, it was an unspoken agreement. Balance.

Hilary was the pretty one.

Shara had gotten out of the car with Hil and stood on the passenger side of the car. Hilary had been sorting photos on her Mac. The computer was on her seat.

Hilary had gone about twenty feet into the forest and squatted, her skirt held around her waist.

And then she said –

(with her mouth twisted up into that *duh bitch* –)

– *you're not the only smart one* –

There's a plant genus *Artemisia* – wormwood – that has all sorts of applications and uses in real life, but which is bitter and sometimes even poisonous. Their first year Botany prof had made them put a little on their tongues. Butterflies eat them, jamming their proboscis into the veins of the plant and sucking out the marrow. To the human tongue, however, the taste is repellant regardless of preparation or benefit.

Like poison.

That was what it was like when Hilary said:

You can stay with me in the apartment off-camp

I work as hard as you

Duh

You're not the only smart one –

It had tasted like wormwood.

There had been nothing to say then. There had been no breeze and no traffic. It had been quiet enough that Shara heard Hilary's urine splash on to the Bishops weed and ivy.

What had she even been thinking?

Hil's Mac was brand new. Shara reached in through the window and picked it up. It was surprisingly heavy. Peripherally she saw Hil drop a tissue to the ground, it bright white on the brown-green covered earth.

There had a been a snap of panty elastic.

I'm not in love with this skirt I don't even know why I bought it –

She saw her life like in a single thought in that moment. Not so much a picture as an ugly knowledge, the feel of cancer growing inside you. Nothing good was every going to happen to her. That she was going to be trapped in an ordinary life: no schooling, no money, no future, no boys.

Shara *had* to kill her.

When Hil got close enough she brought the Mac down on her head with a godawfulsatisfying *thunk*! And she dropped elegantly to the forest floor.

She'd had to do it. It was about balance. One pretty, one smart; one live, one dead.

Shara had dragged her body through the trees, leaves clinging, being pushed aside even as they dropped on both of them, from above. Her heels dug shallow furrows into the damp ground. Her head bobbed with every step Shara took. Like the Mac, she was heavier than she looked.

She'd dropped her and she hit the ground, her head lolled to the side a little, like when they posed for photos fooling around at keggers in first year, chin down, eyes wide, head tilted; that was before all of this shit started before Shara was a thing to be carried, before her father lost everything before her life was shit and poverty.

They'd vamp for the camera. *Smile! Say . . . Paris Hilton!*

The rustling to her right sounded closer; a curious something coming closer to see. It would start with animals, more drawn to her as her body putrified, if it lasted long enough to putrify. The forest was unforgiving. Fauna, flora, all of it starving.

Most people don't think about it, but an ecosystem is like the human body, with every part having function, every function requiring fuel to operate. The forest floor was a series of systems, intricately involved, consuming whatever fell prey to it, to feed its parts to function, every function requiring fuel.

She left her there like that, for the forest to eat.

Shara parked Hilary's car on the street outside the apartment building. She sat a moment, gathering herself. The building and the street was popular with student renters. The front of the building was lit with a set of spots on either side of the front lobby. *Heathrow.* Everyone called it Deathrow. Funny, that.

Now.

They'd always had a system, in case one of them needed the car. Shara put the keys on the top of the tire under the wheel well on the passenger side and left them there. A girl crossed the street a few yards away, lugging a book bag. She didn't even glance in Shara's direction. Nonetheless, Shara's knees were shaking when she walked across the lot. She made three trips, each time watching for watchers, dragging up both their luggage, her own lap top as well and the bloody Mac.

On the last trip up, her eyes darted back and forth across the lot, but it was practically deserted. There was a couple standing at the trunk of a car, unloading; two girls dragged wheeled suitcases somewhere. Further away yet she could see the front of the school. There was a canopy set up, lit with tiny white fairy lights. She could hear faint music. First Nights had started, first years were picking up Welcome Student packages, and in the quad there would be a mixer. There would be a half dozen activities going on, no one close enough to see her, what she was doing.

Hilary would have been rushing to get there. Wanting to change to borrow something. She would have coaxed Shara into going. Shara would have gone. Would have spent the evening watching Hil tart around.

No more.

In the hall another girl passed. She looked at Shara a moment, a pause before saying *hello* and passing her on the stairs.

Hello Shara said back, and wondered how it sounded.

When Hil lost her virginity in first year she came to Shara's dorm. *Do I look different? Can you tell?*

That was how she felt as the girl passed her by. She couldn't help it, she looked back at the girl as she swept out the doors, the night air breezing in through the building. It smelled like cut grass and faintly, wood smoke from the quad.

Sweat trailed down her spine and under her arms. Absently she swiped at it, as if an itch.

She'd studied Hil that morning, for signs of sex and there had been none. *Can't tell at all* she'd said. It would be the same now.

No one would be able to tell.

Her body itched, between her shoulder blades, under her hair line, even between her legs. She was probably covered in bits of grass, dirt. Hilary didn't exactly drag herself into the woods.

Shara scratched under her hair and headed for her dorm.

Do I look different?

Of course she didn't.

Shara didn't go to the quad, skipped out on the First Days festivities all together. She put Hilary's bags in and around the other bed in the room, as they might be if someone had run in and ran out again without unpacking.

157

That's what she would say.

"Oh, yeah. She dropped her stuff off and ran out again. I guess she went to First Days," Shara practiced it in the mirror. Twice. And then she fell into an exhausted sleep.

She slept heavily, waking only once. She sat up in the dark, thinking she'd heard a rustling, and a tug, on her foot.

Dream.

"Hey, I know you," said a boy. Shara turned. "You used to study in the library, every night. Last term, right? I'm Donald Keele. I stocked shelves."

Shara stared without recognition.

"That's okay," he said. His cheeks got red. "You hardly looked up from the books. And it paid off. You won that award, didn't you? The big money?"

"It's not been announced yet," she said automatically. She'd been saying it for months. What did Hil say? *They haven't contacted me yet.* As if she was just waiting to hear.

She blinked. Her eyes were dry as sandpaper. A shower and a nap had not refreshed her the way she'd hoped. She'd missed a meeting with her advisor already, but she'd had a terrible time getting out of bed.

She was off; just *off*.

"I'm strictly a C student. I wouldn't know much about prizes," he laughed.

The girl at the table asked her for her student card. Shara gave it to her.

"Oh," Shara said anyway. The boy, Donald, wore his hair longer than Shara normally thought was attractive. His shirt was thin from washing and the collar was fraying. Whether this was student affectation or genuine poverty she couldn't know, but it was disconcerting, distracting.

She could smell herself. She woken to a smell. At first she'd believed it was coming from outside the window, something in the street, dropped and left to spoil. But it was it back. She could still smell it. She tried, discreetly, to smell her body. The boy was staring at her, waiting for her to say something.

"Do you still work at the library?" she asked politely.

"Yup. And at the cafeteria in the morning, and I'm a TA for Professor Lange. Philosophy. I'm a Philosophy major." He blushed, as if this were an embarrassing thing. She nodded. She had no electives and so did not take Philosophy.

"Here you are," the girl said.

"A couple of us are going to the Cub for tacos, you should join us," he said. The girl at the desk smiled and gave Shara a fat envelope. She handed her student card back. A space in the small of her back was sore. She rubbed it, closing her eyes. There was a note clipped to her envelope. *See me, P. Duggan.* Her advisor.

"I don't think so," she said. "I have something I have to do."

"Are you okay?"

Do I look different? Can you tell?

She nodded. "Yes, just a little –" it trailed off. She was exhausted again. No matter how she slept, she was still dead on her feet. She finished with the registration and went back to the apartment to fall into bed. She didn't call Duggan. Or answer the phone when it rang.

Scrapbook moment: whenever Hilary's mother noted something significant in their lives, she would say, *oh my a scrapbook moment, girls!*

The summer previous, when her own home had been tense and nervous and filled with sweaty fear, Shara had spent most of her days over at Hil's, beside the pool, drinking cosmos and sometimes secretly sneaking a cigarette out of Adonia's stash in the kitchen under the recycling. The first time she'd caught them, Hil gave her a side-eye and said *bitch please you're not supposed to smoke here* and Adonia just went back into the kitchen. Later they agreed that having something on the maid was a good thing, especially when Hil started sleeping with the guy who came to clean the pool. In her defense, it was practically the only guy they saw all summer.

Boredom and monotony had made them childish and they spent a lot of time looking for the old croquet set, their NSync playing cards for 21, the Spin Magic. They found hardly any of the things they looked for, but they delighted in talking about them, spent whole days doing it. They'd been floating in the pool on their childhood blow up rafts, Hil's shaped like a shark, Shara on the turtle. Hil's mom had come out of the house and said

Scrapbook moment! And snapped a photo.

Scrapbook moment: Playing Miss California when they were about ten, California being the apex of glamour to them at ten, and deciding that Shara came in second and Hil first because it was a beauty contest, after all. *You're the smart one,* Hilary had said. Shara agreed. Hilary could be the pretty one if she wanted.

Scrapbook moment: Kevin Murdock kissing Shara at riding, behind the tack shed, and Hilary finding them *he's supposed to be mine* she said, her delicate features twisted into a transparent expression of anger and surprise, at the injustice of it *I liked him! Cheater cheater –*

More than before, Shara understood that look now, the wide-eyed shock, the fish pout speechlessness, the *unfairness* of trounced expectations.

The Canadian Shield Fellowship for instance, in Botany.

Shara was the smart one.

Scrapbook moment: in the arc between overhead and Hil's skull, when the Mac was on its trajectory, too late to stop, Hil had looked dubiously at Shara and said what sounded like *seriously?*

The memories flickered through Shara's memory like a slide show, the Mac, the pool, N Sync 21, Uno, the flare of blood, Hilary's eyes wide open staring up into the canopy of Red Mulberry, leaves stuck to her pale skin –

The pictures flickered and flipped over fading and disappearing while Shara fell asleep, now and then scratching absently at a place on her body, her lower back, the soft inside of her thighs, under her arms.

She fell asleep, woke up and fell back to sleep, her sleep fitful, noise filtering up into the bedroom from other rooms, the street; feet crunching on leaves, rustling. Sound.

In the night Shara dreamed she opened her eyes and over her head was purple morning light dappled unevenly and the room smelled very bad, like something-dropped-and-left-to-spoil except for a breeze that blew gently over her and carried the smell away. Hilary's eyes, wide-open, stared down at her.

"Something's wrong with my arm," she told the big nurse. There were two nurses, a big one and a little one. The big one wore a name tag. It said University Medical Staff. But the place where her name would be was blank.

"A sprain? Is there swelling?" She reached out and took Shara's left arm gingerly in hers. She was surprisingly gentle for a large woman, and the surprise of that made Shara feel like crying.

"It's like a rash, I guess," she said. She raised her arm up over her head to expose her tricep to the woman. "Here," she said. She ran her hand over the place on her arm where it was so itchy – one of the places where it itched, the itch driving her mad – and where it was discoloured.

The nurse squinted and leaned over the counter. She tried to get close and lost patience.

"Come around this side of the counter, please," she said sharply. Shara did. She ran the back of her hand over the flesh that was itchy. The skin felt clammy, maybe even soft, with a scent that reminded her of something

(pleasant *scrapbook memory* of hikes and camping and the underside of the dock at Providence Bay)

"Don't scratch," came the auto-response from the nurse.

She looked at her arm. Peered, stared, stroked, prodded, examined and finally stood back and shook her head. She reached into a cupboard and took out a container of wet wipes, yanking one out.

"Lemme see this –" again she was very gentle and looked to Shara once for confirmation that it didn't hurt as she lightly stroked the afflicted underside of her arm with the wipe. It was cold.

The nurse held it out to show Shara.

"It's green," she said. They looked at it. It was. Green.

"It itches," Shara said. The nurse shrugged and had to go into the little room to wait for the doctor.

Hilary's dad called on the third day. Shara had forgotten that this might happen, her mind on other things

The flies, for instance.

She stared at the call display, their name coming up not as J. Peale, her dad, or even E & J. Peale, but the jaunty "The Peales." Of course they were jaunty. Why wouldn't they be? They were also jovial, cheerful and self-satisfied, any number of kindly, happy adjectives.

Why wouldn't they be?

Scrapbook moment: Shara went home from Hilary's house every few days, the summer before last, but only because she had to. On one of those days, she went home and found her mother crying in the kitchen, standing at the new island, the reno so new the range top had yet to be used. Her mother only cooked a couple of times a week. They'd all gotten used to eating out.

What's going on? She asked her mother. She had to say something, even if they weren't really a talky-touchy family. The woman was right there, though. She had to say something.

Her mother didn't look at her, but she took her hands off her face. Her face was tear-stained. She turned her face away.

Daddy can't pay tuition next year. You'll have to get a job or transfer to another school, okay?

And then she went outside through the living room. The patio door squealed open and then shut again.

She didn't answer the call from The Peales, but stood there and listened to the message, staring at Hilary's luggage, still piled in front of the bed, as if waiting for her to come and unpack. This would be what she said, if someone asked her.

"Hi Hilsy-Punkin, it's Daddy. Just checking in, we haven't heard from you and your cell is off. I know you're busy sweetheart but just give Mommy and me – "

And so on.

The rash spread along her left side. Shara turned slightly to her right and tried to see it all in the small bathroom mirror, foggy from her shower.

The doctor had gently and carefully talked to her about hygiene before sending her back to the apartment with a sample-sized bottle of hand sanitizer. He told her not to let herself get so preoccupied with school that she forgets to shower.

It was moss. Ordinary moss. Garden-variety moss – pardon the pun – *bryophyta.*

That had been a few days earlier. She'd showered and used the sanitizer. Like he'd said.

The rash ran from the soft underside of her arm, down her left side, lesser in the slope of her waistline, but spreading in a jagged circle over her hip on to the rise of her buttock. It continued down the length of her leg, although she couldn't see it in the mirror, she could see it by looking down. She did not look down just then.

It still had a greenish tinge to it, but if she took a rag and wiped at it, the green came off on the rag and underneath the skin was mottled and discoloured. If she ran her hand over it, it felt soft, spongey.

A fly buzzed around her head, landing and flying off when she swatted at it disinterestedly.

The apartment was full of them. It was the smell.

Donald waved her down in the hall. At the very last second Shara thought she would run away, pretend she hadn't seen him, but she was too slow. He grinned, an armload of books leading the way through the scores of students on their way to classes.

"Hey!" he called, waving, but he knew she'd seen him.

She smiled wanly.

Today he wore a suit jacket, something from the second hand store, she thought, because the lapels were wider than was fashionable. His shirt underneath was crispy-looking, purely white against his pink skin. He was very fair.

"Hi," he said, out of breath. "I thought I might see you in this wing."

She smiled and swallowed. Her mouth and throat seemed full of fluid. "Oh," she said. Again she was at a loss. "Donald," she added.

"Yeah. You remember. I wanted to ask you if you felt like going to the First Days Fair tonight. I wanted to hear Gibby Chuck play – he used to play jazz for Dizzy Gillespie, back in the day. You like jazz?" He looked at her. Her hair was uncombed and she was wearing dirty jeans and a sweater that had been on the floor for . . . how long? She might have slept in it. She couldn't seem to keep track of things.

She kept thinking about the woods.

"I don't know," she said. She'd had a terrible dream.

"I think you would. You wanna go?" She didn't answer. He said, "He has a young band. It's new. This is their first tour –"

Hilary had been in her dream.

They had been in the woods. It must have been just at dawn because she remembered the birds were loud, braying, swooping around her head. Hilary would speak, her voice oddly coming from all angles, above, across the big rock, from far away; but Shara wouldn't look at her.

Hilary only said one thing in the whole dream.

Look at me, Shar. Look at me.

"You look like you could use a night out –" Donald said. He stood close and she could feel his body heat. He seemed to vibrate with vitality. She would have like to lean in and melt against him.

"I have to see my advisor," Shara said. The last message had been for her. *Miss Troit I expect to see you at 2 pm, and this time your absence indicates –*

"Okay . . . but you'll go?"

Look at me, Shar.

"All right."

"Good." The two of them stood in the hall while the numbers dwindled around them. He overstood her by a foot and a half, his dark hair dangled in his eyes when he looked down at her. His eyes were blue.

Shara ached to scratch, all over, most worst between her legs, around her eyes, in the deepest part of her ears, where the itching rash had become something unbearable, something practically living. It was not Donald's presence that kept her from scratching, but rather an agreement with herself that she was not going to give in to it.

His mouth was his best feature. His lips were plump and bow-shaped like a baby's.

She'd seen a program on television the other night – a back to school thing with all kinds of experts – and they said student stress was at epidemic levels and caused all kinds of illness, from headaches and rashes to cancer and yeast infections.

It was stress doing this to her.

Maybe it was a yeast infection. She imagined tiny grains of yeast multiplying, into so many millions of grains that it was a moving, shifting mass."Are you okay?"

"I have a headache." She almost said yeast infection.

"You look a little tired."

"I'm under stress," she said. Her stomach rolled uncomfortably. She put her hand over her mouth, ducking her head forward. Her hair spilled over her face.

He reached out and gently-so-gently, pushed it back. She looked up at him and he was smiling softly at her, with affection and interest.

"I'll pick you up at 7, good?"

She gave him the address, conflicted. Confused by his attention. She had a sudden new feeling in the pit of stomach, heated raw feeling of panic. Like she's misunderstood the whole lesson and now there was the exam. Where had he been last semester? *I'm not the pretty one.*

Now I'm the pretty one and the smart one.

She started to go to Duggan's meeting, but gave up about halfway to the office.

Shara was tired all the time, but didn't sleep. The phone rang so much now, and it wasn't just the Peale's. There were other calls, mysterious calls from Out Of Area and Private Number. She didn't answer those. Hil had family everywhere. Everyone was calling Hil.

Her own mom called one night. *Shara it's your mother. Pick up the phone. Shar? Fine. Diana hasn't heard from Hilary either. You two are up to something. Someone give someone a call.*

She fretted about that for a long time.

(*scrapbook moment*: her mother screaming at her that it wasn't just about her they were all suffering over daddy's economic turn around *not Hilary; she wasn't*)

No matter what she did, the apartment smelled. It was gassy. She was gassy, her stomach stretching over bloated organs. She took Tums but nothing helped for long.

Her mind would wander to terrible places. Exhaustion. She would think of the forest floor, of the life cycles of bacteria and bugs that reclaimed what fell, for its own. The relentlessness. Of Hilary, slowly dissolving into the woods. The forest was uncompromising.

She tried to clean.

The vacuum was sitting in the middle of the bedroom. It was still plugged in, although Shara had given up trying to keep up with the dirt that seemed to come out of nowhere: soil and twigs and bits of wood rot and leaves. Everywhere.

She would just get it vacuumed and there would be more.

She was losing it.

Look at me, Shara, Hilary had said.

Scrapbook moment: Her mother called them into the living room for a family meeting. She said the words as though "family meeting" had been something they'd done always, since their early days of red-checkered-family-picnic-frisbee-throwing-sing-a-longs. Proof that there'd never been anything like that was in the way the three children sat three abreast on the Montauk while their parents roamed or sat, alternately, the blocking like an Agatha Christie play at the summer theatre.

Things have taken a turn their mother said and she continued in a convoluted, complex series of practically non-sequitors, talking one minute about Shara's car insurance and the next about the kitchen cabinets being loose and then to their father's recent bad luck.

Your father's had some bad luck.

Her younger sister Cherie, beside Shara on the sofa, whispered *did you pvr Apprentice?* just as her father spoke for the first time, smoking nervously beside their mother's chair.

I've lost my job he said. Her mother cried.

Shara leaned into her sister and said *No. I forgot.*

And they sat like that for a few minutes more, the three kids on the sofa, their dad standing, their mother crying.

Scrapbook moment, as Mrs. Peale would say.

Who wouldn't be stressed after that? The rest of the story came out in dribs and drabs as her grandmother used to say, before giving them $500 for their birthday *you're getting your inheritance in dribs and drabs* ha ha ha.

Three of the six cars were sold, the kids were to share one. The maid disappeared. The pool went uncleaned. The fucking paper stopped.

There was no money for school. When she finally got the nerve to ask about school her mother threw up her hands and screeched *school? School? I knew you would come at me with school I'm not dealing with this right now can't you see I'm upset —*

It might all have been all right if not for Hilary throwing it all in her face. *You can stay with me at the apartment.*

She was not a charity case. She was the smart one.

Shara belched and wiped spittle off her lips with a tissue. She peeked at it. Yellow-gray matter, with substance and weight. She balled the tissue up and tossed it towards the waste basket by the desk. It missed and landed on the floor.

She sucked up the fluid that seemed to continually pool under her tongue. It was foul, tasting as it smelled, like the shore of Lake Winnipeg in August when everyone was going home.

Doctors Google, Wiki and Yahoo mentioned stress frequently. But also everything else.

The Mac was open on the desk, with numerous opened tabs featuring her symptoms.

With all the mucus

(what she decided was mucus, in spite of its odd colour and texture)

– smell –

because of that, it could be a flu or cold. She did not cough, but her throat and mouth stung with the taste of it. It could be gastrointestinal bugs like a flu or a tapeworm or her period, especially with the bloating.

It could be cancer, of the esophagus, pancreas, lungs, or stomach.

Excessive belching was caused by so very many things.

Clammy, cold hands and feet also had a variety of causes.

The patches of bubbling flesh that seemed to have sprung up in the last few hours, was a mystery. When she touched them, the flesh was warm, where everywhere else she was cold; and there was something like a pulse beat under there, but not steady. Writhing. Living.

She pulled a sweat shirt on over her jeans to cover up as much of her skin as possible. She was pale. Very pale. She looked *unwell*.

Just before leaving the apartment to meet Donald, she did two things. She closed the lid on the Mac (a tiny bit of blood could still be seen in the seam, if you were looking).

And she brushed red leaves off the bed. They were everywhere. Like the flies.

Dancing in her head over and over, on a loop: *Look at me, Shar.*

Donald slipped an elasticized yellow band around her wrist and shouted over the music into her ear *we missed the first set* but he was grinning when he took her hand and they ploughed through the crowd, all of them eyes forward, heads bouncing, some of them fingers snapping like jazz daddies. The noise was overwhelmingly distracting – a blessing, even when a bad thought or two popped up in her head, like thinking how much the base line sounded like the noise of the Mac making contact with Hil's skull –

– it was fleeting though and Donald's enthusiasm made her both tired and happy. He leaned into her and said something loudly into her ear, but the music covered it up. He laughed, his face close to hers. In the lull between the chorus and verse she heard him shout *the drummer used to go to McGill* his face solemn just briefly at this bit of abutment, then he smiled down at her as he started mouthing the words to the song along with most everyone in the crowd. Shara didn't know the words, but tried the chorus (throat feeling in pieces with every vibrato) and felt herself grinning like a madman.

He'd picked her up outside the apartment, getting out to open the door for her and as he came around the car she was embarrassed for her thick jeans and heavy sweatshirt *RTSD Science Camp Counselor 2008.* He wore his other jacket, with the unfashionable narrow lapels and looked handsome.

He seemed shy opening her door and waiting until she got inside.

In the parking lot of A Building where the First Days concert was – what had he said jazz Dizzy Gillespie, except Dizzy was dead like so many people lately – he didn't get out right away but instead touched her hair *I had a crush on you last year you don't remember. You hardly looked at me but we talked about plants.*

I remember she said, surprised that she did.

I asked you about bella donna – he laughed. *I was trying to be flip and cool but you said*

Bella donna is an example of god's hand in nature – poison, but that it's taste gave you fair warning. I liked that.

(why didn't you say something last year)

I bet you get the Canadian Shield award.

Then the car went quiet. He thought she was embarrassed and he tried to make a joke –

But in fact that feeling was back, the unrealized point, a missed message, some kind of impending trip to the Dean. But he touched her hair then and said *what happened to your head* –

The room pulsed like the itching-moving-writhing that seemed to be her body now, inside, in her organs, under her flesh, under her hair. It was distracting and she couldn't get on top of the

look at me, Shar –

Bad memory of the dream. Seemed so real. Hilary's eyes, boring into her *look at me* and she wouldn't couldn't didn't.

Did she? It was hard, now, to remember. She struggled to do that and then Donald was beside her. He took her hand and held it. His hand was warm and hers was so cold. He squeezed it with affection and –

There was a brief moment of clarity when she turned and looked up into his face and thought *big deal about money I can do this*

But seconds later his grin faded. He let go of her. Backed away, surprised.

She stared too. *What?*

And the music thumped around them and he raised his hand between them – turned it palm out to show, to see.

He shrieked into the pounding, musical air – and jerked his hand, face twisting into disgust, mouth a grimace, as bits of something scattered around him.

A piece of something hit the back of a girl in front of them, her blonde hair pulled back into a neat tail, and stuck there. Lights flashed as people walked back and forth through the stage lights shining from the back of the club and Shara leaned in to peer at what Donald had shaken off his hand.

He shouted something but she couldn't hear it.

The thing on the back of the girl's sweater was a sphinx, a cipher, a non-sequitor, enigma, puzzlement, poser, conundrum, entirely illogical.

A finger.

She looked down at her hand, in the dark where bodies blocked most of the murky light from the ceiling anyway and turned it over and over and it seemed that maybe –

Some of her hand . . . invisible in the dark. Or gone.

Look at me, Shara.

No one would have heard her scream, not over the music, they were too close to the speakers, but Donald saw her face, the expression and he reached out to her, grabbing her around the arms and just squeezing like you would if you were wanting to help to

see god's hand in nature

And through the jersey of her grey sweatshirt through his fingers seeped some kind of fluid and she felt a kind of collapse inside herself, inside her arms, to the bone inside her chest. And Donald screamed.

And no one heard him over the music, but around them people twisted toward her, their bodies swiveling in mid writhe pretty young faces smooth tortured into grimaces jerking away from the swollen, sweet-hot, molten stench and over the music there was a collected sound of surprise and repulsion.

When Donald turned away from her in revulsion, Shara pushed away and made her way through the crowd, each and every one of whom turned to look – not at her, but at whatever that horrible –

Something

Was.

Shara plodded through the parking lot from Building A screaming passing First Days celebrants, most of them already drunk, most of them hardly seeing her not caring. No one noticed her wake.

The dream had been so vivid. The scents of the last of the periwinkle, of all the summer dying on the stem, on the vine, shrinking, dying, seeping, melting into rich soil. It was pernicious that smell.

It filled the car.

Slowly as the student buildings and campus gave way to town gave way to blank fields and car repair shops and wooden estates hidden, marked only by lit up numbers on posts, gave way to vast fields of scrub and empty neatly tilled fall-hardened earth gave way to

A twisting gravel road.

And if it was light even on the horizon, she would be able to see a geographical anomaly a copse of *morus rubra*.

Hilary hadn't even known that.

Shara, now so much closer to the earth, felt that she could smell them.

Red Mulberry. They were poisonous.

I work just as hard as you do.

Her pretty, pretty face, always so pretty, grinned and she thought it was funny – she was teasing even if Shara wasn't in the mood for teasing and she said

Maybe I'm the smart one, too.

The moon made everything grey but the leaves of the mulberry were distinctive. She parked and got out of the car. Hilary's car.

And from the road, she peered into the woods, at the figure that stood through a break, and in a clearing, about a hundred metres away. Her skin was pale and soft, a slight tan from tennis camp. There would a perfectly shaped, dark mole on the direct centre of her shoulder. Her hair swept over it most of the time; her eye were blue.

And she was pretty.

Shara walked towards her, every step wet and near collapse.

Halfway, she could sense Hilary's vitality. Her life.

The two girls stood together under the trees.

"Look at me, Shara," Hilary said.

Shara did. And *saw*.

Her reflection lay dead on the soft damp forest floor, and must have for the whole week that had passed. Her flesh was mottled and gray, still bloated slightly through the middle, but internally collapsing into the ground, soft with fallen leaves and twigs and green moss and damp with body fluid.

Hilary stood over her.

"It's about balance," she said. "Now you're dead and I'm alive."

The two girls met eyes. Brains and cranial fluid seeped from Shara's head on to the leaves her body torpid, flesh pallid and as cool as the ground cover. Just faintly she could smell the moss under her rotting, ending self.

When Hilary got to the apartment, she did two things: she opened the window and shooed out some curious flies. Then she called her dad. She didn't know *what* could have become of Shara. She was such a smart girl.

While the phone rang she flipped through mail she picked up on the way in.

The Canadian Shield Award for Botany was announced and Hilary did not win. The award was announced long before they found Shara Troit's body, making it all the more poignant.

Shara's paper won: *Reclamation on the Forest Floor in the Canadian Shield*.

Hilary was still the pretty one.

She erased the history from the Mac. It was nothing she would ever need:

Google
"symptoms" + "rotting flesh"

RADIO NOWHERE

BY DOUGLAS SMITH

On the anniversary of the worst night of his life, Liam stood outside the darkened control room of the campus radio station. Over the speakers, the Tragically Hip's "Boots and Hearts" was just winding down. Behind the glass in the studio, Ziggy's small triangular face glowed like some night angel, lit from below by her laptop screen. She looked up, her eyes finding Liam's in the darkness. Smiling, she wrinkled her nose at him. His own smile slid away, falling into the dark place inside him, the place that was always darker on this night.

Ziggy turned back to the mike as the song ended. "I'm closing with a request from an old friend, to an old friend. This one's for Jackie, from Liam. A hurtin' song, cuz he's still hurtin'. Fifteen years ago tonight . . ." She looked at him through the glass.

Fifteen years. He closed his eyes. Fifteen years, and it still hurt this much.

". . . but he still misses you, girl. I miss you. Hell, we all miss you. Too young, too young." She shook her head. "This is Radio Waterloo, CKNW 100.3. Ziggy C, signing off. Back tomorrow night. Stay tuned for Dawg and his Midnight Mayhem show."

Ziggy hit a button, and Springsteen's "Downbound Train" wailed from the speakers. Pulling off her headphones, she ran her fingers through her short, black and green-dyed locks as she stood up. She shrugged on her worn, black leather UW jacket, wearing it as comfortably as she wore every year that had passed since the "1993" emblazoned on the jacket's shoulder.

She stepped out of the studio and snaked an arm around Liam's waist, pulling him into a hug. They stood there holding each other for a moment. Breaking it off, she slapped him on the bum and headed towards the door, squeezing past the crammed shelves of vinyl and CD's. "Let us rock."

He sighed, and forced a smile. "Let us roll."

Outside the old warehouse that housed the station, Ziggy lit up a joint, took a deep toke, and then handed it to Liam. Looking up at a crescent moon hanging above the broadcast tower in a star-specked, cloud-streaked October night sky, she let the toke out and nodded. "So you and your Beast haven't blown the world up yet. Good to know."

He smiled, despite it being the night that it was. The "Beast" was the particle accelerator buried deep below, ringing the campus underground. "If you're going to believe urban legends, at least get them right. That's the one at CERN. Ours is different."

"Nanotech-morphed, which you can't talk about, which is fine cuz I wouldn't understand anyway. Not that it'll make any difference if I understand when we all blow up."

"Implosion, not explosion. We're all supposed to get sucked into a black hole." He took a toke, holding it in, waiting to feel the rush. Waiting to feel anything.

Ziggy shrugged, classic Ziggy, and took the joint from him. "Fuck, Lee, you've been fallin' into one of those for fifteen years. Wouldn't make any diff to you."

They walked in silence, sharing the joint all the way down to Columbia. Tonight, the silence suited him fine. And silence with Ziggy was always comfortable. They turned west onto the Ring Road circling the center of the campus, what used to be almost the entire campus back when Jackie was . . .

Back when.

He remembered, trying not to.

The road bore south. They walked past Village One on their right, lying jumbled like a giant set of children's blocks. Children's blocks. Jackie had wanted to start a family . . .

They walked past the Village Green rolling dark and empty, its grass silvery in the moonlight. He'd made love to Jackie there, one hot August night . . .

They walked until they reached Sick Bay. A single Mallard duck paddled slowly across the small pond, trembling its brown surface. Overhanging the far side of the pond, white and boxy, sat Medical Services. Liam had carried Jackie there when she'd sprained her ankle coming down the steps of the Math building. That's how he'd met her.

They stopped. They'd reached The Spot. The Spot, he thought, feeling the capitalization that he'd given it over the years.

Across the Ring Road lay the rambling one story red-brick of the Student Life Center, what had been the Campus Center back then, before a Tim Horton's had been grafted onto it, and before the QNC-- the huge Quantum-Nanotechnology Center--had risen to loom over it from the south, brightly lit in silver-blue-grey.

Jackie had been waiting in there, in the Campus Center, at the Bombshelter pub, that night. Waiting for him. He'd been late. She'd just left the pub, just started walking back to their home in the Tutor's Houses past Village One. This is where she'd crossed the Ring Road.

Or started to cross.

Reaching into his denim jacket, he pulled out a single red rose. He kissed the still-closed bud, breathing in its thick sweetness, and then knelt to place the flower gently on the curb. Standing, he started to cry.

He should've been there for her. She shouldn't have died. They should still be together. Ziggy's hand found his, and they stood in silence, until his sobs died away.

"Y'okay?" she asked quietly.

"Yeah," he lied, wiping his eyes.

"Me neither," she said. Her arm circled his waist again. "Let's go get drunk."

They turned south, heading for the Grad Club, but had only taken a couple of steps when Ziggy stopped. "Hang on a sec." Pulling out a little silver radio, she stuck one ear bud in her far ear, leaving the other bud dangling down her chest. She started thumbing the dial. "Dawg's show. I like Dawg. He plays all the old shit."

"Glad I have your attention," he said, resenting the intrusion of the mundane into this night. Tonight was about Jackie, not some fucking radio show.

She shot him a look. "Don't start, Lee. I'm here for you, boy. Been here every year."

"Sorry." But he didn't feel sorry. No one understood, not even Ziggy. No one understood his pain, his guilt. Fifteen years.

"Always been here for you," she muttered.

He sighed. Fighting with her wouldn't help this night. "Look, I'm sorry . . ." Overhead, the streetlight flickered. He looked up. The streetlights all along the Ring Road flickered. He blinked. All the lights on campus were flickering. On. Off. On. Off.

"What the fuck?" Ziggy said.

"Oh. Right." He checked his watch.

"What?"

"We're running some tests of the accelerator tonight. That's the first."

"At night?"

"Power's cheaper off peak. And the Beast draws a lot of power."

"Oh, just fuckin' A, Lee. So you're not going to blow up the world, but I'll have to reset all my clocks. Thanks a bunch." She punched him in the arm, grinning.

He laughed, forgetting his anger with her. The lights kept flickering on and off, like a campus-wide stroboscope. When they reached the south end of Sick Bay, Ziggy stopped, looking over at the pond.

He followed her gaze, just as the lights flicked back on and stayed on. On the pond, the same Mallard was still paddling lazily back and forth. "What?"

She kept staring at the duck. "Could've sworn . . ." She shook her head. "That must've been good shit. Could've sworn that duck was walkin' on the water."

He shook his head. "A Mallard with a Jesus complex. God won't like that."

She laughed and pulled out another joint. "So I'm either very stoned or not stoned enough. Either way, this will help." She started to light up, and then stopped, putting her hand up to the radio ear bud.

"What?"

She handed him the other bud, and he leaned in close to her to fit it into his ear. She smelled of soap, warm skin, and marijuana. "Recognize that?" she asked.

It did sound familiar. After a few seconds, it came to him. "Shit, that's from 'Moon over Morocco.' That old radio serial."

She nodded, still looking puzzled. "Not like Dawg to play something like that. And it cut from Jefferson Airplane to this, mid-Gracie Slick."

181

"You change the station by mistake?"

She checked the dial. "Nope. Weird." She grinned. "Man, 'Moon Over Morocco.' That takes me back. Remember when we first heard it? It was on Radio Waterloo then, too. Start of the term, us all sittin' around your apartment, totally stoned."

He nodded, remembering. Then he swallowed, remembering more. He pulled the bud from his ear. "That was just before Jackie died."

Her grin ran away. "Oh. Shit. Yeah, it was." She stared at the radio in her palm, as if it was going to bite her. "Weird. Sorry."

He tried to close the memories out, but they'd already pushed through the door. Fifteen years ago, in the tiny apartment he and Jackie had in the Tutor's Houses. With Ziggy and X-Ray, her drummer boyfriend of the time. Screech, Liam's best bud back then, and that blonde he'd been going with. What was her name? Passing the hookah around, laughing. Jackie cuddling warm and soft next to him. And listening to a crazy radio serial that now suddenly decided to replay on this night of all nights. And replay these memories with it. Jackie. Oh, god, when would the pain stop? He started walking.

"Lee."

He turned. Ziggy still stood there, listening to the radio. Behind her, the streetlights rising along the curve of the Ring Road were flickering once more. Off. On. Off. On. "Shit. This is even weirder." She walked up to him, her face pale. She handed him the other ear bud again.

Static. Buzzing. Then a voice. Male. The static hid what he was saying at first. Then the words became clear, and along with them, the sense of desperation.

"*Can anybody hear me?*" cried the voice. " *...<static> ... anybody out there? Oh, god, is there ... <static> ... left alive?*"

"Jeezus," Ziggy whispered, as the street lights flicked off and stayed off. "That's not 'Moon Over Morocco'."

"*Anybody? Anyone at all? If you're alive...<static>...can hear me, then...<static>*"

The streetlights flicked back on, staying on. The voice disappeared, and Liam flinched as the ending crescendo of the Stone's "You Can't Always Get What You Want" exploded into his ear. He yanked the bud out.

"Sorry," Ziggy said, wincing herself. "Cranked the volume, trying to hear what that guy was saying. That was freaky. He sounded, y'know, serious. Like it was real." She looked up at him, biting her lip.

"You change stations?" he asked, trying to forget the emptiness in the voice.

She checked the dial. "Nope."

"Maybe they switched to another radio play."

She tilted her head, listening. "It's Dawg again. No mention of 'Moon,' nothing about that guy. And that 'Moon' ep had just started. Why would he only play a few minutes of it? Then switch to something else, then back to music?"

The loneliness in the man's words came back to him, and he shivered, but covered it with a shrug. He really didn't give a shit, especially tonight. He had his own loneliness to worry about.

She looked at him, shrugged back. Pulling out the ear bud, she wrapped the headphones around the radio and shoved it in her pocket. "Yeah. You're right. Let's go get drunk. Large quantities of alcohol will make all of this so much clearer." She lit the joint she'd been holding and handed it to him.

#

Three hours later, they sat slumped against the wall of South Campus Hall, after exiting the Grad Club at the suggestion of the bartender. Liam leaned his head back, letting the cold of the brick soothe his pounding head. "It didn't, you know," he mumbled. "The alcohol . . ."

"What?"

"Didn't make it clearer. Nothing's clear to me."

"I was being sarcastic . . ."

"Nothing's been clear to me since that night. Except my work."

Ziggy sighed. "So you bury yourself down there. You and your Big Giant Ring." She laughed. "Liam and his little particles – all of you goin' round in a circle, getting nowhere."

"Fuck off." He didn't need one of her moods.

"Just saying, Lee." She chuckled. "At least your particles get to bump into each other."

"Fuck off, Zig."

"You need to bump into something." She elbowed him. "Or somebody. When was the last time you did any bumping with anybody?"

He did the math. "Two weeks ago." Bumping. That's all it had been. No real contact.

She snorted. "Yeah, right. With who?"

"Whom."

"Fuck off."

"Ginny."

Something flickered across her face. "That skinny little tech? The mousey blonde?"

"Yeah. So there. Take that," he said, happy to make her grin disappear.

She looked away and didn't say anything for a while. "Is it serious?"

He laughed. Serious. He'd felt nothing. All it had done was make him miss Jackie even more. It always did, no matter who it was. "No. Just sex. Just that once, too."

"Good," she muttered.

"What?"

Pause. "Good you're gettin' some."

"Didn't know you were worried about my love life."

That flicker ran over her face again. "Always worried about you." She turned away. "That's what friends are for," she added quietly. She leaned against him, resting her head on his shoulder and reaching out to touch the wedding ring that he still wore, her hand warm on his. "My Liam and his rings. His big one that will end the world, and this little one that was his world, his world that really did end. Liam caught in the middle of his rings, going round and round, getting nowhere."

He closed his eyes against his tears. "You gonna ask when I'm going to stop wearing it?"

Ziggy shook her head, rocking it on his shoulder, her hair tickling his cheek. "Nope. Not tonight."

"I will, you know," he said, trying to sound convincing. "When I meet the right girl."

She pulled her hand suddenly from his, and pushed herself up, her face unreadable. "Great. Hopefully, I'll be the first to know. Just so long as it's not that skinny little shit Ginny." She held up a hand, a key dangling from her fingertips. "Up and at 'em, dude. Next phase of tonight's festivities."

He considered the key through his alcohol and marijuana haze.

"The Tunnels?"

She grinned. "The Tunnels."

#

The Tunnels. Legendary underground labyrinth running under the centre of campus linking all the buildings inside the Ring Road. Not the public tunnels accessible to anyone, like those between the Arts buildings, or Math & Computer and Chem II.

The Tunnels. Capital T. The ones used by plant operations personnel, but not open to the public.

Well, not *officially* open.

Unless you knew where the entrances were.

And had a key.

In a stairwell in the basement of Chem II, Ziggy swore as she wiggled the key in the lock of an unmarked, pale green, metal door. "This night'd be a fuck of a lot easier if they'd stop changin' the locks," she muttered.

"Uh, maybe that's why you can't get it open?"

Something clicked, and she yanked the door open with a grin. "Nah, just a new key. They change the locks, but never their locksmith, who likes my product. Speaking of product . . ." She lit another joint and handed it to him. "After the Minotaur, dude." She slipped inside.

Liam sighed. The dope and the booze hadn't dulled the pain of this night. It never really did. He hesitated, seriously considering calling her back, calling it a night. But the pain would still be there when he returned alone to his empty apartment, and he wasn't ready to be alone yet. Not tonight. "Fuck it." Taking a toke, he followed her inside. The door closed behind them.

He spent the next hour wandering the tunnels behind Ziggy, gradually growing less drunk but more stoned. He found he was okay, Jackie-wise, as long as he kept moving, kept walking, concentrating on the twists and turns of the tunnels, and not on Jackie.

Most of the tunnels were about eight feet high and across, with grey concrete block walls. They ran at right-angles and were often connected by sets of metal stairs, since the campus sloped down from north to south. Large pipes of various sizes and colors ran along one wall, with tubing carrying electrical and communication cables covering most of the opposite wall and ceiling. This left only about three feet of clear space, forcing single-file walking most of the time. Every twenty-five feet, a single overhead fluorescent bulb, often partially blocked by adjacent tubing, provided the only illumination, turning the tunnels into rivers of dimness connecting islands of light.

"I remember the first time I brought Jackie down here," Liam said, swallowing down a memory. "This is the first place I ever kissed her. She said—"

"She said 'Let's play a game,'" Ziggy interrupted. "She'd go hide, and if you found her, she'd give you a kiss. You tell me every fuckin' year." She looked around the dark, dreary tunnel. "Such a romantic spot, too. X-Ray brought me down here once. Asshole wanted more than a kiss."

"She let me catch her," he whispered, remembering that first kiss, how Jackie's lips had felt, tasted. How she'd smelled, how she'd felt in his arms, her body pressed warm against his. He remembered what she wore that night, too. Yellow sweater. Black jeans.

Yellow sweater. Black jeans. He slumped against a wall. Fuck. When would it end?

"Y'okay?" Ziggy asked.

"Memories . . ."

"Are overrated." She handed him a lit joint.

"Jeezus, another?"

Shrug. "Whatever gets you through the night, my BFF. Whatever gets *you* through *this* night. This is my mission. And fool that I am, I decided to accept it. Again."

They turned a corner and stopped. Ahead, this tunnel ended five paces away in a bricked-up wall. "Shit," he said. "Wrong turn."

"Must be under Engineering II," Ziggy said, squinting at the wall. "That old stretch they closed in '98 after that dumb-ass kid died." She turned around. "Time to rewind."

Liam stared at the bricked up wall, thinking of the dead kid, thinking of dead Jackie, staring, thinking, staring . . .

Until the lights – all the lights, not just the one in this shortened tunnel – suddenly died, plunging them into complete darkness.

"Fuck," Ziggy said from somewhere behind him.

He pressed the light button on his watch and checked the time. "Shit. It's the Beast again. We're running the second test."

"Oh, great, Lee. These tunnels are tough enough when we can see." She sounded a little scared.

The lights came back on for an eye blink, then flicked off again. In that quantum of visibility, it seemed to Liam that the bricked-up wall in front of him had disappeared, that he was looking down the old tunnel, the way it had been when he'd first explored down here. The way it had been when he'd brought Jackie down here that first time. That first kiss. Jackie . . .

He jumped as Ziggy grabbed his arm in the dark. "Liam, I'm starting to freak," she said. "I'm too stoned for this shit."

The lights flicked back on. Then off. On. Off. On. Off. The lights kept flickering, and with them, the tunnel ahead flashed in and out of light. And with each flash, the scene before him strobed between showing him the bricked-up wall and then, on the next flicker, showing instead the full length of the tunnel as it once was.

The lights flickered. On. Off. On. Off.

The scene flickered. Wall. Tunnel. Wall. Tunnel.

Ziggy's grip on his arm tightened. "What the fuck?"

"You see it, too?"

And then, in one heartbeat long pulse of dim fluorescent luminescence, the wall disappeared again. Time slowed, and Liam caught a flash of someone moving past the now unblocked end of the tunnel. The image burned into his eyes and his brain. And his heart.

Her face. Her hair. Yellow sweater. Black jeans.

"No," he whispered, falling to his knees. Behind him, Ziggy gave a little cry. The lights flicked off again, only to return a second later, staying on this time. Ahead of him, the bricked-up wall loomed, the tunnel gone once more.

He stared at the wall, not believing but knowing what he'd seen.

"Jackie . . ." he whispered.

#

The next night, Liam was waiting again outside the darkened control room of Radio Waterloo as Ziggy signed off. She stepped out of the studio and saw him standing there. She stared at him for a breath, then shrugged. "Come to walk me home? That's sweet, Lee." Shrugging on her leather jacket, she threw a "g'night" to Dawg as she passed him in the hall, and then walked out the front door. Liam followed her.

"Can we talk?" he asked as he caught up to her on the road.

"Long as it's talk and walk. Gotta get home. Papers to grade."

"Yeah, sure." But he fell silent, unsure of how to start, and aware that Ziggy was in one of her moods, the kind that he'd never figured out.

They'd reached the Ring Road before Ziggy herself finally broke the silence. "Freaky night last night, eh? Gonna lay off the dope for a while."

"It was her, Zig."

"Ah, fuck," she snapped, smashing her fists into the sides of her thighs. "Don't start again." She quickened her pace, pulling ahead.

"It was her," he called to her back. "I saw her. She was right in front of my eyes."

"You can't see shit, Lee!" she flung over her shoulder. "That's your problem. You can't see what's right in front of your own eyes."

What was she talking about? "You saw her, too. I know you did."

She spun around. "I didn't see shit, Liam!" she screamed at him. A couple of first years turned to stare, then quickly looked away when she glared at them. She stalked back to him. "I told you last night. *I* didn't see shit. *You* didn't see shit," she said, poking him in the chest. "That was the grass. The brew. Fuck, we were stoned out of our skulls."

"No. That was her! Back when I first took her down there. We were there, Zig. For that moment, we were back there." He was shouting himself now, trying to make her believe. Trying to make himself believe.

She looked up at him. Suddenly, the anger drained from her face, and he thought she was going to cry. Shaking her head, she turned away again. "You are un-fucking-believable."

He caught up to her. She kept walking, eyes straight ahead. "There's more," he said. "The lights flickering matched against both tests of the Beast last night – the first time when we heard 'Moon over Morocco', and the second time when that wall disappeared, when we saw the old tunnel." He hesitated. "When we saw Jackie."

"I didn't see her, Lee," she repeated, her voice rising. They walked in silence down to the Village Green. Finally, she spoke again. "So? So the Beast was running. So what?"

"So the Beast creates temporary black holes," he answered, trying to control his excitement. "Black holes affect time. I think the accelerator somehow created a time distortion. A window into the past. The tunnels are underground, even closer to the accelerator. Any effect would be greater there."

"Again, so?"

They reached Sick Bay, where the same Mallard duck paddled lazily. A few more steps brought them to the Spot. He stopped, imagining Jackie crossing that road right there that night as he had a million times before. He checked his watch. Almost time. He turned back to Ziggy. "Look, please just humor me."

She folded her arms, staring at him, her jaw working, face unreadable. Something softened in her expression. She sighed and threw her arms up in mock exasperation. "Fine. Fuck it. What?"

"Got your little radio?"

"Yeah?"

"Tune it to Radio Waterloo. And give me a bud."

She fished the radio from her pocket, and handed him an ear bud. She stepped closer so he could put it in, squeezing his arm. "Oh, Lee, Lee, Lee," she whispered. "What am I going to do with you?"

He ignored her. Dawg was talking, introducing the next song. The

Doors' "Break on Through to the Other Side" began.

Ziggy shrugged. "And I repeat – so? That's Dawg."

"Wait." He checked his watch again. "Now." The streetlights on the Ring Road and in the campus buildings began flickering again. Off. On. Off. On.

"Oh, great," she said. "I just reset my clocks, asshole."

On the radio, Dawg faded, replaced by static at first, then gradually, another "Moon over Morocco" episode rose from the hissing into crystal clarity.

Ziggy's eyes widened into something that might have been surprise, might have been fear. "Shit," she whispered.

"That episode – is it earlier or later than the one we heard last night?"

She bit her lip, listening. "Later."

That's what he'd thought, too. "How much?"

"Hafta check, but I'd say about ten, fifteen eps."

"'Moon' played every night when they ran it that year, right?"

She nodded.

He pulled out the ear bud, thinking. It had moved later, by ten to fifteen days. Right direction, but not enough. "Okay," he muttered. "I can fix that."

"Wanna tell me what this is about?"

He looked at her, not sure if he should tell her. "The first test of the Beast last night produced a radio broadcast from two months before Jackie died. The second test gave us a scene from about a year earlier, when Jackie and I'd just met. Two tests, two points in time. I used the settings from those two tests to extrapolate for the test they just ran now."

She stared at him, and that thing peeked from her eyes again. This time, he could tell. It was fear. "Extrapolate . . ." She swallowed. "You're trying to move the time window."

He nodded.

She stepped back from him. "Trying to move it later . . ." To his amazement, tears formed in her eyes. "To when, Lee?" she said, wiping the tears away. "Wait, don't tell me. Late October that year, right? Last night to be precise. Fifteen years ago, last night." She stared at him, the tears returning. "You stupid fuck."

"I can change it, Zig."

"You dumb, stupid fuck," she said, shaking her head.

"I can save her. I can find that night. If I run the Beast longer, the window should last longer. I can be *here*. Here, when she's going to cross the road. I can save her. Don't you understand?"

"I *do* understand!" she cried. "I understand fucking perfectly! *You* don't understand."

He swallowed. "I don't understand you, that's for sure. Why are you acting like this?"

She laughed, a bitter sound. "First smart thing you've said. No, you don't understand me." She looked away, wiping her face. "Never have," she whispered.

He swallowed, lost for a response, finally settling on the only one he knew. "But I love her, Zig."

She spun to face him again, her body rigid, her hands clenched into fists at her side. She screamed her next words. "SHE'S . . . FUCKING . . . DEAD!" She stepped back, hugging herself, sobbing. "Fifteen years. Dead for fifteen fucking years. Fifteen years you've wasted, Lee. Fifteen years in your life. Going around in your fucking circles. Ring around the rosey. Going *nowhere*."

They stood there, facing each other, but suddenly more distant than the few steps between them. He didn't know what to say. He didn't know what to do. He shook his head. "I . . . I still love her."

She wiped her eyes with a fist, shaking her head, her face unreadable again. "That ain't love, Lee. That's obsession."

The lights on campus flickered again. On. Off. On. Off. Ziggy put a hand up to the single ear bud she still had in. She looked at him, her jaw working, then shoved the other ear bud at him. He put it in.

"This is Radio <static> . . . Can anybody hear me? Is there anybody out there? Anybody? Is anybody alive? Oh god, if you can hear me <static> . . ."

Ziggy stood there, staring a mute accusation at him, her back to Sick Bay. He looked past her. The duck . . .

Following his stare, she turned to see what he saw, what he saw but didn't believe.

The duck was walking across the water. Not swimming, not wading, but walking, its orange feet brilliant and visible above the pond's black surface in the lights from Med Services. The night sky above was suddenly dark, starless, moonless.

The static from the radio ear bud faded again, and from it rose that lost, lonely voice. *"<static>nowhere, nothing. Please, is there anybody out there? Isn't there anyone left alive? I'm still here at <static> . . ."* The voice died into noise again.

The campus lights kept flickering.

Off. On. The duck was walking. The stars were gone.

Off. On. The duck was swimming. The stars shone bright.

Off. On. Off. On.

Walk. Swim. Walk. Swim.

No stars. Stars. No stars. Stars.

The flickering finally stopped. The lights returned. The duck was swimming. Stars shone again in the cold night sky.

Ziggy shot another look at the duck, then turned to him. "That duck's not the only one with a Jesus complex, Lee. Go ahead. Resurrect your Jackie. Raise her from the dead. Just keep me out of it."

She shoved the little radio into his hand, then stalked across the Ring Road. On the other side, she turned back, her hands jammed into the pockets of her leather jacket. "What if your precious Beast opens other windows?" she called. "That guy we're hearing on the radio? What if that's the future? The future you're making for us while you're trying to play God?"

He watched her walk away, disappearing behind the QNC. He looked back to the now-swimming duck, then down at the little radio lying like a cold dead thing in his palm. Turning his back on Sick Bay and the duck, he jammed the radio into his pocket, and stared instead at The Spot. He shook his head. Only one thing mattered.

"Jackie," he whispered.

He walked back to his apartment, working the calculations in his head.

#

The next week was even lonelier for him than usual. He'd never realized what a huge part of his life Ziggy had become. For fifteen years, she'd just always been there when he needed her. Part of his day. Part of his world.

Suddenly, she'd disappeared from that world, as if he'd lost her like he'd lost Jackie. She wouldn't answer her phone, wouldn't come to the door, didn't return messages. He finally gave up, not in trying to contact her, but in expecting any response. Ziggy was Ziggy. She'd talk to him again only when she was ready to. That much about her he understood.

So he resigned himself to carrying on a one-sided conversation via phone and text and email messages, hoping that she'd at least listen to or read them even if she didn't respond. Every day, message by message, he explained how his tests were proceeding, his successes, his failures. And with every message, he waited for her to pick up the phone, to see a reply in his inbox, a "message waiting" flashing on his phone.

But no reply came. His loneliness grew, but instead of making him want to give up his quest and to reconcile with his friend, the loss of Ziggy from his life only made him yearn for Jackie even more.

Finally, he was ready, every calculation checked and rechecked, every test confirming expectations. That night, sitting in his small, cramped apartment, he dialed Ziggy one more time. Three rings and it bounced to voice mail.

"This is Ziggy. I'm not here. In apology, I give you this beep." Beep.

"Ziggy, pick up." He waited. Silence. "C'mon Zig." Ziggy's little silver radio, ear buds wrapped around it, lay beside his phone. *Is anybody out there? Can anybody hear me?* "Okay, well, anyway, I'm ready. To try it. Tomorrow. Midnight. At the Spot. I hope . . ." He hoped – what? Fuck it. "Hope you'll be there." He hung up.

He stared at the radio. *Is anybody out there?* Yeah, he thought. My Jackie.

Tomorrow night. Tomorrow night, his life would change. Tomorrow night, he'd have Jackie back. Yet somehow, without Ziggy, it just didn't feel right.

#

The next night. On the Day. At the Spot. Just before midnight.

The night air was cold, the dark sky cloudless and star-spotted. No cars travelled the Ring Road, and the few students who drifted by ignored Liam where he sat on the grass. Down the slope behind him, what he assumed was the same duck slept with its head tucked under one wing, floating lazily on the muddy water in Sick Bay.

For one last time, he looked up the road in the direction of the radio station. He sighed. No point in waiting for her any longer. He stood up.

He turned on Ziggy's little silver radio. Dawg was introducing R.E.M.'s "The End of the World as We Know It." Pulling out his Blackberry, he established a secure VPN connection into the QNC network and the computer controlling the Beast. Opening his test program, he typed "Run / Scenario = Jackie7.3" into the device. His thumb hovered above the Send key. He looked up at the Spot. And stopped.

A familiar small figure, hands shoved deep into the pockets of her worn leather UW jacket, was walking towards him from the SLC. She crossed the road at the Spot, and he felt his guts clench as the memory of Jackie being struck down here melted into a sudden unbidden image of Ziggy dying in this same place. Shivering, he pushed the thought away.

Stopping in front of him, she looked up at him, her jaw working. Then she kicked him lightly on the leg. "Asshole."

He smiled. "Bitch." He swallowed down the sudden lump in his throat. Ziggy was here. Everything seemed right again. This was going to work.

She looked away, then back again. "Still gonna do this thing?"

He hesitated. Right, the test. How could he have forgotten? He nodded. She nodded back, then shook her head. "So what's the plan?"

He waved his Blackberry. "I start the Beast running, with my tested settings."

Another headshake. "And shit gets weird here. How do you know you'll hit The Night?"

He tapped the ear bud. "These settings brought in the same episode of 'Moon over Morocco' that was playing when . . ." He looked down. ". . . that was playing that night. I checked the station's broadcast records."

"You mean you've already gone back to that night?"

"Just low energy tests, enough to affect radio signals. But tonight I'll crank up the volume. Higher energy. Try to recreate what happened in the tunnels, only hold the window open longer."

She looked at the ear bud. "Hear anything else in your tests?"

He hesitated, remembering. *Is there anybody out there?* He shook his head.

She snorted. "Liar." She sighed. "So do the deed." She nodded at the duck. "Me? I'm going to wait with my new buddy."

He swallowed. "Aren't you, you know, going to be here with me?"

She smiled up at him, as tender a look as he'd ever seen on her face. "Been here with you for fifteen years. Now . . ." She glanced across the road to The Spot. "Now, you're hitting RESET. You're getting your Jackie back. You don't need me anymore." She looked at him. "Do you, Lee?" When he didn't answer, she nodded. "Yeah. Thought so." She walked down the slope to the edge of Sick Bay. Sitting down on the grass, her back to him, she lit up a joint and stared at the duck.

Angry, he started to call to her, then stopped. What did it matter if

Ziggy was in one of her moods? Turning away from her, he faced the Spot. His thumb hovered again above the Send key.

You're hitting RESET.

Reset? He swallowed, understanding. If this worked, Jackie would be alive, but these past fifteen years would never have happened.

Been here fifteen years for you . . .

So? He'd dreamed of this moment, right? To finally end the ache that had lived in his heart since Jackie's death. His Jackie. His life. But another ache was growing inside him, one that he couldn't name.

Reset. Start over. Rewind fifteen years. Fifteen years of memories.

You don't need me anymore. Do you?

He looked at the Spot. Fifteen years. Reset. Jackie . . .

That ain't love, Lee. That's obsession.

With a sob, no longer knowing why he was doing it, more because he didn't know what else to do, he pressed the key.

For a heartbeat, nothing happened. Then everything went black, as if he'd just flipped the light switch for the universe. The lights along the Ring Road disappeared. The lights in the Student Life Centre, the QNC, every light on campus disappeared. Above, the stars in the cold night sky disappeared. Complete darkness fell, a darkness that seemed less a loss of light, and more a palpable presence of something else, something that had never known light. Behind him, he heard Ziggy cry out in fear.

On the little radio, R.E.M. faded. A chill ran up his spine, knowing what he'd hear next.

"*. . . body alive out there? <static> . . . hear me? Anybody? If you can <static> . . .*"

What if that's the future? The future you're making . . .

The radio cut out. The stars, the lights, the world returned. Or rather, *a* world returned.

A different world.

Reset.

He gasped. The huge QNC had vanished, replaced by an expanse of grass and criss-crossing walkways between Chem II on the south and Math and the SLC on the north. The Tim Horton's was gone, and the SLC was once again the old Campus Centre as it had been back then, back when . . .

Reset.

Back when Jackie had died.

The static faded from the radio, and "Moon over Morocco" flared to clarity, the same episode that had been on that night. He'd hit the date! He checked his watch. 12:04am.

There'd been witnesses, people who'd known the time when she'd been hit – 12:07am.

Three minutes. Could the Beast hold the window open that long? Could the Universe grant him that much?

As if to mock him, the lights began to flicker. The lights strobed off and on, and with them, the scene before him. Off. On. The Tim Horton's and the QNC returned. Off. On. They vanished again, and the old Campus Centre lay before him.

Off. On. The world where Jackie still lived disappeared.

Off. On. That world returned, and with it, his dream of fifteen years.

He checked his watch. Two minutes. Still wanting Ziggy beside him, he turned to where she sat beside Sick Bay. Except that Ziggy was no longer sitting beside the pond.

She was walking across it. Walking calmly towards where the duck still slept with its head under a wing, only now it stood on one brilliant

200

orange foot on the surface of the water.

Ziggy sat down beside the duck. She was crying, tears glistening her cheeks, her pale face shining like the impossible surface of the pond on which she now sat.

Reset. Fifteen years of memories.

Without thinking, he started down the slope towards her before he remembered. He stopped, looking at his watch. 12:06am. Across the Ring Road, a group of students poured out of the Campus Centre. A familiar slim figure detached itself from the group, hurrying ahead, hurrying home. Hurrying to her death. He gasped, and he had to force his next breath in.

"Jackie," he whispered, unable to believe that it was her. He looked down the road. The blue Toyota that would strike her down had just appeared around the corner of the Psych building. Ahead of him, head down, Jackie rushed towards the road.

The lights on campus flickered. His heart skipped. Was he going to lose his chance to save her? "Moon over Morocco" faded from the radio, replaced again by that desperate lonely voice. *"Can't anybody hear me out there? Isn't there anyone left alive <static>..."*

He stepped onto the road, and as he did so, other noises rose, but not through the ear bud of the little radio.

A splash. A duck squawking. A scream.

Ziggy's scream.

He spun around. Below him, the duck was no longer standing on the water. It was swimming rapidly away from where Ziggy flailed in the murky brown water of the pond. She opened her mouth but her words died in a gurgling sound as she slipped beneath the surface. Ziggy couldn't swim.

Dropping the radio, he leapt down the slope. He was halfway

down before he realized what he was doing, what he'd just left behind.

Jackie . . .

But then Ziggy disappeared under the water again, and he forgot everything else. He dove into the pond, the cold hitting him like an electric shock. Three strokes brought him to where she'd gone under. He dove, kicking, pulling himself deeper. His hand brushed against something. He grabbed, his fingers closing around the leather of her jacket. Gripping tight, he pulled her to him and kicked for the surface. In the air once more, he stroked for the shore, cradling her in one arm. She wasn't breathing. Oh, god, she wasn't breathing.

The pond bottom at the edge was like quicksand, and he seemed to sink deeper with each step, Ziggy hanging like a dead weight in his arms. Finally reaching the grassy bank, he laid her down. She wasn't breathing. She really wasn't breathing. Oh god. He started mouth-to-mouth. Once. Twice. Oh god, please. Three times.

Suddenly, she coughed, spewing dirty pond water into his face. She rolled onto her hands and knees, retching and coughing. She kept coughing until she finally fell back down onto the grass. He lay beside her, cradling her to him, not wanting to let go of her, not then, not ever.

She opened her eyes and stared at him for several seconds without speaking, as if she was trying to remember who he was. Then she grinned. "I walked on water."

"You dumb ass," he said, as relief washed over him. "You almost drowned."

"Oh," she said, then her eyes widened. "Oh, shit! Jackie! Did it work? Did you save her?"

He shook his head. "Saved you instead."

"Oh. Thanks." She frowned. "So go get her now."

He looked back to where the QNC once more rose into the sky. He shook his head again. "The window's gone."

She put a hand to her mouth. "Oh god, Lee. I'm sorry." She started to cry.

"It's okay." He thought about it. *Reset. Fifteen years of memories.* He nodded, as much to himself as to her. "Really."

She looked at him, sniffling. "Really?"

He shrugged. "You were drowning."

She considered that. "So . . . possibly destroying the world didn't stop you, but having to save me did." She grinned. "Cool." Suddenly, she grabbed his hand. "Shit, you've lost your wedding ring."

He stared at his empty ring finger. "Must've come off in the pond."

"Want to try to find it?" she asked, not meeting his eyes.

He thought about that, then slowly shook his head. "No." He swallowed, looking at her. "I think I, like, you know . . . love you."

She stared at him. Then she started to laugh.

"Not quite the reaction I expected."

"Oh, Lee. You dumb fuck. Fifteen years." She kept laughing. "God, you're slow."

He laughed with her, and then pulled her to him into a deep, long kiss. *Is there anybody out there?* Yeah, he thought, I am. Finally.

Somewhere nearby, he could hear a duck quacking.

RED CAGE

BY BRIT TROGEN

The corridor leading up to the common room was horribly quiet.

"Hello?" Kevin walked slowly down the hall, his footsteps echoing on the tiles. The emergency lights on the ceiling rotated soundlessly, casting flashing red beams across the hallway. Directly in front of him, the windows looking out onto the river valley were dark.

He drew closer to the opening of the room, an uncomfortable tingling feeling in his stomach. For a moment he thought he heard a faint scratching sound, but when he stopped to listen it was gone. He stepped into the room.

He waited, dead still, scanning the counter and the far door for any sign that someone had been there. He was about to turn and leave when his eyes passed over a dark mass at the far side of the room, and he felt his entire body freeze.

Staring out at him from a crumpled pile on the floor were empty blue eyes set in a pale, bloodless face.

\#

Kevin Lambert stood at the main doors of the NINT, hoping with every ounce of his being that no one was watching him. Glancing over his shoulder, he swiped his security card through the electronic reader and gave another half-hearted push at the door. It didn't budge.

Great, he thought, checking his watch. *Defeat by door. Perfect start to the new job.* He shifted his weight, and the shoulder bag stuffed with his new uniform brushed up against his hip. He'd tried to put it on earlier but somehow it had felt uncomfortably tight, even though he knew it was the right size.

Taking a few steps back, he stared up at the mirrored windows covering the side of the building.

The National Institute of Nanotechnology was only a few years old, and it stood out as one of the more attractive buildings on campus. Six floors of gleaming metal frame glinted in the sun. Past the reflection of the pink-tinted sky he could see tables lined up near the glass on each floor with upside down chairs set on top of them. There didn't seem to be anyone there.

Swallowing his pride, Kevin waved up at the windows and pointed helplessly at the front door. No response. Embarrassed, he walked to the door again, and kicked it sharply. "Come on, let me *in*."

As if on cue, a tall, gangly man in a navy blue uniform appeared inside from around the corner and began walking towards him. The man looked slightly concerned, and eyed Kevin warily as he approached the door but didn't make any move to open it, instead pointing in the direction of the card reader.

"It won't work," Kevin said loudly, not sure how soundproof the glass was. He held his card up against the glass, and shrugged helplessly.

The man seemed to relax when he saw the card, and after peering at it for a moment he pushed the latch on the door, and it swung open.

"Hi." He spoke in a slow drawl, smiling widely. "You're the new day shift? I saw you from upstairs." He stood in the opening of the door, staring at Kevin with wide eyes. He was young, perhaps late twenties, with dark brown hair and pale, freckled skin. "We gave up on you hours ago."

"Yeah," Kevin began, running a hand through his hair, which seemed to be getting thinner every day. "I was supposed to start this afternoon. I – um – I had car trouble." He felt his face grow warm as he spoke at the ground, hoping to hide the sour hint of liquor on his breath. He'd always been a terrible liar.

The man gave him a strange look, raising his eyebrows quizzically, but stepped back to let him in. "I know. Sheila was waiting for you earlier but there's hardly anyone left now. I'm Jude."

"Hi." Kevin stepped inside and let the door close behind him, feeling a vague sense of suffocation. "I'm Kevin. Sorry I'm so late."

"Not a problem." Jude began walking back through the lobby, gesturing for Kevin to follow him. "Though in the future you should know that kicking the doors won't accomplish much." He glared at Kevin in mock annoyance, then winked. "They're steel plated." Kevin smiled sheepishly as he followed Jude around the corner.

Jude was still staring at Kevin with a strange, wide-eyed expression. "So I hear you used to be a cop?"

"Yeah." Kevin tried to avoid eye contact. *Used to be.*

"So why'd you come here? Seems like a bit of a step down. No offense."

Thanks, Kevin thought, but nodded. "Personal reasons." He couldn't see any benefit in explaining the details of his private life to a total stranger. And phrases like *nervous breakdown* and *indefinite leave of absence* probably wouldn't do much in endearing him to new coworkers.

The lobby of the building was spacious, with a high ceiling and shining, marble floors. At the far end of the room a large counter was set in front of an open door. A visitor's log sat open on the counter, and

Kevin could see rows of dark computer monitors lined up in the room behind it.

Jude nodded to the counter. "This is our main station. Everyone who comes in has to sign in here. Sheila's usually here until six, but she's going on mat leave next week so now it's your shift. All the doors lock down before the night shift starts."

Kevin picked up a pen on the counter and signed the open book. "Seems like a lot of precautions for a biology lab."

Jude shrugged, grinning. "The fifth and sixth floors are biocontainment level four, which means you could pretty much destroy the world with the goodies up there." He smiled, showing his gums. "Technically, you can't go there until you've taken a BCL-4 training course. But even on the BCL-3 floors there's some fun stuff going on. Bird flu, meningitis. I think there's a girl working on anthrax, too. Pretty cool."

Unsure of how to respond to this, Kevin nodded. Jude led the way towards the elevators and punched the up button. The doors slid open almost soundlessly.

"Look," Jude turned to Kevin as they stepped in. "How about I just give you a quick tour and we'll get you started tomorrow?" He pushed the button for the fourth floor.

"Sure." Kevin tried to sound grateful. It was bad enough making the guy wait for five hours. The fact that he was still going to get to look around was more than he'd expected.

The elevator stopped with a lurch at the third floor. As the doors slid open, Kevin felt his heart stop in his chest.

A beautiful, dark haired woman was staring at him with familiar, bloodshot eyes, and an expression of unfathomable sadness.

Cara. A sharp pain shot across his head, and he covered his eyes with one hand, but when he looked again a moment later the familiar face was gone.

The woman was middle-aged, and a stranger. She looked exhausted, as if she'd just been crying, and while her eyes seemed familiar Kevin had never seen her before.

She immediately made as if to get in, but froze when she saw them. She stared at Kevin for a moment before mumbling something about stairs and turning back in the opposite direction. The doors closed again, and the elevator continued its climb.

Kevin tried to steady his voice, feeling sick. "Who was that?"

Jude didn't seem to have noticed his reaction. "Rachel Harding. One of the lab supervisors in genetics. Her husband Peter works here too – goofy looking guy with big glasses, fifth floor – but rumor has it there's trouble at home." The elevator reached the fourth floor and they stepped out. "I hate to gossip," Jude continued in a whisper, smiling manically, "but apparently they've been trying to have a kid and it's not going well. And I heard he's got a questionable relationship going with one of the grad students, too. They're here all the time."

As Jude led the way down a bright, wide hallway, Kevin tried to shake off the feeling of nausea that had swept over his body, wishing he could somehow get at the flask buried in his bag.

Aside from that one strange encounter, the whole building really did seem to be deserted. A heavy silence blanketed the hallway, broken only by the muffled sounds of their footsteps. Kevin got the uneasy feeling that he was intruding.

"It's really quiet here." Kevin was about to say 'creepy', but decided against it.

Jude nodded, his blue, bug-like eyes shining as if he were telling a joke. "It's a *Quiet* building."

Kevin watched as they passed several closed doors, nodding uncertainly. "Probably because everyone's gone home."

Jude shook his head, seeming amused. "It's more than that. All the walls here have been reinforced to stop sound and radiation from passing through them. The work here is so precise that even the slightest disturbance could set everything off." Jude pulled a set of key cards from his pocket and started flipping through them. "It's kind of weird at first, never hearing anybody, but you get used to it." He stepped up to one of the closed doors and swiped his card at the scanner. "This is the shared office where we meet with the researchers every other week. Just stay put for a second while I get you a new clearance card."

Jude slipped inside, leaving Kevin in the empty hall.

#

Kevin sprinted back down the corridor, breathing heavily, trying uselessly to rid his lungs of the smell of death that hung in the air. He should call for help--he tried to yell, to catch his breath--but his throat was dry and no sound came out. And he knew that it wouldn't make any difference. No one would hear him.

He ran toward the stairwell, slamming his shoulder against the door, which swung open effortlessly. He ran, half falling down the stairs until he reached the ground floor, then flung himself back through the stairwell door and towards the main entrance.

On the grass outside the window a multitude of sirens and lights blinded him. He shielded his eyes with one hand, slamming the other into the glass of the door.

"Somebody help!" He screamed at the people clustered around one of the police cruisers. Three figures in biohazard suits and a vaguely familiar uniformed officer turned at the sound and stared at him. *"Please*--get a medic in here." He pressed his open palms against the window.

The policeman looked back at him with pity, and shook his head slowly. Kevin felt his eyes burn with anger and fear. He could almost hear the words running through their heads. *Breach, outbreak, pandemic.* They wouldn't send help. They couldn't, he knew, until the threat, whatever it was, had been identified. But he still couldn't stop himself from hitting, punching, kicking at the door.

"Please," he said again, feeling the walls closing in on him. "Let me out." Exhausted, adrenaline pumping through his body, he slumped to the floor and pressed his hands into his eyes. The image was burned into his mind – Jude's wide eyes, his face swollen with edema, dark blood seeping from his nose, a scarlet rash blossoming across his throat.

It looked like some type of hemorrhagic fever, but Kevin couldn't imagine where he might have been exposed to it. If it was an airborne virus, they would have been exposed at the same time.

The image of Jude's broken body melded with another image – the vision he saw every time he closed his eyes. A mass of long dark hair, a pale wasted face. *Cara.* He hadn't been able to save her either.

The silent red lights seemed to beat down on his head and face, burning into him. He was trapped here, with a nameless guilt he was never able to turn away from.

But this time was different, he realized, as another thought flitted through his mind. *There's someone in here.*

Kevin knew this wouldn't make any sense to the people outside. Of course there were people inside; himself and the few scientists who had been unlucky enough to be locked in when the alarm had sounded. But there was another person too, Kevin thought, someone who wasn't so innocent.

Jude would never have intentionally come into contact with a viral fluid. Someone could have forced him into contact with it. Maybe he had screamed, tried to run only after it was too late.

If that was true, then this time it wasn't his fault. This time there was someone else to blame.

Barely thinking, Kevin lifted himself off the floor and took off for the stairs again, Jude's voice ringing hauntingly in his ears. *The fifth and sixth floors* . . .

He might finally be able to redeem himself, to try to make amends for what he'd done. If there was anything in here that was worth killing for, that was where it would be.

#

Kevin took a deep breath, trying to shake the feeling of foreboding that had settled over him since his arrival. He wandered over to one of the bulletin boards on the opposite wall and skimmed the colorful notices of seminars that would be taking place in the next few weeks.

"Hey!" A loud, sharp voice cut through the quiet, making Kevin jump. He turned to see a young woman with shiny brown hair come striding towards him. She pointed at him, one hand groping in her pocket. "Don't move! Get away from that door!"

Kevin held his hands up in front of him, and glanced at the door that was a few feet to his left. "Wait – What? Which do you want me to do?"

"*Don't move.*" Repeated the girl. She pulled a silver cell phone from her pocket and held it up with her other hand. "Show me your ID or I'm calling the cops."

I am a cop, Kevin almost blurted out, but quickly remembered that this was no longer true. Instead he scrambled to pull his security card from his wallet. Jude came running from the opposite door. "Lisa, calm down! He's with me, okay? He's the new security guard." Kevin feebly held up his ID card.

The girl's face flushed red, in what Kevin thought could either be anger or embarrassment. "Well he shouldn't be wandering around here unattended." She walked to the door Kevin had been standing beside, brushing past him roughly, and swiped her card. "He can't just poke around in places he doesn't know." She pushed the door open and looked around inside, as if expecting someone to jump out at her.

Kevin felt again the stifling sense of humiliation he'd felt when he tried on the uniform. This girl was probably half his age, and was speaking to him like a misbehaving child.

"*And*," she began again, turning towards them as if something had just occurred to her. "Did you leave the main door open? I had to go check on an alarm that was going off. It hadn't been shut completely. Which means *anybody* could have just strolled in."

Jude shook his head, but looked unsure. "I don't think we—"

She cut him off. "You *know* I just finished isolating the high potency strain." Her anger was directed at both of them now. "I don't need this kind of stress right now. I can't risk anybody getting close to it. So *don't do it again*." She stepped in, closing the door behind her, and Kevin and Jude were left gaping at it in silence.

"Wow." Kevin finally said.

"Yeah." Jude shook his head. "Lisa's in the Kaufman lab. They work on avian flu, and get weekly meetings about bioterrorism prevention.

Seems to get them all a little wound up." He winked at Kevin again. "I think she likes you. Come on."

Jude closed up the office and led the way further down the hall, describing the different areas as they passed. They walked through one of the common rooms Kevin had seen from outside, complete with a small kitchen and tables for private meetings or lunches. Jude pointed out a dark room with a spinning, cylindrical door, a microscope room that had taken up almost a quarter of the budget for the building, and finally brought him to a sprawling lab filled with clean, dark counter tops scattered with molecular biology equipment.

"This is one of the secure labs. Pretty standard. You can take a look around if you want."

Kevin wandered past several lab benches, further in to the room.

"That's pretty much it for this floor." Jude's voice carried across the room. "They keep most of the biological samples frozen in the minus eighty down the hall."

A large glass plated container sitting on a counter caught Kevin's eye, and he moved over to it. It looked like some type of incubator, the bottom lined with paper towels and bench cote, and a large, metallic container propped up in the middle. It seemed like an incubator for animal storage, but there didn't seem to be anything inside.

He reached out and tapped gently on the side of the glass.

Immediately, a brilliant red light that had been dormant on the wall above him flashed on. He cried out and covered his eyes, startled by the flare.

"Oh my god." Jude's voice rang out loudly, followed quickly by running footsteps. "What did you do?" He appeared at Kevin's side and stared at him with complete disbelief, his eyes flicking between the incubator and Kevin's hands.

"Nothing!" Kevin was still in shock. "I tapped the side, I didn't know it would do anything." He held up his hands, feeling completely foolish. "I'm sorry – I didn't know."

Jude shook his head, speaking confusedly to himself. "There's no way . . . I can't imagine they'd be running a drill right now." He stared at the light. "There's all kinds of sensors throughout the building that detect output from the labs, but I don't see how you could possibly have set them off. We've practiced this dozens of times; it's what happens if something leaks." He was silent for several seconds, the red light flashing over his face. Finally, he sighed. "Well, settle in. The whole building's gone into lockdown. It'll probably take the emergency team a few hours to get us out of here."

Kevin balked. "You mean something's leaking in here? What are we supposed to do in the meantime?"

Jude shrugged, a mixture of frustration and attempted composure on his face. "I need to marshal each floor. There's a few rooms that have really sensitive material and don't have alarm lights, so I have to make sure that if there's anyone in there they know to get evacuated when the cavalry get here."

"But what am I supposed to do?"

"Go wait in the fourth floor meeting room. I'll come by and get you in a couple minutes when I'm finished. We can wait it out there until this is over."

#

Kevin sprinted up the first three flights of stairs, then stopped, panting. He had no idea what he planned to do. Sneak up behind the possible intruder, who may or may not be armed with some sort of

215

biological weapon, and ask him politely to turn himself in? He'd call that Plan B.

Trying to be as quiet as possible, he began the ascent to the next floor, cursing the fact that he no longer carried a gun. He tried not to think about what was lying in the common room just down the hall.

When he came level to the door he paused again, listening, and stared through the glass down the hallway. There was no movement, no sound. Whatever that was worth. He wouldn't have been able to hear anything through the soundproof walls.

Cautiously, he started up towards the fifth floor. He tried to listen for movement, but his heart was pounding in his ears, making it difficult to focus. As he reached the final step and prepared to cross the platform to the stairwell door, his eyes immediately fell upon the patch of darkness on the tiled floor.

He felt his skin crawl. Blood. Gleaming in the red lights of the stairwell, the dark sheen was unmistakable. There wasn't much; it looked like a small pool had been spread by passing footprints. But it was enough to tell him that he was getting close.

For a moment the stairwell looked different to him, like the setting of a dream. He saw a different room, a different time. He imagined Cara's face, he last time he'd seen it, brilliant with anger and despair.

I didn't know, he willed her to know. *I didn't think you'd do it.* He hadn't stopped her, hadn't known she needed saving. But tonight things could end differently. And then maybe he could finally find peace, and rest.

Stepping around the blood, he pushed through the fifth floor doorway, breath baited.

#

"Hey!" A voice called out sharply, this time in a low whisper. "Excuse me, guard? Where's Jude?" Turning away from the office door he'd been about to open, Kevin recognized Lisa peering out from her lab door.

"Um – he's checking all the rooms for people. He should be back here soon." *Or half an hour ago*, he added silently. "What's up?"

She looked nervous, even more so than a simple alarm would warrant. *No*, he realized, stepping closer. It was more than that; she looked *scared*.

Her eyes widened as Kevin approached, and it looked for a moment like she was about to close the door on him. "I think something's going on." She stared at him, her face pale. "I—I saw something."

Kevin waited, but she didn't elaborate. "What?" He finally prodded.

She stared at him for a moment uncertainly, as if making up her mind. "There was a man. Right after the alarm went off he was just off down the hall, and—" She broke off, steadying her breath. "I called out to him to stop, but he was carrying something . . . a case. He saw me and ran the other way, and—God, I don't know. It sort of looked like Peter. Dr. Harding. Do you know him? I couldn't really see – his face was covered – it might not have been. I've known him for years! But it looked like he was—" She didn't finish.

"What? Stealing?" Kevin hadn't imagined that anything like that could actually happen here.

"I don't know. I just thought you guys should know." She looked at him again with the same uncertain expression. "When's Jude getting back?"

Kevin tensed. "Actually, I thought he'd be back a while ago. I was supposed to meet him . . ."

Lisa's face darkened. "Listen, I just saw the emergency crews get here a few minutes ago, so it's only a matter of time." She stared at Kevin again, as though his presence seemed more suspicious to her by the minute. "And no offense, but I'm just going to wait here."

There was a silence, which Kevin interpreted as her saying: *alone.* And after another moment and a final glance, she pushed the door closed.

He stared at the door, nodding to himself darkly. *I wouldn't trust me either.* After a few more minutes of waiting, he felt like he couldn't take it any more. The flashing red lights were making him feel frantic, like a caged rat. He had to find Jude, do something, anything.

He left the meeting room and started walking back down the hall, but every closed door seemed to contain some hidden, watching person and he found himself constantly looking backwards. Feeling anxious, he set off towards the common room.

#

Kevin walked down the fifth floor hallway, barely breathing. Light was spilling from one of the labs near the end of the hall, and as he drew nearer he saw that the door was slightly open. He waited, trying to steel his nerve, but instead found that he couldn't move, couldn't take one more step.

There was movement inside. Someone on the other side of the door was moving, and . . . Laughing? A low, convulsive sound was coming from behind the door.

Every ounce of Kevin's body protested frantically as he took one last step, and pushed the door open.

There, hunched over a small, glass sided container, was a balding man with large, black rimmed glasses. A gash on the side of the man's head was seeping blood, and he stood there, bent over the counter, shaking. He wasn't laughing; he was sobbing.

The man looked up suddenly at Kevin, tears mixing with the blood that was running down his face. They stared at each other in silence for several seconds.

"Dr. Harding?" Kevin's voice was shaky as he stepped into the room. "Wh—what are you doing?"

At the sound of his voice, the expression on Harding's face changed from sorrow to utter horror, as if he hadn't believed Kevin was real before hearing his voice. "Who are you?" His voice was thick with tears, and he backed away suddenly, his eyes bulging. "Don't touch me!" His hand snatched out towards the counter, and he held up a large, metal rod. He swung it in Kevin's direction like a scythe. "Stay away from me!"

"What's going on?" Kevin backed away, stunned. "Are you all right?"

"She's upstairs," the man cried, his face contorted in agony. "In the—the autoclave room. *Upstairs*, do you hear me?"

"Who's upstairs?" For a split second Kevin pictured Cara's face again, and felt a chill terror flood his body.

But Dr. Harding seemed to lose all strength in his limbs as he spoke, and the metal rod fell clanging to the floor. Kevin could barely hear him through the choking sobs. "Just do it. *Kill her*. I know you're going to, no matter what I say. Do it then, and *leave me alone*."

"No," Kevin said, feeling suddenly cold and intolerably tired, as though he'd been carrying an unbearable burden. "I didn't –I'm not—"

"Killer," Dr. Harding whispered, but he was no longer looking at Kevin. "I didn't mean to. I only touched him."

Kevin moved closer, barely able to hear, but at that moment Dr. Harding lurched forward. *"Don't touch me,"* he choked, pushing the lab door shut with a pitiful moan that was cut off with total silence as the door slammed shut.

And Kevin was left alone once again, his ears ringing, standing alone in the flashing red lights of the hallway.

He moved without awareness, barely seeing as he made his way back to the stairs and began climbing, tracking blood on his shoes, Dr. Harding's words echoing in his ears, drawn inexorably to the sixth floor.

The autoclave room was empty when he arrived.

On two sides of the room, large, shoulder height ovens gaped like dark, hungry mouths. Kevin edged his way inside, trying to stay as far from the ovens as he could. The room was filled with rolling carts and trays, and was eerily silent, like the rest of the building.

Kevin began to distantly wonder whether Dr. Harding might just be insane. Whoever he had been referring to, if anyone, didn't seem to be here. He walked further in to the room, keeping one eye on the door.

As he neared the back of the room, he heard something; a faint sloshing sound, like water lapping against the side of a pool. It had come from the direction of one of the carts. Kevin cautiously stepped toward it.

A large, silver tray with raised edges was sitting on the cart, and as Kevin crept closer he saw that it was filled with a thick, yellow liquid. He peered inside, leaning close, squinting to see in the strange red lighting, then recoiled instantly.

Near one edge of the tray, almost invisible in the thick liquid was a small creature, no bigger than his fist. It was alien looking, shiny and smooth, and curled up in a tight ball. He wouldn't have known it was alive, but it twitched every few seconds, and sometimes rolled over causing waves in the shallow pool of liquid. Large blue veins showed through its transparent skin, pulsing gently.

"Don't touch her." A voice from behind him made Kevin jump. Turning, he saw Rachel Harding standing in the doorway, her right hand holding something concealed at her side. Her face was pale, and void of expression.

"Her?" Kevin felt his skin crawl as he looked back at the tiny thing in the tray.

Rachel nodded, stony-faced. "She's contagious." She walked towards Kevin and placed both of her hands on the cart beside the tray. He saw that she was holding a small syringe, filled with a clear liquid. She stared down at the tray, her face drained and stoic, her eyes out of focus. "We tried so hard, Peter and I. We wanted it so badly." She shook her head slowly. "It just wasn't meant to be."

Kevin felt a wave of nausea run through his body. *They've been trying to have a kid.* His mind fought desperately to avoid the thought, but finally, horrible understanding dawned on him.

He felt sick as he looked back at the tray, at the thing that was supposed to be a child. "Why did you do this?" He couldn't bring himself to look at Rachel.

"It was our last hope." Her voice seemed distant, as if she were speaking from very far away. "Everything else failed. And we thought if we could only do it ourselves, watch over every step, take it into our own hands . . ."

The lights of the room reflected in her eyes, making them glow red.

Kevin could see it clearly; the two of them, bent over a microscope, a Petri dish, an incubator. Watching as if an experiment were progressing.

Rachel spoke softly, almost murmuring. "We failed again. Something went wrong, got in. Everything she touches dies – some sort of hybrid virus. We're both immune, but . . . I knew before Peter what we would have to do. She can't live in this world."

Everything she touches dies. He looked down at the tray; first Jude's then Cara's face flashing before his eyes. "Did you pull the alarm?" His voice felt hoarse. He stared at Rachel, who nodded, and Kevin fought down the nausea that was rising in his throat as his mind raced. "And Jude found her."

For the first time, Rachel's face contorted with grief, her eyes welling instantly. "She was in a private room. Only Peter and I could access it. I brought her up here after I triggered the alarm, but Peter took her, tried to hide her away." Tears were flowing freely across her cheeks. "Jude found them and got infected. By the time I found out it was too late."

She dropped her head, eyes closed. Her knuckles on the side of the cart were white with tension. "I had to fight to get her back."

She was silent for several minutes as Kevin waited, unable to say or do anything more.

Finally, she looked up again, her face composed. "It has to end now." She looked at Kevin, her eyes cold.

Kevin couldn't speak, couldn't move. He knew what was about to happen but was unable to stop it, to fix it.

Rachel seemed to take his silence as consent. Without another word, she reached into the tray and touched the creature lightly, pulling it closer with steady hands. It was gentle, a motherly touch.

222

Then, in one smooth movement, she pushed the syringe lightly through the thin layer of skin into one of the pulsing veins, and compressed it halfway.

The twitching stopped almost instantly, and a few moments later the pulsing veins were still. Kevin heard Rachel's breath catch in her throat as she pushed the tray into the autoclave and pressed the start button. The door began to slowly roll shut. And the next moment she had fallen, crying out in anguish, her hand clutching at the floor as she raised the needle to her own arm.

Kevin fell to the floor beside her, his head spinning, wrenching the needle from her in an instant before she could use it again. He threw it with all the strength left to him against the nearest wall and watched it shatter, the needle point bouncing across the room with a crystal ringing.

A piteous wail rose from her lips, an inhuman sound in the silent room.

"It's over," he whispered, to her, to himself, not able to fully comprehend what had just happened. He felt his stomach churning, his vision blurring. The blood rushed from his head in a wave as he watched the flashing lights of the autoclave.

"It's over."

#

Hours later, the front doors of the NINT were swarmed with plastic-suited officials. The handful of shaken people who had been trapped inside were carefully evacuated, decontaminated and moved to quarantined areas where they would be kept as a precaution for the next forty-eight hours.

Kevin was one of the last people to leave after being found in a state of shock, crumpled in a heap on the sixth floor. An orange-suited medic wrapped him in a large woolen blanket, and two others came to assist him in the shaky descent back down to the ground floor.

Supported on either side by, what seemed to Kevin, faceless plastic figures, he slowly exited the building. News reporters and camera crews were standing just beyond the yellow police tape circling the building, and the dark night was filled with light from the enormous flood lamps that had been set up around the white decontamination tents.

He looked back at the gleaming building, now forbidding and sepulcher-like. The red lights were still flashing inside, shining through the windows and illuminating the outlines of people on the fourth floor. He watched as they lifted a dark shape from the floor onto a metal gurney.

For a moment the entire building seemed to him like a cage; a trap from which he would never fully escape. A place none of them would ever really leave. He hoped that wasn't true, that this time he would find a way out. That he would find a way to forget, to find peace.

Turning, he walked away and didn't look back.

THE SYPHER

BY EDO VAN BELKOM

Monday morning.

First Day. Second Semester.

Richard LaPorte walked the halls of Founders College looking for room 206. It was just a Humanities course in "The Evolution of Feminism" but it had come highly recommended to him from a couple of his friends. The class was filled with chicks and the reading list was peppered with short stories and magazine articles that took a fraction of the time to read than the novels on the reading lists of other courses. He'd probably ace this one, which would be a good thing since he needed a B-Plus or higher if he wanted to keep his grade-point average up and graduate with honors.

He reached 206 and glanced around at the people in the hallway waiting for class to start. As he expected, there were plenty of girls wearing khaki pants and matching Crocs, carrying well-worn backpacks with plenty of pens and pencils in all the right compartments, and looking the world straight in the eye through stylish square-rimmed glasses. They weren't dirty, but a few of them could do with a bath, or at least a comb through their hair.

Whoever had told him the class was loaded with chicks had lied. Sure these were girls and women, but they were all the type who had taken feminism and equality between the sexes to mean they could dress themselves like men and leave their femininity behind.

Richard sighed. It would still be a bird course, only now it wouldn't be as much fun as it would have been with a few pretty girls in the class.

But then he turned the corner and saw her.

She was already seated at the far end of the room. She had blonde hair that seemed to flow over her shoulders like silk. Her arms were bare and slender, ending at dainty wrists that were ringed by thin golden bracelets and similarly slender fingers that were devoid of any rings. The t-shirt she wore was tight, showing off her perfect breasts – just large enough to be noticed, but not so large as to be out of proportion with the rest of her body.

Richard made a beeline to the seat next to her.

"Hi," he said, coolly.

"Hey," she answered with a slight wave.

"My name's Richard," he said.

She smiled at him.

Up close, she was even prettier, with big blue eyes, high cheekbones, a small pert nose, and lips that looked naturally plump and inviting.

This class is *it*, Richard thought. An easy reading list, a room full of girls, and the most beautiful woman in the school. No – check that – the most beautiful woman that he'd ever seen in his life. Just like that this class had instantly become his favorite for the semester, and quite possibly the year.

While Richard had been staring at her – watching her, but trying to make it seem like he *wasn't* watching her – the professor had been taking attendance.

"Richard LaPorte!"

"Huh?"

"Are you Richard LaPorte?"

Richard looked around the room. There were only two other guys in the room and he knew both their last names started with B, which made the professor's question kind of dumb. "Yes," he said.

"I called your name four times," she said. "You're not deaf, are you?"

Everyone in the room laughed.

"No," he said.

"You just weren't paying attention."

Laughter again.

He decided not to reply.

She continued on down the list of names.

Richard looked around the room. A lot of the women were staring at him with smirks on their faces, like they were better than him or something. That's when it occurred to him that the class might turn out to be a bit tougher than he first thought.

But then he looked at her again, and saw her smiling at him like they'd shared a joke that the rest of the class hadn't been in on.

Fuck it, he thought. This is going to be the best class ever!

#

Thursday.

The class after after the first quiz.

The mark on the test paper didn't make sense. There, in bold red ink was his score – 12/25. It was a failing mark and way below any mark he'd ever received in university. The last time he failed a test like this was . . . well, in the third grade.

"For those of you who got a fail, don't be too discouraged," the professor said. "It's only a quiz and you'll have plenty of chances to make up the marks with regular written and oral tests in the coming weeks."

Easy for her to say, Richard thought. She was one of *them*, with her short spiky hair, Capri pants and those big brown sandals. So what if one of the guys got a failing grade. The girls all did well. Shit, they all spoke the same language. Probably got together the night before class and handed out the questions, just to make sure the right people got the right marks.

He crumpled the quiz paper into a ball and thrust it into his pocket. Outside the class he caught up with the other two guys in the class, Baker and Bertoli, and asked them what mark they got.

"Thirteen," Baker said.

"You passed."

Baker shook his head. "Barely. If this keeps up, you know what it'll do to my grade-point average."

"At least you passed," Bertoli said. "I got ten. Can you believe it? A measly ten."

Suddenly, Richard's twelve didn't seem all that bad.

"I don't know how it happened," Bertoli mused. "See, I know this stuff. I knew it so well I didn't even study for the test."

"Maybe that was your problem," Richard suggested.

"No." Bertoli was emphatic. "I knew the material cold. Something happened when I stepped into the room. It was like . . . I dunno, like everything I knew was suddenly gone, you know. My mind was a blank. I tried to recall it, but it . . . it just wasn't there."

Richard nodded slowly. Although he hadn't thought about it at the time, now that Bertoli had explained it, it was the same thing he'd experienced. On the day of the test his mind was suddenly empty.

Just then the blonde-haired beauty who sat next to Richard stepped out of the classroom. She had a smile on her face and her eyes looked even brighter because of it.

"Hey, hi!" Richard said. "I was wondering . . . what did you get on the quiz?"

She tried to hide her smile by pressing her lips together in a thin line, but the exuberance behind them still shone through. "I'm a little embarrassed to say because a lot of people struggled with it." A pause. "But I got perfect."

Richard could feel his jaw drop. This girl didn't seem all that bright, but here she was acing a quiz where straight A students like Baker and Bertoli were getting failing marks.

Richard did his best to sound happy for her. "Perfect, huh? That's great."

"Yeah. Thanks. Bye!" And in a second she was walking down the hallway toward her next class.

Richard's eyes, and those of Baker and Bertoli followed her walk until she turned the corner and she was gone from sight.

"She looks good coming *and* going," Baker said. "Well, from any angle, really."

"That doesn't explain how she got perfect," Richard said.

"Don't worry about it," Bertoli said. "It was just a quiz. No big deal."

"It is to me," Richard said.

Baker looked him in the eye. "You know what's a big deal to me? A pitcher of beer that I'm not drinking cuz I'm standing here talking to you. C'mon. I'll buy."

#

They were halfway through their first pitcher of MGD and Richard was still shaking his head.

"What's bugging you?" Baker asked.

"This quiz." He still had the crumpled test sheet in his hand.

"Are you still on that?"

"I don't fail tests," Richard said. "You don't either for that matter."

Baker shrugged. "It happens. It's only a quiz, anyway. There's plenty of time to make it up before the semester's over."

"But how could we all do so poorly?"

Bertoli topped up his glass, then said. "This is just an observation, Rick, but maybe you're spending too much time concentrating on that hot blonde and not enough on the professor."

"The blond is easier to look at," Baker offered.

Richard shrugged. "We all look at her."

"Exactly."

"What are you getting at?" he asked.

"Maybe she's got something to do with it." Bertoli took a sip of his beer. "We do fine in all our classes except this one . . . the one she's in."

"Okay," Richard said, following.

"And she doesn't seem that smart to talk to, but she aced the test."

"Right."

"So . . . maybe she's a sypher."

"What?" Baker sat up in his chair. "A cipher is a person of no influence. A non-entity."

"Not c-i-p-h-e-r, but sypher with an 's.' S-y-p-h-e-r."

Richard was lost. Baker and Bertoli were English Literature majors and his background in applied sciences was leaving him a bit confused. "However you spell it, what does it mean?"

"Sypher, from the word siphon. "With her blond hair, blue eyes, perfect body and disarming smile, I wouldn't be surprised if she's able

230

to suck the intelligence out of everyone in the room, making herself smarter and the rest of us dumb as hammers."

Richard was silent thinking about it. It made so much sense. Didn't he feel stupid around her, always saying the wrong thing and sounding like an idiot every time he opened his mouth? And she always seemed oh so smart when he knew, he *knew* she wasn't. Nobody could be that good looking *and* that smart. It wasn't natural.

"I think you might be onto something," Richard said at last.

"What?" Bertoli said, watching an undergrad fitness student walk past their table.

"Maybe she is a sypher."

Bertoli laughed. "Relax man, there's no such thing . . . I was just playing with words and made it up."

Richard smiled awkwardly. "I knew that," he said.

But he couldn't get the thought out of his mind.

#

The following week.

Over the course of the next few days, Richard saw various students from the feminism class in the hallways and in York's Central Square and each time he approached them to ask how they did on the quiz.

All of the females did fine on the test, scoring what they usually do on tests in other classes. All except for one. He spotted her in the cafeteria as she was laying a thick coat of cream cheese onto a sesame seed bagel. She was unmistakable in her well-worn army jacket, black boots, short spiky hair and numerous piercings in her ears and eyebrows.

"Hi," he said.

She looked over at him and nodded. "Hi."

"You look familiar," he said. "I think you're in my feminism class."

"Yeah," she admitted.

"I was wondering how you did on that quiz. I failed it and it's not like me to fail a test. Especially when I've got the material down, you know."

The admission seemed to bring her to life. "The exact same thing happened to me," she said, licking some cream cheese off her fingers. "There isn't a bigger feminist in the class than me and I tanked on the first quiz. It's crazy!"

He walked her over to a table and they sat down.

"It's definitely weird," Richard said. "All the other women I asked aced the test. Said it was easy."

"It was an easy test," she said around a bite of her bagel. "I don't know . . . it was like all my knowledge was gone the moment I started trying to answer the questions."

"That's exactly how it felt for me."

A shrug. "I can't explain it."

"A friend of mine had a theory," Richard suggested.

"What?"

"He thinks the blonde has something to do with it."

She laughed heartily at that.

"What's so funny?"

"I do tend to lose my train of thought whenever she's in the room."

"Why's that?"

She stared at him with a confused look on her face. "Because she's hot!"

"You find her attractive?"

"Duh. I'm a lesbian."

Richard could feel his face turning red, but he tried to play it cool. "I knew that."

But all he could think about was that Bertoli's theory was standing up to scrutiny.

#

Over the course of several weeks.

It looked as if Bertoli might be wrong a few weeks later when Richard got back the results of the second quiz. He aced it with a near perfect score and all at once all was right with the world again.

But when he asked the blond how she did on the test, she said, "I was away that day. I'm writing a make-up quiz after class.

She'd been away.

Of course she'd been away. How else could he have received a great mark? She was out of the room, out of his sight and out of his mind. She hadn't been there to reach inside his head and pull out the knowledge for herself.

The third quiz confirmed it.

A failing mark again, and she got every question right.

After that, Richard was in freefall.

He was failing the class and no matter how hard he studied, or how much he looked away from the blond during class, the stupidest things were still coming out of his mouth.

Like the time he was asked for a defining moment in the women's liberation movement, and he'd answered by saying, "The publication of *Playboy* magazine." He'd meant it as an introduction of an icon women could gather around and protest against, but of course he was just laughed at by the rest of the class. Then the blond put up her hand and said, "The publication of *Cosmopolitan*," and stole all of his thunder.

Later, an essay on pay equity didn't help matters when he questioned why women working on construction crews or in manufacturing plants earned the same money as men, but all the heavy lifting was still being left to the men. The professor explained that his poor mark on the paper was not because his claims went counter to the prevailing winds in the classroom, but because he hadn't provided any specific examples to back-up the claims.

That was bullshit. Everyone knew that men were stronger than women and while women's lib and equal rights were all well and good – and women were all in favor of equal pay – whenever it came to moving a heavy box or dealing with something that required strength or brute force, men were called in to handle the problem. And if you balked at it, suggesting that women who earned the same as men should be required to do *all* the same work, well then you were just labeled a misogynist.

And now he had to prove it.

If you wanted proof, all you had to do was get out of the sheltered environment of the classroom and get out into the real world. How many women did you see holding "Stop" and "Slow" signs on road construction sites while men were digging holes in the ground and moving dirt with shovels and wheel barrows?

He should have known . . . The classroom was theory and principal, morals and ethics. It had little to do with the workings of the world. Women had no trouble fighting for their rights in North America where they already had all the rights they need, but how many were willing to travel to the other side of the world and risk death or stoning or mutilation by standing up for their sister's rights in places like Iran, or Afghanistan.

234

It was all so unfair.

Men were over there dying to make a better life for people in those countries, women included. How many women were doing their part?

And now, to top it all off, he was taking a feminism course that had a sypher in it, using her beauty and charm to take all of his knowledge from him, leaving him with barely a mind of his own.

He couldn't fail this course.

If he did, he wouldn't graduate. That would mean four years of his life down the tubes, not to mention the money he spent along the way. And without graduation, how would he get a job in his field, or any job that paid a decent wage? Finally, there were his parents to consider. They had paid for all his tuition and books, had given him money for food and travel to and from school. They'd done all this, despite the fact that his younger sister had been the smarter of their two children. She was bright and got nothing but A's in school, but the family had sent him to university because he was the oldest and their son. His sister would go to school when he was done – when he graduated – and even then he would be expected to help pay *her* tuition.

The pressure on Richard to do well, coming at him from all sides, was too much for him to bear.

Something had to be done about it.

But what?

He'd thought about it for weeks and in the end it was obvious to him what he must do.

He had to get rid of *her*.

She wasn't the cause of all his problems, but she was the reason for most of them. If she were no longer in the class – or even not as beautiful anymore – then he'd be able to concentrate, get a better mark, graduate as planned and his life would be back on track.

It was all that simple to him.

#

Thursday. After class.

He'd made it through another humiliating class.

He'd put his hand up once to answer a question, and another time the professor just said his name expecting an answer, but both times he'd said something stupid and everyone in the class had laughed at him.

Laughed at him like he was some dumb kid who'd wandered into the wrong room, or who was trying to hang out with the grown-ups but not knowing anything about grown-up things.

It made him so angry.

But not for long.

It was her fault; that was obvious. From the moment he walked into the classroom his eyes were on her. She knew he was looking at her and used it to her advantage. There was the batting of the eyes, the flip of the hair and whenever she knew he was staring at her she would uncross and cross her legs, making sure he got a good look at her long tanned legs and three-inch heels.

He never had a chance.

Which was why he was going to do something about it.

Once class was dismissed, he hung around the room until she left. He'd watched her after class a few times before and knew that she walked all the way from Founders College to her dorm room at Stong, practically the entire length of the campus. She made some of the trip indoors, but the majority of the time she was outside . . . and alone.

The acid was pretty basic stuff that he'd gotten from a friend who took some chemistry courses. He'd told the guy he needed something really strong to clean his toilet boil after a party and he'd given him the stuff in a bottle marked for hazardous waste. The bottle had a narrow opening, too narrow to get the liquid out quickly, so he poured it into a jar with a wide mouth that would allow him to eject the entire amount in one quick throw.

That way he'd be able to get the acid all over her face at once and be done with it.

When she was halfway between the gymnasium and Stong College there were bushes by the side of the walkway that were covered in shadow . . . perfect for what he had in mind.

In one quick motion he rushed up behind her, grabbed her around the waist and pulled her in behind the bushes. Then he wrestled her to the ground, straddling her so she couldn't get away.

"What's going on?" she said, resisting a little, but not putting up too much of a fight.

"I know what you are?" he said.

"What? What are you talking about?"

Her face was beautiful and innocent and at another time he would have no trouble believing she was unaware, but he knew better. Despite her questions and "Who me?" attitude, she knew exactly what he was talking about.

"You're a sypher," he said. "I can feel you inside my head every class taking the answers and knowledge you need. You make yourself smart by making me stupid and it's going to end now."

"You're crazy!"

He shook his head. "No I'm not. I'm the only one who knows the truth about you. I can even feel you now, feeling around inside my head wondering what it is I have in mind."

"I'm going to start screaming."

"No you won't. You're not afraid of me. There hasn't been a situation in your life that your good looks haven't got you out of." He raised his voice to a falsetto. "I'm sorry officer, I didn't see the stop sign. Please don't give me a ticket. Boo . . . hoo."

A calm seemed to come over her face then, becoming a complete blank. "What are you going to do?"

He pulled the bottle of acid from his inside jacket pocket. "I figure this," he gestured to the bottle, "all over your face will do the trick . . . It'll take away all your power over me."

She smiled at him. "Don't hate me because I'm beautiful."

"I don't hate you. I just know what you are, and you're evil."

The smile remained on her face, but turned sultry. "You don't understand me," she said, running a lazy finger over her lips. "I'm sure you'd like me a whole lot better if you just got to know me." Her hand moved down her body until her fingers were on the buttons of her blouse. One by one she began to undo them.

Richard could feel himself getting weak. His hands were unsteady and his mind was racing.

"You can't do this to me," he said. "I'm stronger than that . . . stronger than you!"

Her smile widened, becoming a big devilish grin. "I doubt that." She'd undone the top three buttons of her blouse and was now working on the clasp of her bra.

Richard was transfixed. She had gorgeous full breasts and he'd wanted to see them ever since he'd entered the classroom. Now, under these crazy circumstances, he was going to get his wish.

"Put the bottle down and you can touch them . . . and more."

She had control over him. He could feel his resolve slipping away.

If he didn't do something now she'd be gone, the police would become involved and she would have triumphed yet again. He couldn't let that happen.

"No!" he said. "You'll always tease me with more, but never deliver. You'll have absolute power over me and make me look like a fool. Well, I'm not a fool."

He uncapped the bottle of acid and moved to pour its contents onto her face . . .

But the bottle slipped from his hand, hit the ground and the liquid splashed up through the spout in a geyser and struck him directly in the eyes.

Richard put a hand over his face and screamed.

She threw him off and scrambled out of the bushes.

Somehow, he managed to get up, his face and eyes burning. He stepped out from the bushes, took his hand away from his eyes and tried to open them.

Everything was a blur.

And then the pain really hit him. He doubled over and fell face first onto the grass.

#

Four Weeks Later

"You may begin the exam," the professor said.

Richard leaned forward and lowered his head toward the desk until his face was inches from the test paper. It was the only way he could see well enough to read the questions.

He read the first question and knew the answer. The second question was just as easy. In fact, he found all the questions to be easy.

The true and false section seemed a joke and there was only a single obvious answer to each one of the multiple choices.

And the essay? It practically wrote itself.

When he was done writing the exam, Richard lifted his head from the desk and looked around the room, smiling.

It was a hollow gesture since he couldn't really see anyone to gauge their reaction. He knew the blond was there sitting next to him, but now she wasn't a problem.

Since he was legally blind he could look her straight in the eye and still retain all of the knowledge he'd studied a lifetime to learn.

Oh, she'd tried to access his knowledge. At times during the exam he could feel her awkwardly groping at the edges of his mind, but since he couldn't see her she couldn't disarm him with her looks and bypass his defenses.

Ha! he thought. She's powerless against me.

The victory left him beaming with pride.

He would ace this exam, most likely netting a perfect score. A top mark would ensure he would graduate with honors and at the top of his class.

He *would* graduate after all, and hopefully, with his high marks and newly minted degree he'd be able to get a good job, his career started, and his life back on track.

The only problem was – who would hire a blind man whose face looked like fresh road kill?

OLD SPICE LOVE KNOT
BY STEVE VERNON

College is no big deal.

Don't let anyone tell you any different. College is nothing more than a safety net that you jump into from grade twelve. For some of us that safety net became a kind of spider web that you either wove into a cocoon or a burial shroud.

That's how it goes with some folks. Some people like to tiptoe up on life. They sneak at it, with tiny little baby steps, creeping up on the future as if they were afraid that something was about to pounce and grab hold of them from out of the shadows. You start with your basic bachelor degree and step up to your masters – just to be safe. Follow that with a PhD because you want to be sure you'd done everything just right.

College was comfortable, like your bed in the morning.

Sometimes you just didn't want to get out of it.

For those who were very careful or very lucky you never had to leave school at all. You could grow from being a student and get a job with the college administration or possibly even become a professor. That's what college was all about. There was always that chance of getting a degree and getting a real job and maybe one day growing up.

The bait was everywhere.

Why don't you stay and learn?

Why don't you stay and pay our wages?

Why don't you stay and validate our existence?

Why don't you stay and maybe one day we might even let you replace us?

My Dad would have called it chumming the waters.

Of course there were other ways to do this thing. Some of us got bored and quit. Some of us got failed and then quit. Some of us found people with a future and got married and quit.

It happens.

You might find it hard to believe this sort of thing goes on in the 21st century. Well too bad. It happens whether you want to believe it or not. Basically, your average human student is no dumber or smarter than ever before. All of these degrees are nothing more than an expensive set of initials to hang behind your name while you were waiting to get done. It's like you were some kind of fish, deciding on which particular fish hook you were going to bite down on.

There were an awful lot of fish hooks to choose from.

Some of us get pregnant and married.

Some of us get married and pregnant.

And some of us just get pregnant because we're stupid.

Which is right where I came into the picture.

I met William on the first week of school.

You know how it goes. All of the older students lead the new kids on a tour of the campus trying to decide if we were going to make it or not. There were stupid games and stupid tricks and they told us a lot of stupid old stories. They told us all of the history and the folklore, as if they were trying to make us think we were thinking. I mean, come on, who do you think you're fooling? I'm just here for the piece of paper my Dad worked so hard on a fishing boat to pay for.

"This is Shirreff Hall," the tour guide told us. He was a caretaker or something, I guess. He looked like he might have been actually hot at one time at one time in his life, say maybe about a hundred years ago or so.

Come to think of it, he looked a little like my Dad. Not in a creepy way, you understand. More like he might have been able to sit down with my Dad in the Digby Tavern, and the two of them would buy each other cold draught beer until the cows came home and sobered up.

"Was there a real sheriff?" somebody asked. "Like in the cowboy movies?"

"Those are westerns," the guide said. "This is the east."

Okay. So now he totally reminded me of my Dad.

"The hall was named after Jennie Shirreff Eddy, a wealthy widow and former nurse who funded the building of the original Dalhousie University female residence."

What a dummy. Even I knew that and all I had done was skim the college brochures on the bus ride down.

I remembered saying goodbye to Dad at Digby two days ago. It seemed a lifetime. That's corny when you say it that way, but its true none the less.

Dad hung onto my hand, squeezing his fist into a knot like he wasn't going to ever let me go. He reached out his other hand and touched the Nova Scotia tartan neck tie that I was wearing. It was his neck tie and he had tried to tie it that morning, but he had fudged up the knot.

So I tied it for him around my own neck.

The tie smelled of the moth balls that he kept in the dresser drawer and replaced every year or so.

"You're not getting this necktie back," I said. "I'm taking it with me."

He just grinned that Dad grin of his, twisting his face up like he was squeezing a handful of fresh tide-flat mud between his hairline, ears and chin.

"You tie it better, anyways," he said.

"I would have made a hell of a fisherman," I told him. "I can tie every knot on this planet."

I wasn't bragging, not by much.

"Mind your language, girl," he said. "Who in the hell taught you how to speak?"

And then he let slip another wry grin and then he leaned in quick and kissed me hard on the cheek. He stank of fish, even two days off the boat. Fish and Old Spice aftershave, a smell that I'll remember until the day that I die.

Which might be sooner than you might think.

"You're too smart to be a fisherman," Dad told me. "You go to school and make something of yourself."

"I'll always be a fisherman's daughter," I said.

"Well there's hope for you yet," he said.

I smiled and kissed him back.

"Take care, girl."

Just three words, and then he was nothing but a funny old scarecrow of a figure standing on the side of the road, waving goodbye to a bus; receding into a dot in the distance; and then he was gone.

Our guide walked us up to the fourth floor.

"They call this the bell tower," he said. "Only it really is nothing more than an attic."

Didn't they have elevators in here? I might walk myself to death before second year.

"Nearly ninety years ago," the guide went on. "A young girl by the name of Penelope worked as an upstairs maid, right here in Shirreff Hall. She was a drab, lonely girl with straight black hair that was smoked with a hide-and-go-seek gray."

Man, she sounded like a real winner.

I guess they hadn't invented beauty parlours and makeover shows back then.

"She was almost a walking ghost," the tour guide said. "You hardly ever heard her say boo."

Oh my god, please spare me the pain and drop the refrigerator on my head before I have die of interminable boredom. Just how lame can a story get without needing to wear a crutch and a leg cast?

"Her fate wasn't all that unique," the old guy went on. "There are lots of lonely people in this old world. Given time, even the loneliest seem to find someone."

And then he threw us a look that was one part Freddy Krueger and one part dinosaur. He still reminded me a little of my Dad, but the creepiness was winning out over any sort of nostalgia.

"Too bad that Penelope happened to find the likes of Duncan," he went on.

One of the other girls giggled. I wanted to giggle too, but I didn't want to be rude. It was bad enough that this old guy was probably going to have a heart attack any minute now and fossilize to prehistoric long before he got to the end of his story.

"Who was Duncan?" one of the other girls asked.

That's right, I thought. Help old Granddad Moses Methuselah along, why don't you?

"Duncan was a professor who was working at the College at the time. He wooed Penelope."

"What's wooed?" another girl asked. "Is that like a woody?"

Oh my god!

How stupid can you get? Hadn't this girl ever heard of Jane Austen before?

"He sweet talked her," the old guy explained. "And when his teaching term was up he packed his bags and boarded the train leaving Penelope alone and pregnant."

"Gross," one of the girls said.

Stupid, was more like it, but I kept my feelings to myself. That was something that Dad had taught me. You kept your mouth shut no matter what you were thinking. It was better to hold your thoughts to yourself and deal with your problems without anyone else's help.

"Did she tell anyone?" another girl asked.

"Who could she tell?" the old guide answered. "If anyone found out she'd be fired from her job, just that fast. No ladies, this poor girl had come to the end of her rope, right about there."

That's when he pointed up at the tattered end of rope that dangled from one of the roof beams.

"She tied that rope," he said. "Into what she felt was her only possible answer."

"She hung herself?" somebody asked.

"WHAAAAAAAAAAAAAAAAAAAAAAAAAAAAAAAAA!!!!!"

Just that quickly, a girl in a torn wedding dress with pale white skin and dark mascara circles under her eyes, painted blue lips and a

246

rope around her neck jumped out of the shadows, shrieking like a cat who had swallowed a fire siren.

"AAAAAAAAAAAAAAAAAAAAAAAAAAAAH!" I screamed, and jumped right into William's waiting hands.

I have always had a thing for hands.

Hands are important. Hands are how you grab on to life and hang on. I couldn't stand dating a man with pudgy little sausage fingers. I need to be touched by a man who looks like he can handle life.

William had long strong hands.

From the moment I felt him catch me as I jumped backwards from the terrifying sight of that senior co-ed in zombie make-up, rubber noose and a tattered wedding dress.

"Well don't that give your toque a spin," William said. "I got girls falling on me like summer ticks."

When I heard that flat drawn out Cape Breton accent I nearly laughed so hard I almost peed myself.

"I wasn't scared," I said, turning to face him.

"Not much," he said, taking my hands and squeezing them gently.

From the moment that he took my two hands in his, he had me worked like a fist full of putty in his long strong fingers.

"You look scared," was all he said, but what I heard was we ought to go to bed and I will marry you and we will have babies and later on when I have a lawyer's salary I will buy you a fine, fat house and surround you with Cadillacs.

You can hear an awful lot in three little words, even words as insignificant as "You look scared."

Four nights and two dates later William and I snuck back into the Shirreff Hall bell tower.

And then we did it.

Don't play dumb by asking me what "it" is. From high school up until the age of thirty-eight, "doing it" means just one thing only.

Let me tell you, no matter what anyone else says, doing it just wasn't any big deal. He fumbled and I fumbled and I bit his lip only not meaning to and then we bumped heads and swore but not in a nice way.

And then we did it.

It was no big deal.

I won't lie and tell you that the world turned. The truth was that the world was already turning when me and William went ahead and did it.

It's part of the whole college experience, I guess. If you haven't managed to do it in high school then you better get yourself some hurry-up, come college time.

So we did it.

Four days after we did it I threw up before breakfast.

And after breakfast.

And in between.

The flu, I thought. I've got a case of the flu.

Only it wasn't the flu.

"You're pregnant?" William said – using the same intonation that might have better been used to ask me if I'd recently contracted the bubonic plague.

It was shock, I told myself. He was surprised, the same way I had been surprised by that girl jumping out at us up in the bell tower. Any minute now he'd calm down and he'd smile at me the way he did just before we started doing it.

Only he didn't smile.

He called me names. A lot of names and some I hadn't heard before. Speaking as a Digby girl, raised near working men I thought I had heard every name that there was.

Only I hadn't.

"How could you be so stupid?" he asked.

"I'm not stupid," I said.

I was stupid and I knew it but I would be damned before I told him the truth.

"Stupid, stupid, stupid," William said. "Were you born with a hole in your head as big as the one between your legs?"

That hurt.

That was mean and that really hurt.

"Well you were doing it too," I said.

"Weren't you on the pill?"

"You know I wasn't."

He looked at me and he blinked like I'd told him something he'd never heard before in a language that he didn't quite understand.

"Well then this whole thing is your fault," he said.

I opened my mouth.

Closed it.

Nothing fell out in between.

William just shook his head, slow and hard.

"Not my fault," he said.

And then he walked away.

Two nights later I came back up to the bell tower, with a brand new rope.

It was quiet up here. I had heard that some girls liked to come up here and study because it was so quiet. But they never came up here at night.

At least that was what I was counting on.

I had come up here to end my life.

Does that sound extreme to you? Like something a drama queen might pull off?

Maybe so. But I had thought things over long and hard. I did not have it in my heart to kill this baby. Yet I did not have it in my heart to take the bus back to Digby and look at my Dad who had worked so very hard to pay my way into Dalhousie. We hadn't qualified for much in the way of help. Dad had paid the bulk of it. I had seen him go to the bank every week and hand the teller a crumpled bundle of bills, usually stinking of fish and Old Spice.

He'd worked too hard for me to go home and disappoint him. That thought scared me more than any ghost story. The look of quiet disappointment that my Dad would give me as I got off the bus.

And then there would be the years I'd have to spend raising the baby. Dad would pay for that too. I could get a job, the fish plant hired sometimes, but we all knew that the days of the fish plant were coming to an end.

And now, I was too.

I threw the rope up over and tied a slip knot and drew it snug. Once I'd secured the rope I tied the noose.

I was always good at knots.

I carried a chair over to the noose.

This was it, I thought.

I was really going to do it.

I stepped onto the chair. It teetered a little. I found a scrap of cardboard and folded it tight to snug under one of the chair legs to keep it at an even keel. If I was going to hang myself I certainly didn't want to break my neck falling off of a wobbly chair.

I almost smiled at that. Then something softened inside and I had to choke back the tears. I wasn't about to let myself cry. If I started crying now I wouldn't see this whole thing through.

I took two deep breaths and climbed back onto the chair.

A bit of cobweb touched my cheek.

I brushed it away.

"This is it," I said.

I almost scared myself. There, in the silence of the bell tower, those three whispered words sounded as loud as a fog horn.

I nearly fell off of the chair the second time.

Then I calmed myself and pushed my head into the noose. I snugged the noose up tight to my neck. I knew that the knot had to be at one side of my neck or the other. I settled for keeping it close to my ear.

I wondered who would find me up here. I felt bad for who ever it would be. I hope I didn't give them nightmares.

That's when I saw her.

She formed from the shadows, like a whisper of smoke braiding together into a physical form. She was standing there in front of me, a drab and lonely looking girl with long straight black hair that was gently smoked with a hide-and-go-seek of gray.

Penelope.

Shaking her head as if to tell me that this was not the thing to do.

I stared at her.

I could see through her, like she was made out of loose airborne slush that was slowly freezing over. I didn't see any sign of zombie make-up, cheap mascara, or a dollar store rubber noose. She just stood there, with her feet hanging about a half a foot up from off of the floor, shaking her head.

She's right, I thought. This wasn't the thing to do. This was a stupid way of dealing with my problems.

I decided, right then and there that I wasn't going to hang myself.

Then I stepped about a half an inch back and the chair overturned.

I had a half a second to think to myself – I take it back – and then the noose drew tight around my neck. I swung there, kicking in mid-air, trying to wedge my fingers into the hollow of the noose which was snugged so closely to my neck that it felt as if I had swallowed a turtle neck sweater before letting it shrink.

I felt my fingernails breaking. I remember thinking to myself – damn, I've broken my fingernails, and then everything tightened and slowed and it felt as if a great silent vacuum was slowly swallowing what dim light remained.

And then all at once I felt a figure beneath me, leaning up and bearing my weight. A figure, holding me up and not letting the noose draw any tighter.

It was William, I thought crazily, as I clawed the noose free and tumbled to the ground.

Wrong.

I nearly brained myself on the over turned chair. I probably made enough of a racket to wake up half of the graveyards in the city.

Was it Penelope who had helped me?

Wrong again.

I lay there in the attic dust I and looked up and saw the shape of a man standing over me.

It was the tour guide, I decided.

Wrong, wrong, wrong.

I stared up and I could see him as if he were made out of smoke and water. Featureless and yet strangely familiar to me – staring down blankly with all the love that could ever be imagined.

"Take care, girl," the phantom said.

And then, like a candle being blown out, the phantom shape was gone.

And all I could smell was the scent of dead fish, Old Spice aftershave, and sea water.

I went back to my room and showered for a very long time.

Three hours later, freshly towelled and snugged-up in a fuzzy flannel bathrobe, the security guards came to get me.

"Am I in trouble?" I asked, thinking that somehow my suicide attempt had been found out.

"It's a telephone call at the reception desk," the taller of the two guards said.

And then he ducked his head down, like he was embarrassed about something. I worried for a moment that my bathrobe had come undone.

"It's pretty important," he finished.

There was an elevator and we took it down and the girl at the desk handed me the telephone, looking away as if a comet had just flashed through the room.

It was my Aunt Rita on the phone.

She told me about Dad.

About how he'd fallen from the fishing boat and was dragged under and had washed ashore around supper time.

He was wearing his oilskins and his gum rubbers and he'd sunk pretty fast but nobody could quite explain the length of freshly noosed rope that he held in his left hand, squeezed tightly like he was never going to let go.

It took four whole years but I finally graduated.

William dropped out in the second year and went back to Cape Breton. The last I heard he was working at a saw mill.

I took the tour every year. The old caretaker who gave the tour died of a heart attack, at home with his wife. Photos of his six children and fourteen grandchildren were propped upon his casket.

I stepped up to the podium to accept my diploma, wearing the long black robes and the flat black hat of a graduate and a Nova Scotia tartan neck tie around my neck.

IN THE PURSUIT OF DREAMS

BY CAROL WEEKES

The corridors at St. Mary's University are silent in the hours of early morning and dusk. Night classes occur in certain parts of the campus, but in the university's hub, the McNally building dating back to the year 1802 and once run by Jesuit priests, the halls and rooms fall quiet with an almost somber pall at evening. The building is ancient, its stones, polished wood, and arches having borne witness to many visitors over the centuries, many of them dead. From hard to social sciences, and from arts to business, echoes of gained and desired knowledge settle into every room, every crevice of the campus like an ethereal filtered dust coating all. The place reverberates with dreams and hope.

A visitor's kiosk greets those in McNally, past columns of stained glass and an atmosphere of regality. At evening, the kiosk is manned by one person who often sits, shoulders folded over a paperback novel, Tim Horton's coffee at hand as seconds on an impassive clock tick past. It is in these halls, offices, grand rooms, and classes that young and not-so-young minds seek knowledge and destiny in text books, from the seasoned minds of professors, through avid discussion and fervent debate set off by inquisitive questions.

Not all dreams are achieved. Some die on the ground just as the trip begins.

Associate Professor Daryl Hughes set out at a quick pace along a corridor. Today was his first set of classes in the English department and he felt a little nervous as he made his way to his destination. The art of teaching, no matter how seasoned the lecturer (as any professor will tell you) can educe a special kind of apprehension – a metal butterflies effect in the pit of the stomach at the idea of standing, evaluated and vulnerable, in front of fifty or more new students, the likes of which run the gamut from quiet and conservative to downright rowdy and confrontational. You never knew what to expect. A neophyte, his only prior experience had been as a Master's student T.A. with small groups of people. He felt mixed emotions as he neared the classroom door. He mentally rehearsed how he might open the class: possibly with a joke? Perhaps with more firmness about rules such as no cell phones allowed in the classroom and when a break might be permitted during a three hour lecture. He decided he'd gauge the mix of students first.

He rounded a corner and faced the classroom. Its door was shut and locked. A half dozen students, two of them girls with high, glossed hair, one chewing gum with her mouth open and chatting on a cell phone, and four young men, two of them that Hughes recognized as being of that caliber known as 'Goth' regarded him.

"You the teacher?" one of the Goth's asked. His black painted lips looked dusty.

"Yes, I am," Hughes said and forced a cheery smile. The Goth didn't smile back. His eye makeup had been applied to perfection, his skin an eerie taupe. His fingernails were painted ebony. The kid wore a knee length trench coat over faded jeans and a T-shirt with the word 'Metal' scrawled in a vivid yellow swoosh. Below the word Hughes eyed a graphic image of a skull alive with worms, beetles, and other forms of putrefaction emanating from its eye sockets. Charm.

The other students looked at him oddly, as if he'd sprouted a second head. So much for the idea of opening with a joke. He'd just get into the rules; he could *feel* it with these ones.

He unlocked the classroom door, flipped on the lights and regarded the expanse of classroom. The students, as he suspected they would, headed for seats at the back of the classroom, except for the Goth with the skull who, surprisingly, sat at the front, center to the teacher's desk. Perhaps the kid had eyesight problems. A little less mascara, Hughes thought, sarcastic, then cast the mood from his mind so as not to sour the morning. They would be introduced to classic and contemporary short fiction, the likes of Cheever, Carver, Bierce, Hawthorne, Malamud, to name a few. Hughes wanted them to revel in the enactment of characterization, theme, setting, point of view of stories like 'The Enormous Radio', 'An Occurrence at Owl Creek Bridge', 'Young Goodman Brown', 'The Magic Barrel'...Hughes had prepared Power Points, detailed notes, handouts and short in-class exercises meant to develop a keen interest. He had plans, great plans, to inspire most, if not all of them away from the tenets of video games and YTV.

Within minutes the other students arrived and the class filled. He noted the cliques he'd have to break up by week two and the ones he'd have problems with regarding idle chatting during lectures, missed homework assignments and general poor attitude. No matter. He'd handle them all.

#

Shortly into the class Hughes detailed his expectations and had handed out his syllabus. Although he'd experienced some initial unrest, he corralled their attention by asking pointed questions of individual students upon reading short excerpts of the Bierce tale. Ten minutes of the class remained. It had gone quite well and Hughes felt pleased with himself.

"Do you think Farquhar actually perished or did he survive his ordeal?' Hughes asked. As was typical of new classes (and some old ones) no one responded. But the Goth in the front thrust up a tentative hand.

"Yes?" Hughes leaned forward, delighted and a little relieved. Perhaps he'd like this kid after all, mascara or not. Two students sitting directly behind the Goth stared at Hughes. "Do you mean me?" one of two girls, a fat one with bleached hair and too many earrings in one ear, queried him. She looked at her friend, a skinny girl with the same kind of hair and accessories. They giggled, as if sharing a private joke.

Hughes went to respond that the young man at the front of the class had first raised his hand when the skinny girl cut in and said "I think he died. I mean, like, he was about to get his neck stretched and he wanted to get out of there, you know? So he daydreamed, you know?"

Hughes felt his cheeks flame a little. "No, I don't know. You tell me." Circular, ambiguous babblecock.

"It was an internal fantasy," the Goth whispered. "The recounting of a life experienced at the moment of death. It's what Farquhar wanted . . . his hopes, his dreams."

"Very good," he said to the Goth. "Well articulated."

The class snickered. The skinny girl with the earrings gloated a little. Hughes wanted to tell her that he didn't mean her when he realized that he had approximately two minutes left before class let out and he hadn't assigned any readings yet. He flipped through his reader's index and relayed two tales to be covered for discussion in the proceeding class with a focus on theme.

"I suggest everyone invest in a quality dictionary and thesaurus from the campus bookstore while you're at it," he quipped as they gathered their bags. They streamed from the classroom in a ribbon of color and motion. Soon the room was empty, save for the Goth. Hughes regarded him. "Your name wasn't on the attendance list, but then, so weren't a few others. It is?"

"Edward Bannerman. You can call me Eddie." The kid flashed a bit of a smile.

"You enjoy English, don't you? I can sense your excitement with the topic."

Edward shrugged, but his face brightened beneath the shadowy make up. He looked somewhat malnourished and Hughes wondered if the kid was living on a typical strapped student income.

"I want to graduate with my degree in English," Edward said. His breath smelled a little rank and Hughes immediately thought that toothpaste would be a good addition to the next grocery list, but held back.

"Good for you," Hughes said. "I'm sure you'll succeed. Your response contained foresight."

"Thanks," Bannerman said. He gathered his books and Hughes noted that the kid's textbook was a 2nd edition, not the current 5th edition of the reader.

"That book is several years out of date. It will have discrepancies; some stories missing, others on the wrong pages. However, if you can't afford the latest edition, the library contains three new copies."

Bannerman gave him a blank smile. "See you on Thursday."

"Bye Edward."

Hughes watched the kid go and stood pondering for a moment over Edward Bannerman. The kid held an air of *something*. Unease? No, it wasn't that. And it wasn't shyness, either. A shy kid doesn't pop up with an intelligent answer at the front of a class full of strangers on day one of a semester. The exactness of the feeling he sought wouldn't come to him, so Hughes let it go, gathered his materials, and, re-locking the classroom door, headed towards the teacher's lounge where a cafeteria would provide him with a breakfast and coffee. His next class with this group would meet on Thursday evening at 6:30 pm.

#

Thursday evening, September 10th

Only two thirds of the class bothered to show up. Hughes felt annoyed. He had three classes to teach this semester, the other being contemporary Canadian literature and an introduction to poetry. Grant you, the weather today (although not an excuse to miss classes) was likely a reason for so many empty seats. The tail end of one of the season's first hurricanes had beaten its way up the Eastern Seaboard in the early hours of the morning. Hughes had awakened to the steady drum of rain along his windows. Wind screamed around corners of the campus as he'd parked his car and run, briefcase over his head and coat tails flapping, for cover.

"Who *didn't* read the assigned stories?" he asked, looking for attention to detail. Almost all of the hands shot up . . . wavered a little, then flew down with more speed than they'd erected only seconds earlier.

"Ah, good, you're sharp this evening," he said, grinning. "It pays to listen carefully to detail. Now, let's try this again. Who *did* read the stories? " He noted that Bannerman had taken his customary seating arrangement, front and center, while the others sat further away in clots, mid-center to back. Bannerman floated like a lonely, dark island in a sea of indifference. He had his textbook open and Hughes noted that he'd highlighted the pages of a story in bright yellow liner. Good kid; a bit odd perhaps, but he showed initiative. Only Bannerman's and one other person's hands went up this time. Hughes sighed.

"And what did everyone think of 'The Enormous Radio"?" He held chalk poised in front of the board to take quick notes of interest.

"I think a surround-sound system would have gotten her rocks off more," some boy with pimples and wet hair replied.

Hughes decided to humor him. "All the better to play nosy with?"

The boy laughed. A few others tittered along with him. The mood in the room took on the feel of a held breath.

"But what was the theme?" Hughes persisted. "How does the theme and Irene Westcott's character pertain to the events that led up to the story's outcome?"

Ah, pointed question. They stared at him. Someone yawned and stretched their arms above their head. Another glanced through the paned glass that had turned to the color of slate with the rain and dwindling evening.

"How does the word 'enormous' play a dual role in the title?" Hughes persisted. He felt a little perturbed now.

Some kid piped up "Do you want us to think *deep* or something?" Everyone giggled. Now Hughes felt his temper flare.

"Of course I want you to 'think deep'," he enunciated. "This is university. You've paid to be here, or at least, someone did. You're here to think, to advance your minds! What do you expect? That you can go through life, dilly-dallying, only looking at the surface coating of ideas, concepts . . . *living*?" He sputtered, his hands flailing in front of himself. "What are you going to do when you get into your jobs, your careers, where you have to make decisions under pressure or evaluate the validity of any piece of information? What then?" His eyes fell on Edward Bannerman's pale face. The boy's eyes burned into his. Something about the kid gave him the creeps. That was it. Something about the boy wasn't *right*.

"Her paying attention to everyone else's tragedy opened the channel for the imperfections in her own marriage. The word 'enormous' suggests the radio's symbolism of influence in their lives and the breakdown of their fantasy." Bannerman shut his mouth as quickly as he opened it.

Hughes felt stunned.

"You're absolutely right."

The wet-haired boy, whose face had frozen with a half-grimace over Hughes' reprimand, relaxed a little.

"Cool. But chill out, man," the kid told him. "I mean, it's just a story, right? It's fiction."

Hughes felt light-headed, as if the air in the classroom had turned to helium or a mild hallucinogen.

"I wasn't talking to you," Hughes said through clenched teeth.

Students looked at each other. Now no one laughed. Rain trailed along the glass, throwing the reflection of a distant street light into myriad watery diamonds.

"I was talking to Edward, who takes the time to weigh his responses." He motioned with his chin toward the gaunt boy who, as it occurred to Hughes now, wore the same clothes he'd come to class in last Tuesday.

The class observed Hughes, clearly discomforted.

"Who's Edward?" the wet-haired boy inquired.

"Him. *Him!*" Hughes pointed to the boy in black. Bannerman ignored the class, focusing only on Hughes.

A girl snorted. "Nobody's sitting there. It's an empty desk. You high or something, sir?" Oh, Hughes loved the 'sir' attached like a stringy little suffix on the end of the well-salted insult.

"I beg your pardon?" He felt his heart trip-hammer. He saw Bannerman slide his face into his hand and shut his eyes. "I suggest you show some respect to your fellow classmates, as well as to your teacher. Just because someone may be different from you, or quiet, doesn't provide you with the right to make them feel invisible." He heard a chair scrape back. A quiet girl with limp red hair, one who never said a word and whom he'd observed scribbling designs along the edges of her notebook, got up and walked out without a word. A few other students followed suite. He stood, feeling his fingers grip his book as a third group followed, leaving him and only four other students remaining in the room, one of them being Bannerman.

"What's wrong with everyone?" Hughes whispered.

No one answered. The three students who sat great distances apart from each other and from Bannerman, two of them young men, one a young woman, looked at him with expressions of concern and a kind of pitying sadness.

"Are you feeling okay tonight, Professor Hughes?" one of the girls asked.

"I feel just fine," Hughes sputtered, although he honestly didn't now. "Why do you ask?"

"There's really no one sitting in that chair," the girl said. Hughes clearly saw Bannerman seated there, looking bored.

"It's okay," Bannerman told him. "Don't worry about it. I'm here for the education, not the socializing."

Hughes' hovered closer to Edward's desk. "I'm not losing my mind," he told the boy. "You are here. I can see you. I can see your clothes, your books . . . the rain dripping from your hair."

"Okay," one of the other boys said, sarcastic. "We can see you too. What's that got to do with the story?"

Hughes felt panic begin at his ankles, like angry little Chihuahua's nipping at the bone and flesh. It bore up his calves with razor precision and settled into his groin like cold, wet stones. He shut his eyes, counted to ten, and opened them again. The room swam into view, still with Bannerman at its helm.

Somehow, he managed to finish his discussion of Cheever's story then dismissed the class almost an hour early, citing a headache and perhaps the start of a flu bug. At least that explanation seemed to gain him some credence with his remaining audience.

"I hope you feel better soon," one of the girls said as she left the classroom. They seemed delighted and relieved over permission for early departure. It was the end of the week, rainy, and the nearby student pub offered pizza and cheap beer. In a way, he couldn't blame them.

Bannerman remained seated, the only one left in the room. Hughes felt a sense of panic being alone with the kid who gave him the impression that he had no where to go.

"I'm sorry for their blatant rudeness," he told Bannerman. "I was a loner when I was a kid too. I used to get picked on because my mother liked to dress me in sleeveless tweed sweaters. You know the kind, with the diamond pattern over the chest and crisp little shirt collars neatly pressed over. Ignore them. Don't let them get to you." He paused, unable to suspend his curiosity. "Are you from this area?"

"Purcell's Cove," Edward replied.

"Is that home, parents, family?"

"Yup."

"Do you live with your family? I'm sorry if I seem almost as nosy as the Westcott woman, but I feel some concern . . . you seem . . . disenfranchised somehow."

"I want to finish my degree. I want to get on with my life," Bannerman replied.

"You'll do it. I have no doubt that you'll exceed with your studies." He waited for Bannerman's response.

"I live with my family; not that they see me any more than anyone else does."

Hughes felt great pity for this wayward boy.

"All the focus is on my older brother. He's going to be a scientist."

Now Hughes thought he understood what might be going on here; a family forfeiting the dreams of a lad with a creative bent for a sibling more driven towards a conventional and socially acceptable future. It was the blight of the artist, to never fully be understood, to perpetually toil with the demons that sought creativity at the cost of societal scorn. He thought of Poe, dying penniless and discarded, in the gutter; Hughes' heart twisted.

"Pursue your dreams, no matter what anyone thinks," Hughes leaned closer so that he could look Bannerman in the eyes, eyes that, when they glanced back into his, felt like gazing into full moons. "Artistic people like us must strive to meet our desires, no matter the opposition. Not that we want our recognition to arrive posthumously, which is, sadly, often the case for some."

"Better late than never," Bannerman replied, stoic.

This made Hughes snort with laughter, a bright spot in an otherwise languid evening.

"You can always do a little teaching on the side to support your writing. I sense that you want to be a writer."

"I am a writer. Those who call themselves writer must actually write."

"So true. I look forward to your first paper." Hughes gathered his materials together. "Safe drive home."

"How did you know I drive?"

Hughes paused. "Purcell's Cove isn't a stone's throw away. What do you drive?"

Here, Bannerman smiled. It was the first time Hughes had seen the boy's face open up this much.

"Mustang Shelby; candy-apple red, 1967 vintage." Then, he added rather sheepish, "My father's car."

"I love those old cars," Hughes said. "They don't make them like that anymore."

"I can give you a lift to wherever you're going."

For some reason, the statement made Hughes hesitate. "Thanks, but I have my own vehicle here. It's just a little Honda hatchback, but it does the trick . . . to use a cliché."

He shut the lights off in the classroom and waited for Bannerman to walk past before locking the door. "Good night. I'm sorry that tonight's class didn't go so well."

"No problem. I'll see you next week." Bannerman brushed past him.

The key jammed in the door and Hughes had to grapple with it for half a minute before it dislodged itself. When he stood up, he realized he stood alone in the quiet corridor, its rows of polished oak doors silent and filled with shadow. As he turned towards the direction of the parking lot, his shoes squeaking a little on polished surface of the hallway, it occurred to him that he hadn't heard any footsteps as Bannerman had left. "I'm going to have to ask about that kid," Hughes mumbled as he made his way past the entrance kiosk, giving a brief wave to the student helper working the desk.

"Good night," the girl called, cheery.

"Yes, thanks," Hughes said. Then he paused. "Did you see a boy with a long black coat come through here just a minute ago?"

The girl looked puzzled. "No. Some students left a few minutes ago . . . but none wearing a long black coat."

Hughes shut his eyes as the feeling of unreality set in again. It would have been the only way for Bannerman to have exited the building. Perhaps he really was coming down with a virus. "Thanks," he said and moved into the rain towards his car. Cold water flooded his neckline and ran down his back. Something had to be righted. He wasn't sure what, why, or how, but the sensation of unease followed him home. Even a hot shower and a glass of quality bourbon over ice didn't quell the discomfort and Hughes went to bed feeling chilled.

#

An e-mail from the faculty Dean, Mark Fraser, waited for Hughes the next morning. It read *"Daryl, we need to meet to discuss a concern. Please call or IM me. Thanks."* Hughes sighed. He sensed it had everything to do with last evening's class. Someone had lodged a

267

complaint. An hour later, Hughes sat in a hard-back chair in front of Fraser's desk. Sunlight flooded through stained glass windows, throwing Fraser into a fragmented roadmap of color.

"Daryl . . ." Fraser began, "how are the classes going?"

Hughes regarded him, stony. "As far as I'm concerned, just fine. I've had a few problems with student attitude, but I've worked it out."

"Hmm. I'm going to cut to the chase. I had a girl from your short literature class, a Belinda Roberts, arrive at my office last evening with a few of your other students in tow, claiming that they had some concerns about . . ." and here Fraser clasped his hands with difficulty.

Hughes leaned forward. "About what?"

Both men regarded each other.

"About your mental state," Fraser finished. "They said you were talking to an empty desk, claiming that a student actually sat at that desk. Someone you called Edward. No one else saw anyone sitting there, Daryl." Fraser looked pained. He fiddled with a ballpoint pen on his blotter, twirling it about and about in a ragged circle. "I understand that teaching is a challenging, often stressful profession and that this is your first week of new classes—"

"The student named Edward *is* in the class. He's a loner. Perhaps this is their idea of a joke, to try and isolate this kid further, as if he doesn't already have enough problems."

Fraser raised his eyebrows. "Edward *who*, Daryl? What's the kid's last name?"

"Edward Bannerman."

Fraser stopped twirling the pen. He stared at Hughes. He strained forward in his chair. "Did you say 'Bannerman'?"

"Yes, Edward Bannerman. Goth kid; favors black clothes, dyed black hair, even eye makeup, but he's *bright*. He's one of the few who bothers to respond to questions and his answers are thoughtful, weighted with judgment and delivered with precision."

The temperature in Fraser's office seemed to drop a notch despite the sun.

"Daryl . . . unless we have another Edward Bannerman enrolled in this school who just happens to emulate a former student's style, and if we do, I'm not aware of him . . . what you're telling me can't be possible."

Hughes' eyes flared. "Why not? What is wrong with all of you?"

"The kid is *dead*, Daryl. He died two years ago in a car crash while driving home from class. Yes, he was bright. English Honours major with a 4+ GPA. Terrible shame. It was September and we'd gotten hit with torrential rain that day. We shut the campus early because of road flooding. He took a corner too fast, hydroplaned, and the car wrapped itself around a utility pole just blocks from here. The kid died on the scene. Nineteen years old, driving his father's sports car. I honestly don't know what to tell you, except that this boy no longer exists."

Hughes' palms grew clammy and swallowing became difficult. He stuttered.

"M-Mark – I'm seeing this boy as sure as a real person. I can smell the rain in his hair . . . he carries text books with him . . ." Hughes stopped, remembering the older version of the text book; a book that dated back several years.

Fraser looked sympathetic. "I don't know what to say. Perhaps you're picking up on some kind of psychic energy; not that I know anything about that kind of stuff and given that it isn't grounded in hard science, it isn't anything that can be explained. All I know is that it's spooking your class, and for that reason, I have to ask you to refrain from making mention of Bannerman again. Even if you think you see him, ignore him. We have to deliver a quality education here. Our students are our future—"

"I realize that!" Hughes snapped. He felt flabbergasted. "Fine, I won't mention a thing again. But when he shows up again, I'll bring him down here with me!" He saw that Fraser struggled with something and assumed that he wanted to suggest that he, Hughes, might want to seek out psychological help.

"We'll let it go," Fraser said. "Tell the class that you weren't feeling well; apologize for the one evening and then let it slide. Things should resume as per normal, as long as you don't hiccup with this again."

Hughes stood up. "Are we done then?"

"I guess."

Hughes left Fraser's office, frightened and irate. Damned those students for feeling the need to run like scared little sheep to the Dean's office, but worse . . . the idea that he was seeing a dead boy . . .

"I'm going to pretend he isn't there," Hughes' muttered to himself. "He isn't there, he isn't there!"

The short fiction class rolled around again a few days later and, much to Hughes' horror, Bannerman waited in the corridor as Hughes approached. Hughes said nothing.

"Good morning, sir," Bannerman said.

Hughes ignored him. Out of his periphery vision, he saw Bannerman's face drop.

"I said good morning, sir," Bannerman reiterated.

Hughes unlocked the door and strode into the room. He could *smell* the kid, this stale, almost cloying odor like damp clothes forgotten in a trunk. Dead. Dead and walking around campus. Other students filtered into the room, some of them regarding him with curiosity. Within minutes he had two-thirds of his normal enrolment sitting in front of him, with Bannerman at front and center, like some sunken ship's masthead.

Hughes' cleared his voice. "Before we begin the class, I want to apologize for my behavior last week. I had the start of a terrible virus and migraine . . . I actually think it affected my vision processes temporarily and made me see double . . . so sorry for having been short with you. Let's go forward with new material, shall we?"

He saw them relax, many of the faces adopting composure of empathy.

He also saw Bannerman's face harden.

They moved into the discussion of D.H. Lawrence's 'The Rocking Horse Winner'.

"What do you think the rocking horse represented in this story?" he asked the class. He waited for a response. As usual, no one was forthwith in raising a hand.

Except Bannerman.

Hughes ignored him. He felt an air of frost issue towards him and saw Bannerman's anger simmer in his features. For a few seconds Hughes swore he saw his own breath turn to frost. His bladder burned with a new fear.

"Come on, think about it."

"Maybe it was the boy's way of trying to win his mother's love," a normally quiet girl said.

"Very good start," Hughes agreed, glad for this break in the chill. He immediately saw Bannerman's face curl with resentment. Hughes felt himself tremble. Somehow, he got through the class and gathered his books, leaving as the last student stepped out. Except for Bannerman who stood by his desk, watching him.

"You can't let me down," Bannerman told him. "I want my degree. I have the right to achieve my dream."

Hughes' looked about himself and when he saw that the room and corridor were clear, he stared hard at Bannerman. "You're dead. You're somehow a figment of my imagination. I can't help you." Hughes hurried along the corridor. At one point he felt someone rush up behind him, a sensation of being rushed, but when he whirled, he faced an empty hallway save for a row of metal lockers and some plastic chairs pushed up against a wall.

"Go away and leave me alone." He stood alone in the corridor, his heart pounding beneath his cotton shirt.

Upon completion of his second class, Hughes decided to go home early, rather than spend the afternoon correcting papers in his office. He felt shaken. He sensed Bannerman around every corner, behind every piece of furniture, in every shadow. *I want my degree. I have the right to achieve my dream.*

"I can't give you your dream." Hughes locked his office, swallowed two Advil by the water fountain, then hurried to his car.

#

His Honda may not have been what most professors might drive, but it was economical and it served its purpose. His associate professor position would allow him to save enough money over the coming year for a down payment on a small house. He had his future and he wasn't about to let some residual energy from a dead kid ruin his life. If need be, he'd bring a priest into the school. He determined to put Bannerman out of his mind.

"Why me?" he muttered.

"Because you're new and unbiased, because you see my potential, and because you have what it takes to get me where I want to go," a voice said from his right. He glanced to his right and saw Bannerman in the passenger seat. The stench of Bannerman's damp clothes filled the interior of the car.

Hughes froze. "Get out of my car!" He tried to jab his key into the ignition but it wouldn't fit. He stared at the ignition switch. This wasn't his car. He was in an older car, a sports car with black leather seats and a polished dashboard. And, with the same slide of surrealism, realized he was now in the passenger seat.

Bannerman cranked the ignition and the Mustang sprang into life with a roar on a fine-tuned V-8 engine; the car's body trembled as Bannerman slipped the stick shift into first gear. As Hughes sat stunned, his mouth open, heavy drops of rain began to fall. The kid was real; Hughes saw his coat fold over itself, smelled that raw, damp stink of material

(rotting material, the stink of earth worms)

and they surged forward through the parking lot, the torque of the car gaining speed. Rain increased, coating the windshield and turning the landscape to a haze.

"Let me out of this car," Hughes screamed. "It's impossible. Perhaps I have a brain tumor and the hallucinations seem real, but you are not real. You're dead, I'm alive, and I'm still in my own car." He squeezed his eyes shut, hard, hyperventilating. When he opened his eyes again, he was still in the Mustang as it tore into the street towards the center of Halifax.

"Slow down!" Hughes screamed.

"I didn't appreciate the way you ignored me in this morning's class, like I don't exist."

"You *don't* exist!" Hughes shrieked. "That's why your family ignores you – because they don't see you. You're dead and I don't know how I can possibly be riding in a dead man's car, having this discussion."

"Dead isn't gone, you know," Bannerman told him and Hughes noted that Bannerman's gums had deteriorated around his teeth; they were grey and *things* moved in there. A smell of rot wafted at him.

"Dead is just a term for interrupted," Bannerman continued, gripping the steering wheel. He accelerated into third, then fourth gear. "I have things I want to achieve and I need that degree. I want completion. I want closure. You can give it to me. You have what it takes to provide me with the grades so that I can go on and do what I want to do. You can teach me what I need to know. Be my teacher."

Hughes wept. "Please, just stop the car."

The roads became slippery with puddles and Hughes felt the Mustang's tires slip as Bannerman took a curve in the road. They were coming up on an intersection, the light still green.

"We can do it together," Bannerman told him. "I just need someone to help me. The other teachers don't see me anymore because they don't believe . . . you did, until that shit, Fraser, opened his mouth this morning. But it isn't too late. We can still do it."

"Do what?" Hughes babbled, hysterics rising in him like angry bees.

"Student and mentor; we can be a team. We have the time to do it."

The traffic light turned orange. Bannerman stepped on the gas. "It will only hurt for a few seconds, and then we'll be free to pursue my dream."

"Stoooppp!" Hughes screamed. He felt Bannerman stamp down on the gas pedal, felt the car accelerate through the intersection, felt the

274

tires slide as the back end fishtailed. The car hit water and slid, water splashing over the passenger side. To their right, a wooden utility pole containing papers for upcoming concerts, transcendental meditation, and other services, the papers gone soggy in the rain; a pole that grew in size so that Hughes discerned all of its details – the soot of exhaust fumes, the splinters at its base, a clump of dying weeds that had sprung up along an edge.

Suddenly, they were airborne and the pole came at them. Hughes caught sight of one of the papers clinging to the pole's surface. It read: *Consider your dream on campus: visit Student Services at SMU to discuss career options today.*

The pole connected and Hughes felt himself engulfed in pain as glass shattered and metal tore. He saw Bannerman's body shift, then explode into pieces as the pole tore into the Mustang, wrapping the car into the shape of a disfigured crescent. He tasted blood, exhaust fumes, the acrid bite of the rain.

Everything became still.

Hughes realized that he observed the accident scene like a bystander from a distance. Somehow, they were on the sidewalk. Bannerman stood beside him, clasping his school books, whole again.

"My dad was really pissed over losing the car," Bannerman said.

The rain stopped and the sun came out.

"Shall we head back to the campus?" Bannerman nodded his head. "It's within walking distance."

Hughes felt aghast. He glanced down at himself. No blood, no glass. The world looked normal, felt normal; it was as if it had all been a bad dream. "This isn't real," he muttered to himself. "I'm imagining it. I'm going to walk back to the parking lot, find my own car, then I'm going to make a doctor's appointment. It could be a brain tumor."

Bannerman looked sad and amused. "Do whatever it takes to adjust," he said.

Bannerman followed him back to campus.

"Don't follow me," Hughes growled, his tone scathing. He hurried ahead of the Goth, feeling a surge of relief when he reached the university parking lot. There was his Honda, still parked where he'd left it. He got into the car and, hands shaking, started the ignition and drove home. He ignored Bannerman who stood on the sidewalk, watching him go.

#

Hughes showed up for class the next morning, having slept poorly through the night. He tried calling the doctor's office but the line had been perpetually busy. He'd taken some Valerian root to help him sleep and had willed away thoughts of Edward Bannerman. Fraser's conversation with him must have spurred the driving hallucination.

He unlocked the classroom door, eager to move forward with life. He arranged his books as his students filled the room. To his annoyance, he saw Bannerman walk in and sit at the front of the room, to stare at him. Hughes swallowed hard.

"Good morning everyone," Hughes said.

No one responded.

"I said good morning everyone!"

Students continued to ignore him, engaged in their private conversations. Someone's cell phone went off with a familiar hip-hop tune.

"Everyone, sit down and be quiet!" Hughes roared.

Bannerman shook his head and laughed. "Just teach me."

Hughes fumed. "I told you to get away from me," then shut his mouth as he realized he was talking to someone that the rest of the class couldn't see. He'd have Fraser on his ass again.

Speak of the devil, Fraser appeared in the classroom doorway at that moment and Hughes' heart sank at the site of him. What now? Had there been another complaint?

Hughes went to address Fraser, when Fraser walked right past him and stood at the front of the class near to where Hughes waited, speechless and annoyed. Fraser cleared his throat.

"Everyone, may I have your attention please?"

The class noise tittered out. Students, recognizing the department Dean, did as they were told. Fraser looked somber.

"I'm afraid that I have very sad news to report. I'll be taking over your class for the next couple of weeks until we can find a replacement for Professor Hughes. Your teacher was killed in a car accident yesterday afternoon while leaving the campus. His car slid through a puddle . . . he was hurled into a utility pole. He died instantly."

Students gasped. Someone said "I'd heard there'd been an accident, but I didn't know who it was." Someone else began to weep.

Hughes felt his fists clench. "I'm right here!"

"I'm so sorry," Fraser continued to the class, his face ashen. "None of us expect tragedies like this to occur. I promise you that your semester will continue. Our guidance counselors and chapel are on hand for those who require support. Professor Hughes had a lot of potential and I know that he loved his students."

Hughes' mouth wavered. "Are you all crazy?" he screamed. Everyone ignored him, except Bannerman.

"Fun being ignored, isn't it. Never mind. Can we do the Malamud story next?" Sun streamed through the classroom windows and in its essence Hughes noted tiny shards of glass on both Bannerman's clothes and himself, twinkling like myriad diamonds as the day awaited them.

LAB NOTES

A NOTE ABOUT CAMPUS CHILLS

In October 2008 *Titles Bookstore* at McMaster University held a "Haunted McMaster" event featuring 10 horror authors doing readings as well as free custom ghost walks of the McMaster campus performed by the folks from Haunted Hamilton. It was a smashing success and something we knew we would do again in 2009.

But this year, we wanted it to be bigger. So, since *Titles Bookstore* owns an Espresso Book Machine, as do the University of Alberta and University of Waterloo bookstores, we thought it would be interesting to see if we could invest some resources into producing an original anthology of horror fiction. Thus the theme of *Campus Chills* was born.

A good portion of the year was spent soliciting fiction from a group of extremely talented writers of speculative fiction. The goal was to get a range of stories set on different campuses and exploring the gamut of what the horror genre has to offer, while attempting to avoid stories drawn from real world horrors such as the Virginia Tech shootings in 2007 or the Montreal Massacre in 1987.

After reading the incredible tales that came in to me, I can honestly say that the goal was far surpassed. I was utterly impressed with both the quality and the dynamically different approaches each of these talented authors have taken in producing their incredibly chilling tales and I am honoured to be in their fine company.

Interestingly enough, when Robert J. Sawyer first released his novel FLASHFORWARD[1] back in 1997, there was a scene where he has two characters go to their local bookstore and sip coffee while they wait for a book to be printed on demand in the store. Rob's science-fiction scene, dated April 28, 2009 has half of the bookstore's space left to actual pre-printed guaranteed bestsellers and the rest of the facility dedicated to titles that could be printed on demand. His fiction imagined that it would take minutes to produce a single copy of virtually any book and that no title was ever truly out of stock.

Who better, then, to introduce a book created on just such a technology? And if that isn't enough, Sawyer is often fondly referred to as the *Dean of Canadian Science-Fiction*, which, of course, makes him the perfect person to introduce this fine cast of Canadian writers and their speculative campus tales.

The "Lab Notes" section you are about to read is a free-writing style exercise in which the authors have been invited to share whatever they felt like composing in regards to the story they wrote for this anthology, their own campus experiences, etc.

The intent is to add an extra dimension to the book, and for those of you reading this who are disappointed that the tales are now done, you perhaps have a little sense of lingering behind to chat with the authors after the candles are blown out and the evening's ghost stories are over.

Enjoy.

# # #

---

[1] Yes, the same novel that has been adapted into a hit ABC television series in the fall of 2009

AUTHOR NOTE FROM KELLEY ARMSTRONG

When I'm asked how long I've been writing, I say "all my life." And when I'm asked how long I've been writing stories with a paranormal bent, I give the same answer. I've always been fascinated by mythology and even more with the possibilities of supernatural legend. These days, I usually work in paranormal suspense, but I rarely turn down the chance to return to my horror roots.

When Mark first asked me to contribute to *Campus Chills*, I thought "Great! I'll write a story set at my alma mater, the University of Western Ontario." I came up with my story and went to the campus to get the setting details . . . and discovered, once again, the problems with working in a real setting: the layout is rarely exactly the way I need it for my story. So I can either change the story or fudge the details hope no one notices the discrepancies. I picked the third option—don't name the campus. But readers familiar with UWO may recognize the basic layout.

If you'd like more information on my work, you can find details and sample chapters at my website www.KelleyArmstrong.com. Thanks for reading!

AUTHOR NOTE FROM JULIE E. CZERNEDA

After graduating, University of Waterloo Alumnus Julie E. Czerneda (class of '73, Biology) and former staff member of the biology department (SEM technician then senior demonstrator for undergraduate labs) spent fifteen years writing and editing science texts used around the world. Then, she turned fulltime to writing science fiction on biological themes. In fact, 2009 marks twelve years since Julie E. Czerneda's first novel, *A Thousand Words for Stranger*, was published by DAW Books, New York. As for now? Thirteen novels, several anthologies, and short stories later, Julie's just getting started, confessing it's far too much fun to slow down. She's even working on a fantasy novel -- for a challenge. In her spare time, Julie remains involved in science education and literacy, giving public and teacher workshops worldwide. She received the Alumni of Honour Award from the University of Waterloo in 2007 and yes, that is her name on the rock between Biology and Math. How cool is that?

Julie credits UW with more than a great education and memories. She met her best friend and future husband, Roger Czerneda (BSc '73, Chemistry), in her very first class at UW. Which was, as you've likely guessed by now, in Math Lecture Hall Two. 8:30 am Monday. Dr. Smith's calculus class. While the real Dr. Smith was a treasure, the lecture hall doesn't seem to have changed one bit. Leading to the story in this book.

More about Julie and her work can be found online at www.czerneda.com.

AUTHOR NOTE FROM KIMBERLY FOOTTIT

Although I started writing when I was eleven, I really think that my career as a serious writer began when I was doing my undergrad at McMaster. I worked on my first collaboration then – an enjoyable alternative to taking notes in American History class. I suppose that it's only fitting that my second collaboration take place at the university as well. The bonus is that I get the opportunity of working with my good friend and writing guru, Mark Leslie. When I first heard his Prospero's Ghost tale back in the old days at Chapters, the title character stuck with me, even after all the details of the story had faded away. To be a part of giving Prospero a legacy here at McMaster has been a great experience.

Kimberly Foottit lives in Hamilton with her mischievous kitty Ernest. Her published stories include "Walter's Brain" (a science fiction love story set at McMaster) and "The Reverend and Mrs. Owens." She graduated from McMaster in 1997.

AUTHOR NOTE FROM JAMES ALAN GARDNER

My first fiction sale was a horror story set at the University of Waterloo. No, really.

This was back in the early 1980's, and Chris Redmond, editor of the UW Alumni Courier, bought a story from me about a demon messing around with computers in the math building. It was called "The Phantom of the Operator." As you might guess from the title, it was played for laughs rather than trying to be scary. Still, it was about a demon . . . at UW . . . and here I am again.

To be honest, "Truth-Poison" is my first sincere effort at horror. I'm mostly a science fiction guy—all my novels have been sf—with a smattering of fantasy now and then. This reflects my background: a B.Math and M.Math in Applied Mathematics from Waterloo. My

Master's thesis was on black holes, and when I switched to writing fiction, I retained my love of science. Even now, many years later, whenever I start writing, what comes out is almost always sf.

But I like *reading* horror, and once in a while, I've considered actually writing some. The only problem is that I'm congenitally optimistic; when I imagine people confronting some Big Bad, I like to picture them winning. That's not how horror works. Oh sure, in horror *novels*, protagonists may squeak out some sort of victory, even if it's only escaping from whatever is trying to kill them. But in short stories, horror never ends well. The monster always "gets" you . . . and even if the protagonists survive, there are fates worse than death.

Could I write such a story? Nah. I like having people *beat* fate.

However . . . when Mark asked if I wanted to write a horror story taking place at UW, it was an offer I couldn't refuse. Even better, he told me he already had plenty of overtly supernatural stories, so he hoped I might do something with a scientific flavor—an experiment gone wrong or something like that. I kicked around ideas and finally came up with "Truth-Poison": another story about a demon at UW. What goes around, comes around . . .

[Obligatory biographical info: James Alan Gardner. Author of eight novels—beginning with *Expendable*—and numerous short stories. Two-time winner of the Aurora award. Two-time nominee for both the Nebula and Hugo awards. UW alumnus, and also a frequent guest at UW's Waterloo Unlimited program. *http://www.thinkage.ca/~jim*]

AUTHOR NOTE FROM SÈPHERA GIRÓN

I attended York University in the eighties with my eye on Creative Writing but instead, chose to stay in Fine Arts Studies where I earned a B.A. I couldn't decide which discipline to follow so I continued my renaissance life with writing, music, theatre, and dance. For the first two years, I lived in Stong College Residence on the thirteenth floor.

It was at York that I grew as a writer under the fine tutelage of teachers such as b.p. nichol. I also really enjoyed screenwriting and psychology.

I wrote many horror stories while living at Stong and though this isn't one of them, it vaguely reflects the life on the thirteenth floor of residence back in the early eighties. I'm not certain what day to day residence life is like twenty-five years later which is why I chose to set the story in the era that I attended York. The funny thing is, one of my sons is now attending York. Circle of life and all, I guess.

You can take a walk on the wild side with Sèphera online at the following website: http://www.sff.net/people/seph/

AUTHOR NOTE FROM MICHAEL KELLY

Taddle Creek is but a memory. Once, it flourished, meandering through the greenery of aptly named Philosopher's Walk on the campus of The University of Toronto. Pictures from the late 1870's show the creek and a small lake, with campus buildings reflected in the calm waters.

As my tale, Different Skins, notes, the creek was buried, made into a sewer.

I wondered about all this as I toured the University with my daughter, who was thinking about going to the U of T. She did eventually chose Toronto, and loved it. But I wondered, as we walked the pathway, what a gurgling stream would be like in this already idyllic setting.

I wondered about its history, about what watery secrets lay buried beneath the ground.

You see, just south of Bloor St., where the path cuts through a narrow valley, there is a sewer grate. You can lift the grate and hear running water. It is the remains of Taddle Creek. It isn't the soft babble or gurgle. It sounds more like a scream. And perhaps it isn't just the remains of a long buried creek beneath the ground.

Michael's second collection of short stories, *Undertow and Other Laments*, has just been published by Dark Regions Press. Also newly available is *Ouroboros*, a novel co-written with Carol Weekes, from Bloodletting Press. As an editor and publisher, Michael has released his first book, *Apparitions*, an anthology of ghost stories, under his *Undertow Publications* imprint.

His recent fiction has sold to *Campus Chills*, *Tesseracts 13*, *Postscripts*, and *Strange Tales*.

You can find Michael online here:
http://lonesome-crow.livejournal.com/
http://www.facebook.com/michael.kelly2
http://www.undertowbooks.com/

#

AUTHOR NOTE FROM NANCY KILPATRICK

I'm not a McGill alumnus – I attended school in the United States – but I do live in Montréal and have long been fascinated with the Redpath Museum at McGill University. I'm old-school and miss the Victorian-style natural history museums that are fast disappearing and the Redpath has a touch of lingering Victoriana to it, preserved, I believe, because it is part of the university world. Montreal is a city with several universities and colleges in the downtown core, consequently there is quite a night-life here – a friend once asked me if you had to be under thirty to live in Montreal! I wanted to blend all these elements and more and the fact that McGill's Redpath has the Sara exhibit worked out well for my idea.

Award-winning author **Nancy Kilpatrick** has published 18 novels, around 200 short stories, 1 non-fiction book and has edited several anthologies. She writes mainly horror, dark fantasy, mysteries and erotica and has been working on two new novels over the last year. Her most recent short fiction has appeared in: *Blood Lite* (Pocket Books); *Bits of the Dead* (Coscom Entertainment); *The Living Dead* (Nightshade Books); and *Traps* (DarkHart Press). Look for upcoming stories in: *Hellbound Hearts* (Pocket Books); *Darkness on the Edge* (PS Publishing); *The Bleeding Edge* (Dark Discoveries); *The Moonstone Book of Zombies; The Moonstone Book of Vampires* (both Moonstone Books); *By Blood We Live* (Nightshade Books) and *Don Juan and Men* (MLR Press). Her most recently published anthology was co-edited with David Morrell – *Tesseracts 13*, an all horror/dark fantasy anthology (Edge Publishing) – and launched at **Worldcon** in Montreal, 2009. She has just finished editing her 10th anthology, the all-vampire *Evolve*, to be launched at the **World Horror Convention 2010, Brighton, UK**.

You can check out Nancy's latest endeavors at her website: *www.nancykilpatrick.com*

AUTHOR NOTE FROM MARK LESLIE

The concept for "Prospero's Ghost" was originally born on a campus in the early 1990's when I was teaching drama at "Campus Camp" a summer program for 9 to 15 year olds at Carleton University. During a tour of the Alumni Theatre on campus (a space I was intimately familiar with having worked there as a theatre technician, stage-hand and actor during my time as a student at Carleton), I had the students sit on the dimly lit stage while I told them the creepy story of how late one night I was in the theatre alone cleaning up when I encountered the ghost of the theatre, whom I nicknamed "Prospero's Ghost."

I readapted the same tale for a ghost story I told to the staff at the Chapters in Ancaster during the Halloween season of 1997 – explaining how I'd encountered the ghost walking around with a copy of "The Tempest" in his hand one night.

Flash forward more than 10 years and the legend of Prospero's Ghost has found a new life. When I was looking at doing the *Campus Chills* project, I was eager to include a tale set at McMaster University where I work. I thought it would be neat to re-adapt the "Prospero Ghost" story into an academic setting at Mac. But it wasn't until I sat down and started trying to flesh out the background of the ghost with my friend and colleague Kimberly Foottit that the tale took on an entirely new light.

Prospero's Ghost was reborn and more fully fleshed out than ever before thanks to Kim's creative insights. And while we were working on making the ghost more authentic and giving him a good reason for haunting, we figured we would have some fun and incorporate the *Espresso Book Machine* at Titles Bookstore as well as the *Kirtas* scanner at the Mills Library into the storyline – really give Professor Prospero a reason to come back from the dead and seek his revenge on the librarians and booksellers who would dare exploit his precious text.

Working with a talented writer like Kim was just what this tale needed. I could not have pulled off the story so successfully on my own – in retrospect when I look back at it, I see how the story and characters are given greater strength and more rounded dimension with having gone through Kim's imagination and pen.

So, after almost two decades of telling the tale of Prospero's Ghost, I have happily landed, with my talented colleague, on what I think is the penultimate version of this tale.

Though I'll be honest – if the mood catches me, I'll gladly gather a small group together with the lights down low and tell the tale of how late one night, working all by myself at Titles Bookstore, I encountered the ghost of Professor Marshall Emerson and barely lived to tell the tale.

AUTHOR NOTE FROM SUSIE MOLONEY

I got a late start in university, mostly because I got an early start on motherhood, and so I always felt two steps behind everyone else. This was the 80s before being a single mother was cool, or even widely accepted and for about two years I was defensive as hell, and maybe the slightest bit envious of those girls walking in front of me, in the latest fashions, laughing about the weekend, swinging purses that didn't have a small plastic dinosaur, a sippy cup, and a inoculation schedule inside. They didn't have to rush out of their last class to make it to daycare before it closed, they didn't have to haul a bookbag *and* a diaper bag. If someone stared at them, it wasn't at the spit up smeared on their shoulder, it was because they were pretty, young, filled with the *joie de vie* of youth. It was so *easy* for them.

"Sown," my story about an envious girl and her closest frenemy, the girl always a step ahead.

It took a couple of years for me to see the privilege in my own life, the stability offered by responsibility. There was no all-night cramming for me because I wasn't partying all weekend. There were no hang overs (those would come later). And every night I went home to this sweet-smelling, tiny, lovely body, into a house where I was the smartest person in the room, for at least awhile.

But I remembered that maybe sometimes, I wished they were dead.

Envy eats from the inside.

Otherwise I'm a lovely person, with a fourth novel, *Rhymes with B*tch* coming out 2010 from Random House, and currently working on a fifth, my version of those awful girls of the Manson Family.

AUTHOR NOTE FROM DOUGLAS SMITH

I attended the University of Waterloo from the years (mumble mumble) to (mumble mumble), graduating with an Honours B. Math and a computer science major. I loved my UW years – lots of friends around all the time, a beautiful campus within walking distance of Village I (I had no car), and a co-op program that provided ample money for a student lifestyle and also added a year to how long I could stay in that lifestyle before having to face the real world. So when Mark invited me to write a story for this anthology, although I had no idea of what story I would write, I knew that it would be set at UW.

The story necessitated a research trip back to campus. As a writer, I've found that people are wonderfully helpful with your research, and this was no exception. Beth Bonnert and Chris Redmond from the University were both great in pointing me in the right directions. Rick Zalagenas, Director of Maintenance and Utilities, kindly gave me a long guided tour of the infamous steam tunnels, things of legend when I went to UW. I never got into them as a student, so Rick's tour was an unexpected bonus of writing this story.

James "Road Dog" Walker also kindly gave me a tour of the UW campus radio station, the control rooms, and filled me in on the history of the station. Weird side note: Prior to meeting James, I'd already written a draft of the story, which included the deejay named "Dawg." Like I said, weird.

Finally, I had to figure out what visual changes the characters would see from that spot on the Ring Road near Sick Bay as the time flips back and forth over fifteen years. Yes, I was the guy you saw last summer standing in the middle of the road taking pictures in front of the SLC. Thank you for not running me over.

The story is (at least to me) more in the "weird" than the "chills" vein, but it works that way sometimes. And yes, it was partly inspired by the Springsteen song. The story contains many aspects of my UW years, but I won't tell you which ones are true.

Okay, I'll tell you one – the duck is true.

No, really, it is.

Really.

About Me: I'm an award-winning Toronto author of speculative fiction with over a hundred fiction sales in multiple languages around the world. I was a John W. Campbell Award finalist for best new writer, and have twice won Canada's Aurora Award. My first collection of short fiction, *Impossibilia*, was released in 2008 and garnered two more Aurora nominations. A second collection, *Chimerascope*, will be released in January 2010. I recently completed my first novel, an urban fantasy set in Ontario, incorporating Cree and Ojibwa legends. A film based on my story, "By Her Hand, She Draws You Down," is in post-production with TinyCore Pictures in the US. I can be contacted via my web site, *www.smithwriter.com*, and I twitter at *http://twitter.com/dougsmithwriter*.

AUTHOR NOTE FROM BRIT TROGEN

As someone with a background in molecular genetics I tend to focus on the biological side of things. So when the National Institute for Nanotechnology opened on the U of A campus right across from the (considerably less flashy) Biological Sciences building where I work, I immediately imagined it was filled with research just like my own, but with shiny, futuristic tools that weren't three decades old.

So when I stopped in to look around I was surprised to be turned back by building security. There's an aura of mystery surrounding all things science, especially when you're not even allowed to go poking around inside. And even though I later learned that work in the NINT is just as much physics and engineering as biology, my interest was piqued, and the story "Red Cage" is the result.

In addition to writing science fiction I work to make science accessible and entertaining as a Director in the science media company Science in Seconds Ltd. My blog can currently be found at http://scienceinseconds.blogspot.com/

AUTHOR NOTE FROM EDO VAN BELKOM

Everyone knows one . . . the pretty girl who knows she's pretty and uses her looks to her advantage. You really can't blame the girl, though. People use whatever the maker gave them to their advantage, right? The problem actually lies with the male of the species. Have you ever seen a pretty girl walk into the room and suddenly all the guys' attention is on her, acting foolish and doing things that they normally wouldn't be caught dead doing. And for what? A smile, a wink and a little bit of flirting? Sure, it's human nature and it's been that way since the dawn of time, but what if it weren't? What if (and there's the question that's the start of every great fantasy story) it wasn't human nature at all and pretty women actually had control over the weaker sex? That's how I came up with the idea for, "The Sypher."

Edo van Belkom is the author of the Silver Birch and Aurora Award winning "Wolf Pack" series of young adult novels from Tundra books which include *Wolf Pack, Lone Wolf, Wolf Man* and *Cry Wolf*. For Tundra, he has also edited the horror anthologies *Be Afraid* and *Be Very Afraid*.

Apart from this series of novels, Edo is also the author of well over 200 short stories, and 25 novels including *Mark Dalton: Smartdriver*, published by Natural Resources Canada and used as an educational tool to teach long-haul truck drivers fuel-efficient driving practices, as we as the novel *Battle Dragon*.

Edo attended York and has a degree in Creative Writing.

No fooling.

#

AUTHOR NOTE FROM STEVE VERNON

I loved college so much that I attended three of them. I went to King's College as a young fellow and dropped out in my second year to get married and have a child. Twelve years later I went through a divorce and decided to return to college. I chose St. Mary's and stayed in the men's residence at Loyola. At 30 I was the old man on the floor – but I loved the chance to throw myself into the books. I majored in English and minored in Philosophy – both areas of interest that are guaranteed to lead to a fine career selling auto parts at your local Canadian Tire outlet. I took every English and Philosophy course I could and jobbed out the mandatory sociology courses at Dalhousie, in order to fit them around my schedule. So that made three colleges – and I'm ashamed to say that I graduated from none of them. I balked at the mandatory courses, refusing to buckle down on anything that didn't have anything to do with English or Philosophy.

Still, I took what I learned about reading, writing and the art of creative thinking to become a writer of folklore. I have three ghost story collections under my belt – *Haunted Harbours: Ghost Stories from Old Nova Scotia* (2006), *Wicked Woods: Ghost Stories from Old New Brunswick* (2008), and my do-it-yourself ghost tour collection *Halifax Haunts: Exploring the City's Spookiest Spaces* (2009). All of these books are from a regional publisher – Nimbus. In addition, I have a children's picture book coming out in the fall of 2009, *Maritime Monsters,* a field guide to the sea monsters and wood beasts of the maritime provinces – and I am currently working on a young adult novel. I am determined to warp young Canadian minds at any chance I get.

It was during the writing of the Halifax collection that I first came across the Penelope legend. Interestingly enough, there is a similar story told about a young girl who hung herself in a King's College attic. I haven't run into any sort of a ghost story in St. Mary's. Perhaps our football team ran them off the campus. It was fun to take the bones of that old story and build it into something that would speak to college kids today. So, from this old drop-out to the college kids who are reading this collection – have fun and work hard and someday you too might wind up selling auto parts at your local Canadian Tire outlet.

#

AUTHOR NOTE FROM CAROL WEEKES

I attended St. Mary's University in Halifax, Nova Scotia from 1989 to 1993. I graduated with a Bachelor of Arts Degree in English. My first year English professor, Terry Whalen, encouraged me to write where my heart led me and I've never forgotten his words.

St. Mary's dates back to 1802 and its buildings from that era, with their stone walls, rich woodwork, and stained glass windows lend a natural inclination towards the perfect environment in which to build a classical ghost story. I can remember walking the halls during night classes . . . how quiet the corridors could become, how shadows loomed around corners, and how the solitary hum of something like a soda drink machine could seem formidable in the evening pall. I hold St. Mary's University close to my heart, always – my delightful and nostalgic Alma Mater whose subject matter in both my Major and electives taught me to think both objectively and creatively.

In 2007, I released my first novel, *Walter's Crossing* through NSP Books in South Carolina. Prior to that, I'd published myriad short stories since 1995 in numerous venues, from Horror, to Sci-Fi, to Mainstream, to Literary. My work has appeared in two of Canada's well known anthologies, *Northern Frights 4 & 5*, edited by Don Hutchison, in NYC 'Space and Time', and in Canada's literary journal 'The Dalhousie Review', to name a few. A 2nd novel, *Ouroboros*, co-written with Michael Kelly, is slated for an October 31, 2009 release from 'Bloodletting Press' in California (*www.bloodlettingbooks.com*)

Although I write in whatever category happens to appeal to me according to ideas that beg to be developed, I've always held a special place in my heart for Horror fiction, including that sub-genre known as 'the ghost story'. I love to write. I live to write. My background and inspiration heralds from a wide selection of reknowned authors, both classical and contemporary: Poe, Machen, Blackwood, Bierce, James, Dostoyevski, Ballard, King, Straub, Koontz, Steinbeck, Cheever, Faulkner . . . the list could go on and on.

If a young author or writing student were to ask me for some basic advice, this is what I would tell them:

Always believe in yourself. Never let anyone discourage you from the goal of 'getting there' with your writing. Work hard. Learn to listen to advice and to take constructive criticism. Develop a thick skin and also learn to accept rejection when you send your work out. It is the platform upon which you will develop your style, hone your edge, and build the backbone you need when you do start working professionally with editors. Read a lot - as many authors that you can get your hands upon, and learn from them. To write well, you must love words and language. Roll in words. Take a thesaurus to bed and lovingly stroke each page. And most of all - have fun when you write. Yes, you will be challenged - that's the beauty of advancing as a writer and only when you look back over a period of time will you see how far you've come. The 'overnight success' worked years to 'get there'. You can too.

ACKNOWLEDGEMENTS

This book project exists thanks to three pioneering and forward thinking Canadian booksellers. The editor would like to extend a note of sincere thanks to Todd Anderson, Donna Shapiro and May Yan, the directors of University of Alberta, McMaster University and University of Waterloo bookstores and the staff who support them at all levels. Thank you for believing in this book and this project. Additionally, thanks to the eagle eyes of Gordon Higginson, proofreader extraordinaire.

Thank you to the contributors who not only showed great trust in embracing this project, but also investing the time to write a story specific to the theme of *Campus Chills* and delivering truly top quality chilling tales. And a special thanks to Rob Sawyer, our Dean, for supporting us and cheering us all on.

Most of this book was set in *Palatino Linotype*. The *Palatino* family of fonts is an old style serif typeface designed by Hermann Zapf in 1948. In 1999, Zapf revised Palatino for Linotype and Microsoft, called *Palatino Linotype*.

Titles and various sets of header text within this book were set in *Shortcut*, which was designed by Eduardo Recife of www.misprintedtype.com